THEORIES OF EARLY CHILDHOOD EDUCATION

Theories of Early Childhood Education provides a comprehensive introduction to the various theoretical perspectives influential in early childhood education, from developmental psychology to critical studies, Piaget to Freire. Expert chapter authors examine assumptions underpinning the use of theory in the early years and concisely explore the implications of these questions for policy and practice. Every chapter includes applications to practice that will assist students and professionals in seeing the relevance of the theoretical perspective for their teaching.

Lynn E. Cohen is Professor in the Department of Special Education and Literacy at Long Island University, USA.

Sandra Waite-Stupiansky is Professor Emerita of Early Childhood Education and Reading at Edinboro University of Pennsylvania, USA.

THEORIES OF EARLY CHILDHOOD EDUCATION

Developmental, Behaviorist, and Critical

Edited by Lynn E. Cohen and Sandra Waite-Stupiansky

NEW YORK AND LONDON

First published 2017
by Routledge
711 Third Avenue, New York, NY 10017

and by Routledge
2 Park Square, Milton Park, Abingdon, Oxon, OX14 4RN

Routledge is an imprint of the Taylor & Francis Group, an informa business

Library of Congress Cataloging in Publication Data
Names: Cohen, Lynn E., editor. | Waite-Stupiansky, Sandra, editor.
Title: Theories of early childhood education : developmental, behaviorist, and critical / edited by Lynn E. Cohen, Sandra Waite-Stupiansky.
Description: New York : Routledge, 2017.
Identifiers: LCCN 2016035122| ISBN 9781138189478 (hardback) | ISBN 9781138189485 (pbk.) | ISBN 9781315641560 (ebook)
Subjects: LCSH: Early childhood education--Philosophy.
Classification: LCC LB1139.23 .T52 2017 | DDC 372.21--dc23
LC record available at https://lccn.loc.gov/2016035122

ISBN: 978-1-138-18947-8 (hbk)
ISBN: 978-1-138-18948-5 (pbk)
ISBN: 978-1-315-64156-0 (ebk)

Typeset in Sabon
by Saxon Graphics Ltd, Derby

Dedicated to
Kensley Rose Chojnacki (born November 9, 2014)
The second of a new generation of players
L. E. C.

To Nick, my partner in all walks of life
S. W. S.

CONTENTS

List of Illustrations ix
Foreword xi
Preface xiii
About the Editors xv
About the Contributors xvii

PART I
Developmental Theories **1**

1 **Jean Piaget's Constructivist Theory of Learning** 3
SANDRA WAITE-STUPIANSKY

2 **Maria Montessori: Yesterday, Today, and Tomorrow** 18
PHYLLIS POVELL

3 **The Eriksons' Psychosocial Developmental Theory** 31
ELIZABETH JONES AND SANDRA WAITE-STUPIANSKY

4 **The Importance of Urie Bronfenbrenner's Bioecological Theory for Early Childhood Education** 45
JONATHAN R. H. TUDGE, ELISA A. MERÇON-VARGAS, YUE LIANG, AND AYSE PAYIR

5 **The Vygotskian and post-Vygotskian Approach: Focusing on "the Future Child"** 58
ELENA BODROVA AND DEBORAH J. LEONG

PART II
Infant/Toddler Theories **71**

6 **The Educaring Approach of Magda Gerber** 73
RUTH ANNE HAMMOND

7 T. B. Brazelton's Developmental Approach to Learning 87
JOSHUA SPARROW

PART III
Behaviorist Theories 99

8 The Work of B. F. Skinner: Effective Practices within Early Childhood Settings 101
KATHLEEN M. FEELEY

9 Ole Ivar Lovaas: A Legacy of Learning for Children with Disabilities 115
EMILY A. JONES, SALLY M. IZQUIERDO, AND CARALINE KOBEL

PART IV
Critical Theories 129

10 Mikhail Bakhtin: Dialogic Language and the Early Years 131
E. JAYNE WHITE

11 Educative Experiences in Early Childhood: Lessons from Dewey 149
DENISE D. CUNNINGHAM AND DONNA ADAIR BREAULT

12 The Whole World Is a Chorus: Paulo Freire's Influence 165
ELIZABETH P. QUINTERO

13 Working with Deleuze and Guattari in Early Childhood Research and Education 180
GAIL BOLDT

Index 190

ILLUSTRATIONS

Figures

3.1	Erikson's Eight Stages of Psychosocial Development	33
9.1	The A-B-C Model	117
9.2	The Components of DTT Plugged into the A-B-C Model	118
9.3	An Example of DTT Instruction within the Context of the A-B-C Model	118

Table

11.1	Rubric for Educative Experiences in Early Childhood Classrooms	156

FOREWORD

I just read *Theories of Early Childhood Education: Developmental, Behaviorist, and Critical*, and I am happy to offer this foreword. I learned a lot from the chapters in this text. Off and on over the years, I have taught the "early childhood theory" course to master's and doctoral level students, and I wish I had had this book to support my instruction. This edited volume includes an array of important theoretical perspectives that goes beyond what has been traditionally offered in texts on early childhood theory. I think it will be a great resource for university instructors who know the importance of providing students with a solid foundation in theory.

For most of my career, I have worked within the early childhood education and early childhood teacher education fields to try to broaden our thinking about what constitutes appropriate practice and what counts as important knowledge. I have recently focused on expanding the ways we think about early childhood pedagogy. Because it is shortsighted and ill-advised to disconnect theory from pedagogy, the design of *Theories of Early Childhood Education* fits hand in glove with my beliefs about where we need to go in the early childhood field.

It is a noteworthy strength that the editors have included in-depth descriptions of theories that are often left out of discussions of early childhood theory. When teaching early childhood theory, I have had to bring in my own materials and identify my own readings in order to teach what the editors of this book call "critical theories." If our field is to mature, future teachers and teacher educators need to know about alternatives to the narrow conceptions of appropriate theory that are included in virtually all the introductory textbooks designed for preparing future early childhood teachers. I applaud editors Cohen and Waite-Stupiansky for putting together a text that substantively and symbolically provides a broader vision of what's possible in early childhood.

I believe teachers need to be professional decision makers. They are the individuals who know best what the children they work with every day need in order to learn and grow. In order for them to make wise decisions, teachers need a broad knowledge of development, learning, curriculum, teaching, and assessment. My bias is that the early childhood education field's emphasis on development does not give teachers all the tools they need to be successful in real contemporary classrooms. Books like this that include a cross-section of theories provide a model for helping teachers think about using all the knowledge available to help them provide the best learning experiences possible for all of their students.

Overall, the chapter authors did a very good job of describing the important attributes of their theories and then laying out pertinent applications of those theoretical elements to early childhood classrooms. As a reader, the consistent pattern in each chapter made it practicable for me to keep track of some complex information. As an instructor, the parallel organization of each chapter would make it easy to develop activities that encourage students to analyze, compare, and critique across the various perspectives included in the book.

In terms of readability, the editors' choice to frame each chapter around individual theorists (rather than abstract theories) made the book much more engaging. Each chapter starts with a biographical sketch of each of the theorists responsible for generating the theoretical constructs described. Having this information is not just interesting, it adds social, political, and historical context that helps the reader place the theoretical tenets in perspective. The editors and authors should be congratulated for helping early childhood educators see that human beings in particular circumstances during particular times used their experiences, intellect, and research skills to generate theories that have had a powerful impact on the lives of countless children around the globe.

To conclude, I recommend *Theories of Early Childhood Education: Developmental, Behaviorist, and Critical* as a valuable resource for pre-service and in-service teachers, as well as advanced graduate students. Reading the chapter on John Dewey's contributions reminded me of how Dewey's thinking has influenced my approach to processing information and challenged my previously held beliefs. My take on Dewey's philosophy is that we should prepare students to be critical of the status quo, but to not dismiss current understandings and approaches out of hand. Theoretical tenets have applicability to the situations we face in an increasingly complex post-modern world—or they do not. Dewey's pragmatic approach teaches us to look closely at traditional early childhood theories and to carefully consider alternative theories in order to figure out what best informs our professional practice. This book provides the raw material for doing that and for developing the intellectual tools and dispositions for applying a more expansive approach to our work in the early childhood field.

J. Amos Hatch
University of Tennessee

PREFACE

This book was five years in the making. Over those years, we discussed the need for a book that introduces pre-service teachers, in-service teachers, and doctoral candidates to classical and contemporary theories of how children learn. We brainstormed the most notable theories that influenced our own pedagogy, both as early childhood educators and teacher educators. The 13 theories presented in this book were the result of this process. There is a wide range of theories, most of which are not new but might be new to the reader. All of them have something to say to teachers of young children. As we set out to find contributors, we sought authors who had not only studied the theory, but who knew the theory at its deepest levels. The authors who present the theories in this book have written extensively about the theory, studied it at length, and actually *lived* the theory in their own professional careers. As the chapters arrived, we were struck by the depth of knowledge and wisdom that came through the words written by each author. Their voices are unique and different, but the appreciation for and understanding of the theories are in common. Our vision of compiling a book that has strong chapters which can stand alone or together as a coherent whole has been realized in the pages that follow.

The chapters are arranged in four parts. Part I, Developmental Theories, addresses children's learning as a developmental process that progresses from infancy into later ages. The theories of Piaget, Montessori, Erikson, Bronfenbrenner, and Vygotsky are known to all students of early education, but are presented here in fresh ways by contributors who introduce the readers to the originators of the theories, then lead them into the essence of the theories at their core, followed by applications of the theories in early childhood settings. Readers who have read multiple texts on these theorists will see them through new eyes after reading this part.

The second section of the book, Part II, presents two theories that focus specifically on infants and toddlers. Heavily influenced by medical pediatrics, both Gerber's and Brazelton's theories have strong implications for the growing field of early childhood education for the youngest of students, from birth to three years old. As the importance of the youngest years becomes recognized more widely, the genius of these two thinkers takes on new meaning.

Part III focuses on behaviorist theories that, often omitted from early childhood texts, have relevant application to early childhood education, particularly work with special populations. The chapters on Skinner and Lovaas present their approaches in practical, applicable terms, which is a welcome addition to the dialogue about ways to teach children with and without special needs.

Finally, Part IV of the book addresses what we have labeled critical theories because they represent theories that have influenced the way in which the entire educational enterprise works by questioning its traditions. The four theories presented in this section are not new, but they are still relevant today because they force us to reexamine the way we teach in a global, postmodern society. Bakhtin, Dewey, Freire, and Deleuze and Guattari represent a diversity of critiques of the way we view language, pedagogy, and a culturally appropriate view of education.

One of the unique aspects of this book is that each author presents the human side of the theorists. One of the emergent themes throughout the book is that none of these extraordinary men and women created their theories alone. Many of them publicly attributed their ideas to those closest to them, namely their families. In the cases of Piaget, Erikson, and Dewey, their spouses worked with them in developing, disseminating, and continuing their theories. For Skinner, Piaget, and Gerber, their own children were their earliest subjects. And Montessori's son became her lifelong colleague. So, although we often attribute the theories to one person, we recognize that there were many behind and beside him or her whose names we do not often hear, but whose influences are loud and clear.

Our intention was to introduce thinking about theories of early childhood into today's dialogue. Although theories are the main focus, their contribution to policy and practice is not neglected. We are hopeful that reading of the historical and theoretical links between different schools of thought will provide readers with important information that they need to pass standardized and performance assessments required by states for teacher certification. We considered it important to include material in each chapter on the implications for practice. Readers at all levels of preparation, from undergraduates to post-graduates, are at the stage of considering the connections between their course work and the practical applications in real classrooms. The chapters in this book are a timely reminder of the value of theory as it relates to teaching practice.

We thank our Routledge editor, Alex Masulis, for support and encouragement with proceeding with our initial ideas to write a book dealing with classical to contemporary theories of early childhood. Also, Judy Van Hoorn and Olga Jarrett gave timely and insightful reviews to several of the authors. Most importantly, the 19 authors of the 13 chapters on the most influential theorists of the last century have our highest respect and gratitude. As we opened each chapter file, we were amazed at the depth of understanding and ability to communicate abstract ideas and concepts of each and every contributor. The voices contained in this book are those of wise and learned writers whose collective contributions make a chorus worth listening to.

Lynn E. Cohen
Sandra Waite-Stupiansky

ABOUT THE EDITORS

Lynn E. Cohen, Ph.D., is a professor in the department of special education and literacy at Long Island University/Post Campus. She received her Ph.D. from Fordham University. Dr. Cohen teaches courses at the undergraduate, masters, and doctoral levels. Before coming to LIU/Post, she was a preschool, kindergarten, and literacy teacher. Her research interests are related to young children's social and emotional development, oral language skills, emergent literacy, and play. She co-edited two other books with Sandra Waite-Stupiansky: *Play: A Polyphony of Research, Theories, and Issues, Play and Culture Studies, Volume 12* (2012); and *Learning across the Early Childhood Curriculum: Advances in Early Education and Day Care, Volume 17* (2013). Dr. Cohen has published numerous articles in several journals including *Contemporary Issues in Early Childhood Education*, *Young Children*, *International Journal of Early Childhood*, *Early Childhood Development and Care*, and *Journal of Research in Early Childhood.*

Sandra Waite-Stupiansky is Professor Emerita of Early Childhood and Reading at Edinboro University of Pennsylvania. She earned a Ph.D. from Indiana University, Bloomington. Her areas of research include recess in elementary schools, play, and child development. She was the managing editor of *Play, Policy, and Practice Connections,* an online publication of the Play, Policy, and Practice Interest Forum of the National Association for the Education of Young Children, from 1995 to 2013. She co-edited two other books with Lynn Cohen: *Play: A Polyphony of Research, Theories, and Issues, Play and Culture Studies, Volume 12* (2012); and *Learning across the Early Childhood Curriculum: Advances in Early Education and Day Care, Volume 17* (2013). Dr. Waite-Stupiansky assisted the writing team of *Play at the Center of the Curriculum* (6th ed.) (Van Hoorn, Nourot, Scales, & Alward, Pearson, 2015). She has written multiple articles and books for practitioners published by Scholastic.

ABOUT THE CONTRIBUTORS

Elena Bodrova is currently Director for Research and Development at Tools of the Mind and a Research Fellow at the National Institute for Early Education Research at Rutgers University. She holds a Ph.D. in Child Development and Educational Psychology from the Russian Academy of Pedagogical Sciences and an M.A. in Child Development and Educational Psychology from Moscow State University, Russia. In collaboration with Dr. Deborah Leong, she developed the Tools of the Mind program based on Vygotskian and post-Vygotskian theories of learning and Luria's theories of brain development. Her work on applying Lev Vygotsky's theory to education started in Russia, where she worked in the Institute for Preschool Education, and continued in the U.S. where she worked as a visiting professor at the Metropolitan State University of Denver and later as a Principal Researcher at Mid-continent Research for Education and Learning. Dr. Bodrova is the co-author with Dr. Leong of *Tools of the Mind* (2nd ed.) (Pearson, 2007), and multiple articles and book chapters on early literacy, assessment, play, and self-regulation.

Gail Boldt is Professor in Curriculum and Instruction at Penn State University. Her research interests include the intersections of affect, subjectivity, subject positions, and materiality in young children's experiences in families and schools. She teaches undergraduate literacy courses and graduate courses in social theory. Her most recent research has been conducted in a Deleuzo-Guattarian inspired preschool in Paris that serves children with disabilities, and at the psychiatric hospital in France where Guattari practiced. Dr. Boldt is the editor of the "Psychoanalysis" section for Oxford's *Bibliography of Childhood Studies*. She is also a psychotherapist with a practice with children.

Donna Adair Breault is Dean of the Dwight Schar College of Education at Ashland University. She served as chair of the Dewey Studies Special Interest Group of the American Educational Research Association (AERA) from 2014 to 2016. Prior to entering higher education, Dr. Breault was an elementary and middle school teacher and administrator. Since entering higher education, she has taught courses in curriculum, foundations, research, and leadership, and she has coordinated programs in educational leadership. Dr. Breault's research includes applications of Dewey's theory of inquiry in curriculum, research, and organizational systems. She has co-edited *Experiencing Dewey: Insights for Today's Classrooms* (Routledge & Kappa Delti Pi, 2013). Her publications include *Red Light in the Ivory Tower* (with co-author, David Callejo-Perez,

Peter Lang, 2013) and articles in *Educational Theory*, *Educational Studies*, *The International Journal of Leadership in Education*, *Journal of Thought*, *Planning and Change*, and *Scholar-Practitioner Quarterly*.

Denise D. Cunningham is Professor and Program Coordinator of Early Childhood Education at Missouri State University. Dr. Cunningham earned her Ph.D. in Teaching and Learning, with specializations in literacy and early childhood education, from the University of Missouri–St. Louis. She has over 15 years of experience as an administrator of both for-profit and not-for-profit child care facilities and is a former primary teacher and literacy coach for St. Louis Public Schools. Dr. Cunningham teaches the undergraduate methods courses for early childhood teacher education as well as literacy coursework at the graduate level. Dr. Cunningham's research interests include early literacy development, early childhood curriculum, and pre-service teacher preparation.

Kathleen M. Feeley is Associate Professor at Long Island University in Brookville, New York and founding director of the Center for Community Inclusion, home to two New York State Education Department's Technical Assistance Centers for the Long Island region (the Early Childhood Direction Center and the Special Education Parent Center). Dr. Feeley's clinical work and research focuses on demonstrating the effectiveness of behavior analytic interventions to address the needs of children with chromosome disorders. Having worked extensively with young children with autism spectrum disorders, Dr. Feeley is replicating many of these strategies to meet the unique needs of children with Down syndrome. She has co-authored *Augmentative and Alternative Communication Strategies for Individuals with Severe Disabilities* (Brookes Publishing, 2012), co-authored a book chapter in *Enhancing Learning for Children with Down Syndrome* (Faragher & Clarke, Eds., Routledge, 2014), and published articles in the *Journal of Intellectual Disabilities*, *Behavioral Interventions*, and *Research in Developmental Disabilities*.

Ruth Anne Hammond is an RIE Associate and mentor teacher. She has authored *Respecting Babies: A New Look at Magda Gerber's RIE Approach* (Zero to Three, 2009). She was mentored and certified by its founder, Magda Gerber; currently serves on its Board of Directors; and was RIE President from 2005 to 2011. She taught infant studies and led the Infant/Toddler-Parent Program for 17 years at Pacific Oaks College and Children's School in Pasadena, California. She has been a member of Dr. Allan N. Schore's interpersonal neurobiology professional study group since 2008.

Sally M. Izquierdo is a Ph.D. student in psychology in the area of Behavior Analysis at the Graduate Center, City University of New York. She has over 20 years of experience providing services to support children with disabilities in a variety of settings. She holds her B.A. in psychology from SUNY Geneseo and her M.A. from Florida Gulf Coast University. Her current research interests include the effects of sign language and stimulus–stimulus pairing on speech production, intelligibility, and engagement in communication interventions for infants with Down syndrome.

Elizabeth Jones is Faculty Emerita at Pacific Oaks College where she taught early childhood courses. Her studies of child development have served as the basis for understanding human development and learning across the life cycle. Teaching adults, observing children, dialoging with colleagues, and documenting the dialogue have provided her with never-ending adult play experiences in the social construction of knowledge. She has authored and co-authored several books including *The Play's the Thing: Teacher's Roles in Children's Play* (2nd ed.) (Teachers College Press, 2011), *Teaching Adults Revisited* (N.A.E.Y.C., 2007), and *Playing to Get Smart* (Teachers College Press, 2006).

Emily A. Jones is an Associate Professor in the Department of Psychology, Queens College, City University of New York. Dr. Jones's research draws on knowledge about the behavioral phenotype characteristic of a given disorder to determine target intervention resources, even doing so in a preventative way, before impairments become pronounced. She is examining interventions to address joint attention in children with autism and communication, cognitive, and motor skills, as well as aspects of the intensity of intervention in children with Down syndrome. Dr. Jones is also evaluating the effects of support groups and sibling training for families of children with autism. This work has been supported by funds from the Professional Staff Congress, Organization for Autism Research, Doug Flutie Jr. Foundation, and Autism Speaks, and published in peer reviewed journals such as *Behavior Modification*, *Journal of Applied Behavior Analysis*, *Research in Autism Spectrum Disorders*, and *Research in Developmental Disabilities*.

Caraline Kobel holds a B.A. in psychology and sociology from Queens College, City University of New York. She is currently enrolled in the Applied Behavior Analysis master's program at Queens College. Caraline is the Coordinator for Baby Butterflies, an inclusive "Mommy and Me" program. She is also a graduate research assistant in the Developmental Disabilities Lab, under the supervision of Dr. Emily A. Jones. She has over two years of experience working with children with developmental disabilities such as autism and Down syndrome. In the future, Caraline hopes to earn her Ph.D. in Behavior Analysis.

Deborah J. Leong is Professor Emerita of psychology at Metropolitan State University of Denver where she taught for 36 years in the Department of Psychology, and is co-developer of Tools of the Mind ("Tools") with Dr. Elena Bodrova. She received her Ph.D. and B.A. from Stanford University and her M.Ed. from Harvard University. "Tools" is a pre-K and kindergarten program that fosters the development of executive functions and the development of social-emotional and academic skills. She has co-written books, articles, and educational videos with Dr. Bodrova on the Vygotskian approach to psychology, self-regulation, and the development of play, as well as books on assessment in the early childhood classroom with Drs. McAfee and Bodrova.

Yue Liang is a doctoral student at the University of North Carolina–Greensboro. She worked as a research assistant at Beijing Normal University, conducting research on creativity development among children and adolescents. After completing her master's degree in psychology, she moved to the United States to pursue a doctoral degree. She is currently working with Dr. Jonathan Tudge at the Department of Human Development and Family Studies, and studying the development of gratitude among Chinese and Chinese immigrant children and adolescents.

Elisa A. Merçon-Vargas is a doctoral student in the Department of Human Development and Family Studies at the University of North Carolina–Greensboro. She completed her masters in psychology at the Federal University of Espírito Santo, in Brazil, where she worked with national and international adoptive families, using Bronfenbrenner's theory in her master's thesis. She is currently working with Dr. Jonathan Tudge studying the development of gratitude among different cultural groups, including Brazilian immigrant families in the United States.

Ayse Payir is a doctoral student at the University of North Carolina at Greensboro. After completing her degree in journalism at Istanbul University in Turkey, she worked for the production and screen writing of several television series for three years until she decided to have a career in psychology. Upon completing her degree, she won a Fulbright award and moved to the United States to pursue an M.A. in psychology at New York University. Currently she is studying cognitive and emotional development of children under the supervision of Rob Guttentag and Jonathan Tudge. On completing her Ph.D., she will take up a postdoctoral position at Boston University, working with Kathleen Corriveau and Paul Harris.

Phyllis Povell is Professor Emerita and former Director of the Early Childhood Program at Long Island University. She received her Ph.D. from New York University in History of Education/Comparative Education. Her book, *Montessori Comes to America: The Leadership of Maria Montessori and Nancy McCormick Rambusch* (University Press of America, 2010), is required reading in Montessori teacher training courses. Her articles and book reviews have appeared in many academic journals, and include "John McDermott and the Road to Montessori Public Schools," in *Montessori Life*, and the book review, "Maria Montessori Sails to America: A Private Diary 1913" in *Montessori Life*.

Elizabeth P. Quintero is Professor and Coordinator of Early Childhood Studies at California State University Channel Islands. She has worked as a teacher (Pre-K to Grade 2), curriculum specialist, and university teacher educator. Her passion is programs serving families from a variety of histories in multilingual communities. Dr. Quintero's publications include *Storying Learning in Early Childhood: When Children Lead Participatory Curriculum Design, Implementation, and Assessment* (Peter Lang, 2015); *Critical Literacy in Early Childhood Education* (Peter Lang, 2009); and the book chapters, "Conocimiento: Mixtec Youth Sin Fonteras," in Awad Ibrahim & Shirley Steinberg (Eds.), *Talkin' Bout Their Generation* (Peter Lang, 2015); and "Juan, Melina, and Friends: Guides for Reconceptualizing Readiness," in Parnell & Iorio (Eds.) *Reconceptualizing Readiness in Early Childhood Education* (Springer, 2015).

Joshua Sparrow is Director of the Brazelton Touchpoints Center at Boston Children's Hospital and Associate Professor of Psychiatry part-time at the Harvard Medical School. His work at the Brazelton Touchpoints Center focuses on cultural adaptations of family support programs, organizational professional development, and aligning systems of care with community strengths. Dr. Sparrow has collaborated with agencies such as Harlem Children's Zone and American Indian Head Start Programs. He lectures nationally and internationally and consults for media programs for children and parents. He has co-authored with Dr. T. Berry

Brazelton, *Brazelton Touchpoints: Birth to Three* (2nd ed.) (Da Capo Press, 2006), *Nurturing Children and Families: Building on the Legacy of T. B. Brazelton* (Wiley-Blackwell, 2010), and numerous book chapters and journal articles.

Jonathan R. H. Tudge is Professor of Human Development and Family Studies at the University of North Carolina–Greensboro. He gained his B.A. (History) and M.Phil. (Sociology) at the Universities of Lancaster and Oxford in the UK, and taught young children in London and Moscow for seven years before moving to the United States to work on his Ph.D. in Human Development and Family Studies at Cornell University with Urie Bronfenbrenner. Upon completing his doctorate he did post-doctoral work with Barbara Rogoff at the University of Utah, and moved to UNC–Greensboro in 1988. Dr. Tudge's publications include *The Everyday Lives of Young Children* (Cambridge University Press, 2008), and he has co-edited two other books, as well as authoring several papers on Bronfenbrenner's bio-ecological theory. Dr. Tudge is currently studying the development of gratitude in different cultures with funding provided by the John Templeton Foundation.

E. Jayne White is Associate Professor at the University of Waikato, New Zealand. Jayne has a long-standing interest in education, with particular emphasis on early childhood pedagogy, spanning over 30 years. Her interest in various aspects of teaching and learning spans the domains of infant and toddler education, educational philosophy, play and creativity, democracy, environmental education, classroom education, assessment, and evaluation. At the heart of her practice lies a strong emphasis on dialogic pedagogy, and the ways in which teachers can best engage within complex learning relationships—regardless of the age of the learner. She has published numerous articles related to Bakhtin and dialogic pedagogy, and authored books including *Introducing Dialogic Pedagogy: Provocations for the Early Years* (Routledge, 2015), and *Educational Research with Our Youngest: Voices of Infants and Toddlers* (Springer, 2011), and co-edited *Bakhtinian Pedagogy: Opportunities and Challenges for Research, Policy, and Practice in Education Across the Globe*, part of the Global Studies in Education book series (Peter Lang, 2011).

Part I

DEVELOPMENTAL THEORIES

1

JEAN PIAGET'S CONSTRUCTIVIST THEORY OF LEARNING

Sandra Waite-Stupiansky

Jean Piaget revolutionalized the way educators, psychologists, and researchers view children's learning and development (Beilin, 1992). This chapter aims to give a brief history of his ideas and theory as they evolved over his lifetime and beyond, then apply many of Piaget's concepts to the contemporary early childhood classroom. As research on all areas of child development, from brain research to social and moral research, has informed theory and practice, the strength of Piaget's theory is how it has adapted and evolved over the last seven decades in a way that can incorporate these new findings. The first section of the chapter will introduce Piaget as a person and a theorist. An overview of key concepts of his theory will follow, with implications for practice at the end. The challenge is to capture Piaget's theory and implications in one chapter when his work filled approximately 100 books and 600 papers, many of which have not been translated from French into English, and have multiplied exponentially by others who have written about his ideas and theories (Muller, Carpendale, & Smith, 2009). This chapter aims to present the elements of Piaget's theory that are most informative for early childhood educators, and is by no means exhaustive in its coverage of the breadth and depth of Piagetian theory as a whole.

Born in 1896 in Neuchâtel, Switzerland, Jean Piaget was the oldest child and only son of Arthur Piaget (Swiss), a university history professor, and Rebecca Jackson Piaget (French), a school commissioner and political activist. Jean was a serious and precocious student whose interest in biology started young and led to publications on birds and mollusks starting at the age of 10 (Hall, 1987) and a job at the local Natural History Museum (Muller et al., 2009). His lifelong love of biology influenced his ideas for the rest of his life.

In 1918, Piaget graduated from college with a degree in the natural sciences, followed soon after by a Ph.D. with a specialty in mollusks, both from Neuchâtel University. He was offered a faculty position at the same university in 1925. His path to this point was rapid but interspersed with periods of intense questioning of the emerging ideas in philosophy, religion, and evolution, and how these ideas fit into Piaget's unquenchable interest in epistemology, the study of knowledge. Throughout his life, Piaget was adept at studying contrasting views within disciplines and finding a third alternate view or "tertium quid" that transcended the opposing views without contradicting either (Bennour & Voneche, 2009, p. 50). Furthermore, he was a gifted writer who published his ideas regularly for others to consider and debate, which he welcomed.

During his course of study at the university, Piaget spent a semester in Zurich working at a psychological laboratory specializing in psychiatry. He became interested in the ideas of Jung, Freud, and Adler, writing a paper and giving lectures on the relationships among these theories, marking the beginning of his interest in mental development.

Piaget's interest in psychology took him to Paris, where he worked with Theodore Simon on standardizing intelligence tests for children. It was here that Piaget developed his method of questioning children about how they arrived at their answers to the questions on the test, which were often wrong but formed a consistent pattern with other children of the same age range. He developed the method that he called the "clinical interview" that allowed him to follow the child's answers with further questions to try to illuminate the child's reasoning. Piaget continued to use this method throughout his long career.

Another important connection occurred during this period of Piaget's life. He met and married a member of his research team, Valentine Chatenay, with whom he had three children, Jacqueline, Lucienne, and Laurent, between 1925 and 1931. All three of his children's early development was well documented in several books on infant cognitive development (Piaget, 1952/1963; 1954/1971/1986) and instrumental in the formulation of his ideas.

In 1929, Piaget was offered a faculty position at the University of Geneva, which is where he spent most of the rest of his career until his death in 1980. As evidenced in an interview conducted by Elizabeth Hall, he continued to work well into his 70s, experimenting, teaching, and revising his own theories (Hall, 1987). In his last published interview, six months before his death in 1980, Piaget reiterated his roots in biology and the parallels between scientific discoveries and a child's developmental progression (Voyat, 1980/2011). This theme influenced his thinking throughout his lifetime as it appeared again and again as he theorized about children's intellectual, social, and moral development for over 50 years.

Piaget's Theory: Key Concepts

Constructivism is the name Piaget gave to his theory because it represents his idea about how learning occurs. He used the term "constructivism" to convey that people construct their knowledge as a result of constant active interactions between the environment and the structures within the brains of the organism; in other words, the constant balancing and re-balancing between the mental structures of the learner is the result of active engagement with the environment and results in the construction of knowledge for that individual, who can then act upon the environment in light of the new structures. Thus, the learner is an agent of change of both the internal and external realities. Learning proceeds in predictable vectors and patterns, but it is not linear nor lock-step, as stage theory would suggest. There are stops and starts, progressions and regressions, and sudden surges and regressions are expected as an individual moves in the direction of higher levels of functioning. Piaget captured this nonlinear progression profoundly: "There is an adult in every child and a child in every adult" (1932/1965, p. 78).

Most overviews of Piaget's theory emphasize the series of stages through which children proceed, starting with sensorimotor and progressing to preoperational, concrete operational, and formal operational thinking. Unfortunately, these ages and stages make up most of what many educators know about Piaget's theory. Over the years, many researchers, including Piaget himself, challenged the lock-step nature of the stages. Piaget even argued against the notion of homogeneous stages. "This renders arbitrary any attempt to cut mental reality up into stages" (1932/1965, p. 78). Rather, he described "successive phases of regular processes recurring like a rhythm," traces of earlier ways of thinking reappearing at later ages when new problems or experiences confronted an individual. Human development is like the evolutionary processes of a species. The earlier structures give way to more sophisticated ways of adapting, but they do not disappear completely. Through this process intelligence evolves, which, according to Piaget, is "a generic term to indicate the superior forms of organization or equilibrium of cognitive structures" (1947/1950, p. 7).

As this chapter will demonstrate, there is so much more to understanding Piagetian theory beyond the stage components. For the purposes here, the emphasis is on how children learn about their worlds and themselves. They start with coordinating their motor responses from reflexive, involuntary movements to coordinated movements that show premeditation. This occurs in the first two years of life for most infants when children are not fluent in language. Piaget and Inhelder (1969) called this the "sensorimotor period" (p. 3). Then, preoperational thinking, or pre-logical reasoning, starts to include children's budding sense of logic and exploding use of oral language. As children begin to apply logical reasoning, they start with here-and-now interactions with the environment, mostly "on the concrete plane of action. ... until the age of seven or eight, when coordinated actions are converted into operations, admitting of the logical construction of verbal thought and its application to a coherent structure" (Piaget, 1952/1963, pp. ii–iii), leading to the term "concrete operational thinkers" being used to describe children in the primary grades. As their reasoning continues to develop in complexity, accuracy, and application, the learners become more abstract thinkers, which has come to be known as formal operational thinking (Piaget, 1947/1950). The learner is no longer tied to the present, concrete plane, but can think in metaphors and abstractions. He or she moves from "symbolic behavior and memory" to "higher operations of reasoning and formal thoughts" (1947/1950, p. 9). Reference to these planes of development will occur throughout this chapter as the different concepts and ideas of Piaget are presented.

Active Learning and the Nature of Knowledge

Piaget was well aware of theorists in early childhood education who preceded him, such as Maria Montessori and Freidrich Froebel, and their arguments that children are active agents in their learning. Piaget's interest in the nature of knowledge and epistemology led him to theorize that children not only construct their own knowledge, but the types of knowledge they are constructing are not equal, and different knowledge demands different means of construction. Kamii (2014), who studied with Piaget and translated his theory into practice, classified knowledge into three distinguishable but overlapping types: physical knowledge, logico-mathematical knowledge, and social-conventional knowledge.

Physical knowledge emanates from the source or object itself. The child acquires physical knowledge from interacting with the object and taking in the knowledge through his or her senses. When children feel the coldness of an ice cube or the smoothness of a rabbit's fur, they are experiencing knowledge of the physical properties of cold and smooth. Experiencing the brightness of the sun or the smell of chocolate leads to knowledge of the physical attributes of the sun and chocolate. Importantly, the child must discover the physical knowledge directly through his or her senses, not from alternative means such as someone describing the attributes to the child or watching a video about ice or chocolate without having first-hand experience with the objects previously.

Logico-mathematical knowledge is constructed within a learner's mind (Kamii, 2014). It is the logic that a learner constructs from interactions with the external (and later internal) world. Logico-mathematical knowledge involves relationships between and among objects, ideas, and people (Waite-Stupiansky, 1997). So when a child compares the brightness of the sun to the brightness of the moon, the physical knowledge taken in through the direct senses is put into a relationship of greater or lesser brightness (logico-mathematical knowledge). When a child drops a glass bottle on the concrete sidewalk, the resultant shattering of the glass helps the child create an "if ... then" relationship: *If* I drop my bottle on the hard concrete sidewalk, *then* it will shatter and make a shrill sound. When items are put into relationships, such as cause/effect relationships, they are internalized as logico-mathematical knowledge. The source of this type of knowledge is the child's mind and must be constructed through active experiences.

Social-conventional knowledge comes from the collectively agreed upon social conventions of a child's culture. The child memorizes this knowledge from people around him or her who already have the knowledge. Language is a prime example of social-conventional knowledge. The words a child learns are determined by his or her culture and experiences speaking with representatives from that culture. If the child had been born into a culture that speaks a different language, the social-conventional knowledge acquired would be quite different. Another example of social-conventional knowledge are rules of conduct that vary from culture to culture, such as when it is appropriate to wear a hat (outside but not at the dinner table). The source of social-conventional knowledge is a child's social surroundings because it is learned from people who already have the knowledge and it must be memorized by the child.

The reason why the types of knowledge are important for early childhood educators to know is because the way in which children learn each type of knowledge differs, which means that teachers are most effective when they differ the instruction according to the type of knowledge being addressed. If a teacher is addressing physical knowledge, direct sensory experiences are the best modality for instruction. Introducing the concept of cold would be done best with physical objects that have cold attributes (ice cubes, snow). If the knowledge is logico-mathematical, such as arranging items by their temperature from cold to hot, having a variety of objects of different temperatures that can be put into a logical order from cold to hot would be the most effective approach. If learning the names of objects (social-conventional knowledge) such as ice, snow, hot, cold is the goal of instruction, then introducing the new vocabulary as the objects are explored would be in order.

The three types of knowledge overlap and are often hard to separate in the real world. Yet the implications for instruction, which will be addressed later in this chapter, are far reaching and important. If the instruction fits the type of knowledge, the child's learning will be optimized and meaningful.

Operations and Logic

The core of Piaget's theory when addressing all types of development, social, moral, cognitive, or motor, is the notion of operations. In Piaget's (1962) words, operations are "active schemas constructed by the mind" (p. 161). Operations are reversible applications of logic that start with children's explorations of their bodies during the earliest years when sensorimotor operations are prime, leading eventually to formal, abstract applications of logic at the highest levels of reasoning, a process that takes a decade or more of development. As children operate on their environment, they form schemes that can be repeated, varied, tested, and refined. In doing so, children begin to form mental structures that influence future interactions with their environment (Voyat, 1980/2011). In the first few weeks of life, the infant is governed by reflexes such as sucking, but soon thereafter the child starts to explore his or her body, then starts to include objects within reach and people with whom she or he has contact, and progressively moves away from primarily exploring his or her own body and immediate surroundings. These explorations lead to schemes or patterns that move from fortuitous or accidental to exhibiting repetition based on previous experiences and/or imitation of how others have acted in his or her presence. Evidence of the formation of mental structures starts to appear when a child can hold a thought or image in his or her head, such as the presence of an object even when it is out of sight. This appears in the second half of the first year of life and constitutes what Piaget and Inhelder (1969) called the "permanent object" (p. 48), or the more popularized term, "object permanence," as it has come to be known more recently. Piaget argued that when the child continues to look for objects moved out of sight, the first signs of intelligence appear because the child "knows" that the object is still there, even though it is out of sensory range. Thus, the child is holding the image or thought of the object in his or her mind. This was an important milestone for Piaget since it was evidence of the child's thinking.

As a child continues to operate on the environment and construct mental structures, other evidence appears, such as the first symbolic play. A child pretends to start a car with a set of keys or to drink from an empty tea cup. This type of pretending usually appears between the first and second birthdays. Piagetian theory argues that the child is using his or her body and actions to represent a person starting a car or drinking a cup of tea. The important point is that the child is not actually doing these actions, but is *pretending* to do so. He or she is acting out an activity that he or she has never done, but has witnessed others doing. This is a milestone in cognitive development again because it represents the presence of mental structures upon which the child is acting. The child is using real objects as he or she symbolizes actions or activities experienced or witnessed previously in life. Piaget argued that this type of play is based on assimilation of reality for the child and has a ludic, or playful, quality (Piaget, 1962).

Operations and logic continue to develop, first with objects and people in the immediate environment, but as the child acquires language, he or she can talk about items and people outside of the immediate surroundings in time and space (Piaget, 1962). A child can talk about events that occurred in the past or events that are planned for the future. A child can discuss a grandparent he or she hasn't seen for several weeks. The child is moving forward, propelled by various and multiple concrete experiences in order to construct knowledge arising from these experiences. This knowledge forms the foundation upon which future thinking will be based.

As a child grows more sophisticated and can move beyond concrete experiences and start to experience ways of representing objects and ideas in symbols and signs, further operational thinking is possible. A toddler picks up a toy car and says, "Vroom." He or she sees a picture of his or her grandfather and exclaims, "Granddaddy!" or watches a video of a recent holiday and recognizes it as an event that occurred in the past. These are lower levels of representation because the symbols actually look like what they are symbolizing. As the child acquires language, a new level of representation that is further from the actual object is possible. Then, as the child starts to recognize written letters and words that signify the spoken language, a higher form of representation is possible. Reading, writing, denoting numbers with numerals and drawings extend the child's ability to communicate and understand communications about events and notions outside of the here-and-now concrete surroundings. Furthermore, when signs represent operations such as addition, subtraction, or equals (+, –, =), a child who has already constructed operations with concrete materials can understand and abstract the meaning of what these signs represent. Introducing the signs for the operations before the child has constructed an understanding of the actual operations using active manipulation on the concrete plane is contrary to Piaget's theory. Such early introduction of signs leads to surface level learning and rote memorization because the child has not developed the necessary mental structures upon which the operations are based.

Equilibrium and Adaptation

Although he never strayed far from his roots in biology, in the last decades of his life, Piaget returned to his original notion of equilibrium as the most important driver of learning as he distanced himself from the stage theories that he had become known for in American child psychology (Fosnot & Perry, 2005). Fosnot and Perry point out that according to Piaget, equilibrium is "the mechanism at play in any transformational growth process" (p. 16). As humans encounter new experiences and act upon their environment, the disequilibrium they encounter will lead to the self-regulating balancing between what they know and what is new to them, which results in learning new concepts and strengthening what they already know. To Piaget, the processes and dynamics described in biology, evolutionary theory, and construction of knowledge are parallel (Hall, 1987).

In *The Origins of Intelligence*, Piaget (1952/1963) argued that "intelligence is an adaptation" (p. 3) and the "most general biological functions: *organization* and *adaptation*" are at work (italics in original, pp. 4–5). He argued that since the organism is in constant relations with the environment, that organism is in a constant process of adapting to that environment in order to maintain equilibrium between what is within and pressures from without. Furthermore, "adaptation is an equilibrium between assimilation and accommodation" (p. 6). This process of adaptation involves a balancing and re-balancing within the organizational structures of intelligence through incorporating new knowledge into existing structures (assimilation) and changing existing mental structures to incorporate new knowledge (accommodation).

If assimilation occurs when the pressures on the outside (i.e., in the environment) coordinate with or match the structures and organization the organism has constructed on the inside (i.e., mental schema and structures), the environmental elements can be incorporated into the existing structures, or what is known by the child already. For example, if a child is introduced to a dog that is larger than any dog she or he has encountered in the past, but it still meets the child's schema for dog (has four legs, wags tail, barks), the new knowledge can be incorporated into what he or she already knows. On the other hand, if the environment does not match the child's mental structures, a process called accommodation must occur. If accommodation is the result of pressure by the environment for the organism to change, when the child encounters a cow for the first time, his or her notion of dog doesn't fit any more; although the cow has four legs and fur, it has other attributes that do not match the dog's (i.e., it moos instead of barks, it moves differently, it has a peculiar smell). In order to accommodate to the new environmental information, a child must accommodate internal structures and create a new structure or schema for "cow."

Thus, one of the most important concepts contributing to the construction of knowledge is the process of equilibrium, and its inverse, disequilibrium. The pressure to stay in equilibrium between the environment and mental structures is the engine that drives learning, or, in Piaget's (1962) words, intelligence.

Conservation

Arguably one of the most important logical operations in Piaget's theory is the notion of conservation. In its simplest terms, conservation is the understanding that elements that look or appear different are really equal or the same. The famous example of two balls of clay or two vessels of water when transformed in front of a child are thought by a preoperational child to be different amounts when they look different because of their shape or configuration. Piagetian theory explains this by arguing that the child does not keep the image of the original shapes of clay or water in mind and lets the new appearances override the original image. In other words, the child does not conserve the image or notion that the two items are the same when they are changed in shape, even though it occurs right in front of him or her.

Conservation is germane throughout logic, from the notion of equality (e.g., 2 + 2 = 4) in simple mathematical operations to transformations of ideas at the most abstract levels. Conservation cannot be rushed, but is constructed gradually as the child matures and extends experiences with multiple objects. When asked about the "American question" of whether conservation can be taught at earlier ages, Piaget replied, "to accelerate the learning of conservation concepts could be even worse than doing nothing" (Hall, 1987, p. 31).

A child who uses egocentric thought focuses on one viewpoint or one way of solving a problem that may have multiple solutions. A child who is pretending to read a book to his or her "class" and holds it so that only he or she can see the illustrations exhibits egocentrism and does not account for the angle from which others are viewing the book. The child who reasons that there is only one way to classify a bowl of fruit, such as by color, is only considering one solution to the question, "Can you sort the fruit into piles that are alike?" Egocentrism is not selfishness, but it is the natural way in which young children see the world from their singular point of view.

Piaget would never argue that the environment is not important to learning logical operations such as conservation. Importantly, it is the child's interactions with the environment that creates the disequilibrium within the child's thinking and provokes him or her to progress to more accurate conclusions. The four-year-old child who argued that the balls of clay or vessels of water were different amounts when they appeared in different shapes, would be 100% sure that these same objects are the same when confronted with the same problem two years later. What has happened in the meantime? How did the child learn this simple form of conservation to such a high degree of assuredness? A Piagetian would argue that it was the interactions between the child and the environment, coupled with the constant striving for equilibrium between the two, that propelled the child to a more sophisticated application of logical reasoning so that the internal structures matched the external realities. This is accommodation and assimilation in action, which is the only way these two processes develop and adapt.

Moral Development

Although he is not as well known for his theory of moral development, Piaget's extensive research and copious notations of children interacting with each other, particularly in play and games, spawned other research and theories on moral development (e.g., Kohlberg, DeVries, Selman, Damon, Corsaro). Piaget, in collaboration with others, including his wife, Valentine, documented children's understanding of rules in *The Moral Judgment of the Child* (1932/1965). They argued that, "children's games constitute the most admirable social institution. ... a jurisprudence of its own" (p. 1). Further, "all morality consists in a system of rules" (p. 1).

When interviewed at the age of 73 by Elizabeth Hall, Piaget maintained that children progress from accepting rules as given, which he called heteronomous reasoning, to moving toward basing rules on cooperation and mutual reciprocity, which he called autonomous reasoning (Hall, 1987). As children become less egocentric and focused less on their own perspective, they start to take the viewpoints, intentions, and rights of others into consideration. One of the main activities that propel children to move from heteronomous to autonomous reasoning is engaging in playful activities with peers. As children negotiate the rules of play, try to explain their own rights and perspectives, and coordinate their actions with others in order for the play to progress, they are learning the fundamentals of social engagement. In Piaget's words, they reach "a cooperation that liberates individuals from their practical egocentrism and introduces a new and more immanent conception of rules" (1932/1965, p. 76). More applications of Piagetian theory to children's play are presented in the next section of this chapter.

Implications for Early Childhood Educators

Piagetian theory can be applied to the education of all learners, but this section will focus on learners between the ages of birth to eight years, the domain of most early childhood professionals. This emphasis is not meant to downplay the work of Piaget for older learners, which has interesting and important applications as well, but the foundation for all later learning is laid in the early learning experiences, and, for the sake of staying within the parameters of a single chapter, the younger years will be the focus here.

Teaching in accordance with Piagetian theory is predicated on one main assumption: the learner is an active agent in his or her own learning. In other words, all teaching must allow the child to be an active constructor of the knowledge being addressed. On the surface, this seems simple; but in reality, it can mean major changes in the way we educate young children. When defining active learning, it does not mean that the children are always physically active, although with younger children this is probably the case. Active learning means that the child is active mentally as he or she questions, experiments, postulates, tries out new ideas, and changes existing ideas. The challenge for teachers is to provoke and encourage these mental activities by the way the environment is arranged, the time allowed for active explorations, opportunities to work with peers, types of questions posed by adults, and other teaching strategies employed.

Teaching Toward the "Big Ideas"

One of the important implications of Piagetian theory is that logical operations cannot be memorized or taught in a direct way, but that is not to say that they are not learned. A teacher's approach is to teach *toward* the processes and operations, acknowledging that learning is a process not a product. As learners construct more logical ways of ordering and organizing their thoughts, they often go "two steps forward and one step backward" as they progress. For example, a five-year-old may be able to classify shoes into categories such as "ties," "Velcro," and "no fasteners," but when asked if there are more shoes or shoes with ties, replies that there are more shoes with ties. Thus, the child is using some logic in classification, but not so when asked to put the classifications into a hierarchy where one class includes the smaller class. This type of hierarchical reasoning might not appear until six months or a year later. Constructivist teachers continue to present multiple experiences with classifying objects and provoking questions as they teach toward the big idea of classification along multiple dimensions and with a variety of materials. One of the challenges for teachers is to withhold judgment of the children's pre-logical answers, knowing that these are important and expected phases in the construction of knowledge, and, at the same time, provide just the right dose of disequilibrium that will propel the child's thinking and questioning.

Reflecting back to the three types of knowledge as defined in the last section of this chapter, early childhood educators who differentiate instruction according to the type of knowledge they are addressing will naturally teach toward the big ideas. If the focus of instruction is numbers and numerals, the instructional strategies must include at least two types of knowledge: logico-mathematical knowledge in the form of number sense, that is the relationships between and among numbers, and the social-conventional knowledge that includes the culturally determined sign for the numerals and their names. For example, if a child understands the number "five" then she or he will know that five ants is the same number as five elephants, even though one appears to be much larger. Understanding numbers is what Kamii (2013) calls the "mental relationship human beings construct from within" (p. 60). This deeper understanding of numbers would be the logico-mathematical big idea that teachers teach toward. Within the realm of social conventional knowledge, the English word for "five" and the sign used to denote five is 5. Both of these concepts are important for understanding and communicating about numbers and numerals, but they are culturally determined. Other cultures use different words (e.g., *cinco*) and signs (e.g., V). Unfortunately, teachers often focus on the social-conventional aspects of numbers, mainly the names and symbolic representations of the number, without ensuring that the children understand the logico-mathematical knowledge crucial to the concepts.

In the area of science and scientific concepts, physical knowledge plays a crucial part. As children experiment with elements of the physical world from the time they are very young and drop their rattle and hear the clank it produces upon hitting the floor, they are taking in physical knowledge directly through their senses. Piagetian theory argues that the source of physical knowledge is the objects themselves, so the child must have ample opportunities to explore objects surrounding him. The child drops the rattle, then food, and anything else put in front of him or her, each time experiencing a different sound upon impact with the floor. Keeping safety in mind, early childhood teachers can provide these direct sensory experiences by providing multiple objects and opportunities for children both indoors and outdoors. Perhaps it was from Montessori's influence that Piaget stressed the "sensorimotor" experiences that dominate the first two years of life and formulate the basis of intelligence that cannot be overemphasized for all later intelligence. And, as Piaget argued, learners return to earlier modes of learning as they get more sophisticated in their thinking but confront new problems or new materials. Even older children must explore new objects and formulate physical knowledge directly through their senses if they have not had prior experiences with the objects. It is only through direct experience that learners can then move away from the concrete and on to symbolically representing these experiences in words, pictures, symbols, signs, ideas, and so forth. For example, reading about snow and looking at photos of snowy landscapes is not sufficient for a child raised in the tropics to understand the physical characteristics of snow. The teacher must figure out a way to bring snow into the child's direct experience, perhaps by making snow with a snow cone machine or something similar. The children need to stick their hands into the snow, taste it on their tongues, and watch it melt in their warm palms. Only then they can relate to a story about a snowman.

The Importance of Play

One of the most important messages of Piagetian theory for teachers of young children is the importance of play for all areas of development. Piaget spent countless hours watching and recording children's play behaviors from infancy into adolescence. He based many of his experiments on playfully and purposefully manipulating objects within the infant's grasp and observing the reactions, particularly with his own three children (Piaget, 1952/1963; 1954/1971/1986). His copious notes on the infants' reactions led to further experiments and hypotheses about what the children were thinking as they reacted to environmental manipulations. Later, when the children were able to reflect upon their behavior and thinking, he and his team of researchers interviewed children about their play. As described earlier, these interviews led to his theory of moral development that included children's ideas of the origin and application of rules, distribution of justice, and more.

Piaget contended that children learn different concepts when they play with peers as compared to when they play with adults. Peers are their contemporaries and equals on the power hierarchy, so they learn about reciprocity or mutuality in their play interactions with peers. A child who would never dare take an object from an adult would be more prone to do so from another child. The child who has had an object taken is going to react with "mine" and perhaps a physical tug-of-war over the object. This small but common interaction teaches the perpetrator that the other child has rights and claims over the object which he or she has violated. Thus, the perpetrator and the victim have learned an important lesson of reciprocity: others have rights and violators of these rights will hear about it in no uncertain terms. With multiple peer interactions, particularly the types that occur in peer play, the children begin to construct an understanding of not only the rules of social behavior, but the reasons for these rules. As children begin to engage in games with rules, which at first is rather unsuccessful for the egocentric child of four or five years old, they move from the notion that the rules are given by a higher authority (Piaget noted this for seven- and eight-year-olds) (Piaget, 1932/1965) to an understanding that rules are essential for the game to continue and can be negotiated by the players if all agree (Piaget noted this among young adolescents) (Piaget, 1932/1965). Piaget called the notion that rules are unalterable and given by a higher authority, heteronomous reasoning. He called the later-appearing concept of rules being mutually agreed upon and important for maintaining social order, autonomous reasoning based on cooperation (Piaget, 1932/1965).

As early childhood educators, the "big idea" to teach toward is the more sophisticated autonomous reasoning. This is not to say that the teacher needs to usurp authority because that would lead to chaos in the classroom. This is to argue that children need safe contexts within which to practice the skills of negotiation and compromise. These opportunities are inherent in children's play with peers.

The Role of the Teacher in a Piagetian Classroom

According to Piagetian theory, constructivist teachers are co-constructors in an early childhood classroom. They are learners as much as the children. In their role as teachers/learners, they orchestrate a setting that allows for multiple concrete experiences that are planned to provoke children's learning. The setting is full of choice, time for peer play and interactions, stimulating and challenging materials, and lots of encouragement from the adults. Rather than only concentrating on their methods, teachers focus on each child's learning in order to determine the best teaching strategies. When designing best teaching strategies, the teachers consider the type of knowledge addressed, the big ideas and processes to teach toward, the child's prior experiences, culture, and mental structures, among other factors, then determines the best materials and experiences to meet all of the above. Teachers are active processors just like the children. The level of activity is high, but it is planned and orchestrated to help the children construct new concepts in meaningful ways. A constructivist classroom always has a healthy hum as teachers and children move about, interacting with each other and the materials provided. Much of the instruction occurs in small groups and individually, yet there is a time and place for large group meetings and instruction as well. Children's work spaces in the form of tables, floor, and desks, are movable and arranged according to the planned activities. Spaces for children to play with blocks, pretend play themes, art media, science and nature specimens, books, writing materials, and other hands-on materials abound in a constructivist setting. The schedule is predictable yet flexible, with both indoor and outdoor activities on a daily basis.

In order to provide a constructivist classroom, teachers have a variety of items in their toolboxes. These tools include the materials they provide, the questions they ask, and the inclusion of peers in the teaching of new concepts. Each of these will be addressed in more detail.

Materials

To constructivist teachers, exploration and experimentation with concrete materials is essential for the emerging development of a child, especially the young child. But this exploration and experimentation is more than just random manipulation of objects. It is full of thought, prediction, hypothesizing, and testing ideas by manipulating controllable variables. Interacting with objects progresses from fortuitous or accidental to planned and purposeful as a child becomes more sophisticated in his or her thinking. In one of his last interviews, Piaget pushed for schooling that involved more experimentation in the scientific sense when asked how he would change schools (Hall, 1987). Children are natural experimenters as they try to figure out the workings of the world around them. Teachers who share this same curiosity about the world engage the child in joint investigations of whatever interests the child. If the child is fascinated by the caterpillar she or he watched closely on the playground, an investigation of caterpillars and butterflies can teach toward the big ideas of life cycles, habitats, camouflage, and other concepts that can be found in many topics of biology. And it all started with one child's interest in the woolly caterpillar on the playground.

Constructivist teachers approach the materials provided in the curriculum knowing that experiences with real objects must precede representations of these objects such as models, videos, photos, words, and the like. These more symbolic media work when the child has already had direct experiences upon which to build. In other words, a child who has had the experience of having a butterfly swoop past or land on a finger, can relate to a photo of a butterfly because the mental structures that allow him or her to bring meaning to the photographic representation of a butterfly have developed internally. So as much as possible, the constructivist teacher "keeps it real."

Authentic Questions

Authentic questions are queries to which the teacher does not already know the answer. For example, if a teacher holds up an orange and asks the children what color it is, the correct answer is orange. This is a convergent question that has one right answer, and the teacher already knows that answer. Many questions that teachers ask fall into this category. The teachers know the answers and the children must match their answer in order to be correct. There is definitely a time and place for convergent questions, especially if the knowledge in focus is social-conventional knowledge because the children must memorize the culturally determined names of colors, quantities, and letters. Yet there is a very different type of question that teachers often forget to ask. These questions, often called authentic questions, seek the child's perspective. For example, instead of asking what the color name for the orange object is, the teacher can ask what other things are the same color as the selected object. The children have a range of answers that would be acceptable (pumpkins, macaroni and cheese, carrots) and the teacher does not know what the children are going to say. In the interaction about all of the possibilities, the color word for orange is used naturally in a meaningful context. The question provokes much more thinking on the part of the children, as they have to engage logico-mathematical thinking in order to compare all objects to the orange object and those that fall within the parameters of what culture designates as "orange."

A simple rule to keep in mind for teachers is to ask themselves, "Do I already know the answer to this question?" If so, they can try to think of an alternative way to ask the question so that there is more than one right answer and they don't know what that will be. This makes the Q/A sessions that prevail in classrooms much more interesting and thought-provoking than convergent, low level questioning. A culture of joint problem solving emerges as children and teachers ask each other meaningful, authentic questions throughout the day.

Peers

One of the best tools in a constructivist teacher's toolbox is the other children. Whenever there is a class full of children, there will be a range of logical reasoning, vocabulary development, perspectives, and more. Teachers who welcome this range and plan for it in the daily curriculum will expand the teaching staff many times over as the other children become members of the team. When children play together, question each other, argue over small and large issues, they are cross-referencing their own thinking with that of others. This is something teachers cannot offer by nature of the power differential between adults and children. Piaget recognized the essential role of peers, especially in his theory of moral development. The challenge for teachers is to build ways into the curriculum so that children can work and play together.

Communicating with Others about Constructivist Methods

Although constructivist theory is not new, it looks much different than traditional approaches to education. Many adults picture a classroom as neatly arranged desks facing the front of the room where the teacher has a desk. Even with more technology integrated into the classrooms, this physical arrangement is static in most adults' minds and memories. When working with adults, an illuminating exercise is to ask each adult to draw a picture of a classroom. Most will draw the traditional arrangement described above. The ensuing discussion of their drawings can bring forth deeply ingrained notions of what classrooms look like, which is a launching point for discussions of what classrooms of today should look like.

But to communicate effectively about constructivist approaches, active engagement must be involved. If at all possible, engaging adults in a learning experience that is active, full of peer interactions, and provokes new ways of knowing can be very effective. Asking parents to play with blocks, experiment with bubbles, look at objects with a projecting microscope, and other such activities, allows them to experience the curiosity and awe that their children experience. Inviting others to visit the constructivist classroom and participate in activities with the children works well, too. Documenting the children's learning with photos, quotes, and video can communicate the types of learning when words fall short. Thus, just as teaching is more than telling, communicating with other adults about constructivist methods needs to involve more than talk. It needs to include direct experiences with real objects.

Conclusion

Piaget's ideas about how children learn and the nature of knowledge started a paradigm shift in the way educators and psychologists look at children. No longer are children regarded as rote learners who memorize a predetermined set of facts and skills. Rather, children are respected as active constructors of knowledge who act upon their environment as much as or more than the environment acts on them. Learning is an active process that occurs from the inside–out rather than outside–in as children bring meaning to their experiences and thinking in a purposeful, somewhat predictable way along the planes of development that Piaget so richly described through his extensive research and incomparable ability to learn from the children of his research, especially his own offspring.

As with all solid theories, the ideas that Piaget proposed are actively evolving and adapting as researchers and practitioners discover more about the workings of the brain and its enormous capacity for creative, adaptive functioning. Yet the uncanny ability that Piaget had to unite theories from multiple fields—from biology to psychology to philosophy—and apply the ideas to child development and learning is unmatched in its effect on early childhood education and the way early childhood educators view children and their learning.

References

Beilin, H. (1992). Piaget's enduring contribution to developmental psychology. *Developmental Psychology, 28*, 191–204. http://dx.doi.org/10.1037/0012-1649.28.2.191

Bennour, M. & Voneche, J. (2009). The historical context of Piaget's ideas. In U. Muller, J.I.M. Carpendale, & L. Smith (Eds.), *The Cambridge companion to Piaget*. New York: Cambridge University Press.

Fosnot, C.T., & Perry, R.S. (2005). Constructivism: A psychological theory of learning. In C.T. Fosnot (Ed.), *Constructivism: Theory, perspectives, and practice* (2nd ed.). New York: Teachers College Press.

Hall, E. (1987). *Growing and changing: What the experts say*. New York: Random House.

Kamii, C. (2013). Physical-knowledge activities: Play before the differentiation of knowledge into subjects. In L.E. Cohen & S. Waite-Stupiansky (Eds.), *Learning across the early childhood curriculum*. Advances in Early Education and Day Care (Volume 17). UK: Emerald Group Publishing.

Kamii, C. (2014). The importance of thinking: Direct vs. indirect understanding of number concepts for ages 4–6. *Young Children, 69*(5), 72–77. Available at www.naeyc.org

Muller, U., Carpendale, J.I.M., & Smith, L. (2009). Introduction: Overview. In U. Muller, L.I.M. Carpendale, & L. Smith (Eds.) *The Cambridge companion to Piaget*. New York: Cambridge University Press.

Piaget, J. (1932/1965). *The moral judgment of the child*. Glencoe, IL: The Free Press.

Piaget, J. (1947/1950). *The psychology of intelligence*. London: Routledge and Kegan Paul.

Piaget, J. (1952/1963). *Origins of intelligence in children*. New York: W.W. Norton.

Piaget, J. (1954/1971/1986). *The construction of reality in the child*. New York: Ballantine Books.

Piaget, J. (1962). *Play, dreams, and imitation in childhood*. New York: W.W. Norton.

Piaget, J., & Inhelder, B. (1969). *The psychology of the child*. New York: Basic Books.

Voyat, G. (1980/2011). Interview with Jean Piaget: Translation, appendix, notes, and references by Leslie Smith. Retrieved from www.fondationjeanpiaget.ch

Waite-Stupiansky, S. (1997). *Building understanding together: A constructivist approach to early childhood education*. Albany, NY: Delmar.

Suggested Websites

www.foundationjeanpiaget.ch
www.piaget.org
www.tasplay.org
www.museumofplay.cog
www.naeyc.org

2

MARIA MONTESSORI

Yesterday, Today, and Tomorrow

Phyllis Povell

Biographical Background

On August 31, 1870, Maria Tecla Artemisia Montessori, now known as Maria Montessori for the method of education she developed, was born in Chiaravalle, Italy, to Alessandro Montessori and the former Renilde Stoppani.

After his military service and five years of employment in the finance department of the Papal State, Alessandro Montessori began working in the salt and tobacco industry, where he quickly rose to a management position. In 1865, his promotion required a transfer to Chiaravalle, a small tobacco growing town, where he met Renilde Stoppani, a cultured and well-read woman whose passion was for autonomy and a united Italy. Similar beliefs bonded them, and they were married in the spring of 1866. In 1867, he was reassigned to Venice and subsequently back to Chiaravalle in 1869, where the couple awaited the birth of their daughter. The first five years of Maria's life were spent in this small town by the sea, until 1875, when her father had to relocate his family. This time it was to Rome.

At this time, Italy had only been unified for fourteen years. Geographically and religiously, Italy had always been one country, but politically it was composed of many separate entities. Ten years after the unification of Italy, which took place on March 17, 1861, the Italian capital was moved to Rome and the Risorgimento (resurgence) was complete. Yet, there was still much work to be done to bring together the disparate factions in Italy. One of the most important pieces was a national educational system to give its population a sense of nationalism and a similar cultural outlook. Fortunately, this new national system would provide greater educational opportunities for Maria.

The Casati Law of 1859, which made four years of education compulsory, was later extended by Education Minister Baccelli to enable girls to attend *liceo* (high school) and technical institutes. When Maria was thirteen years old, she showed an interest in mathematics and chose to go to a technical institute with only one other girl. Legend tells of their harassment by the boys and the necessity to isolate them during recess. Maria did not seem to be discouraged by these annoyances and later enrolled in the Leonardo da Vinci Technical Institute for her secondary studies. She could not attend the classical high school because of her lack of the classical prerequisites. She graduated in 1890 with a newly found desire to attend medical school.

There are many tales of her efforts to attend medical school which include her rejection by Dr. Guido Baccelli, professor of clinical medicine, to whom she responded, "I know I will become a doctor" (Povell, 2009, p. 42). Another tale alludes to the intervention of the pope on her behalf; while a third version talks about another religious figure who made it possible for her to study Greek and Latin behind a hidden bookcase so as not to distract the seminarians. This third account may be the most accurate since her mother's brother, Antonio Stoppani, was a scholar-priest at the University of Milan, and he may have intervened to allow her to complete the courses she lacked for entrance to medical school. Much of the research for the biographical background of Montessori and its documentation can be found in my book, *Montessori Comes to America: The Leadership of Maria Montessori and Nancy McCormick Rambusch* (2009).

Montessori entered the university as a part-time student for two years, which enabled her to complete the medical school entrance requirements. In 1892, she began her course of study at the University of Rome Medical School. She graduated in 1896, and was among a handful of women doctors in Italy. Many biographies, both for adults and children, credit her as being the first woman doctor in Italy. My previous research indicates otherwise:

> In 1877, Ernestine Paper of Florence was the first woman to become a physician after the unification of Italy, followed by Velleda Maria Farni from the University of Turin in 1878. In 1882, Osmilda Ferraresi earned the degree in Medicine and Surgery at the University of Modena. Succeeding them were Giuseppina Cattani in 1884 at the University of Bologna and then Avalle Paola in Cristoforis from Cagliari University a year later. Two women graduated from the University of Rome Medical School, Edvige Benigni in 1890 and four years later Marcellina Corio Viola, in 1894. One year before Montessori received her medical degree yet another woman, Deco Afra, earned her degree at the University of Parma. Two more women graduated as doctors the same year as Montessori, Emilia Concornotti from Pavia and Adelina Rossi from Turin.
>
> (Povell, 2009, pp. 30–31)

But although it appears that many women were graduating with medical degrees in Italy at this time, this was not really the case. From the time of the first woman who graduated until the beginning of the twentieth century, there were only twenty-four who graduated with a degree in medicine (Rava, 1902).

The decade in which Montessori was in medical school was an exhilarating one worldwide. The importance of childhood was recognized, as were the fields of anthropology, hygiene, and pedagogy which were being researched all over Europe and the United States. Education became the new word of the times, and it was seen as a method of strengthening the body and the mind of children of the future. Later, Montessori would call this period "The Discovery of Childhood" (Montessori, 1976).

Her four years in medical school were greatly influenced by her liberal professors, who were attracted by the new sciences. Their interest lay in what they termed "degenerate" children. Professors Molischott and Celli introduced new ideas to Montessori at a time when she was just beginning to formulate her own professional philosophy. Babini described the 1870s as the:

> years that medicine begins to claim for itself the ability and the competence to enlarge its own field of intervention to the point that it would actually promote a kind of physical, moral and social regeneration of the young Italian state.
>
> (Babini & Lama, 2000, p. 37)

Professor Moliscott was one of the faculty who influenced Montessori's studies. His lectures focused on the new discipline of social medicine, which targeted the conditions of life in the lower classes. This same interest was expressed by Professor Celli in experimental hygiene, who believed diseases such as tuberculosis and malaria could be eliminated from the lower classes. These two men also took a very active role in their commitment to schools, children, and the equality of women. Their passion and sense of obligation to this community came at a time when the young Montessori was prone to these liberal ideas.

These beliefs led her to serve as an intern at the university's psychiatric clinic, where she encountered Professor Bonfigli, who also took an interest in social medicine and the development of children's moral sense and character, all ideas which resonated with Montessori. It was here that she collected data for her dissertation on antagonistic hallucinations. She could have chosen to study pediatrics or gynecology, fields that might have been more hospitable to women, but she had been predisposed to these ideas by her professors and it appears she wanted to work closer to Giuseppe Montesano, who was working at the same clinic. Their interests were compatible as were they. They published articles together on an equal basis, which was an impressive occurrence for a woman at that time. In 1898 they established a group called Per la Donna (For the Woman), whose mission was for collaboration between men and women in both the scientific and social fields.

Giuseppe and Montessori were attuned to each other intellectually, socially, politically, and intimately. From this relationship, a son, Mario, was born on March 31, 1898. After his birth, he was sent to live in the countryside with a wet nurse until he was 12 years old. The couple never married, and anecdotes suggest they swore undying love for each other and promised never to marry anyone else. Some authors claim Giuseppe's mother was against the marriage because Maria was not the kind of woman she wanted for her son. I contend that Maria chose not to marry because she did not want to let down her mother, who encouraged her to be more than she had been: an intellectual housewife. It does not seem coincidental that after her mother's death Montessori took Mario to live with her. They became collaborators in the Montessori Method for the rest of their lives.

Another plausible explanation is mentioned by Fellini, who suggests that this was a time of free unions between lovers (as cited in Babini & Lama, 2000, pp. 108–109). Maria had previously lectured on "the unions of love and collaboration as a means of power. This momentous decision to give up her son was the 'watershed of her life'" (Povell, 2009, p. 50). She believed social progress depended on women's emancipation, and this conviction was bolstered by her own educational struggles and successes. The decisions she made enabled her to overcome the vast restrictions put on a woman in Italy just prior to the turn of the twentieth century.

In addition to her interest in medical reform, Montessori began to focus on feminist issues. Prior to her graduation in March, 1896, the feminist organization Associazione Femminile di Roma was established in Rome with Maria serving as its vice-secretary.

The mission of this group was to not only inspire women to stand together but to urge them to follow their own roles in society.

Germany, also, was forming numerous women's organizations. In 1896, the Association for Women's Weal, one of the more active groups, decided to hold an international women's conference at the Berlin Exposition called "Women's Achievements and Women's Endeavors," to which Montessori was an invited speaker from Italy. She was supported by Italian women of all social strata and by the aforenamed Roman association in her efforts to raise money to attend. She spoke to various groups of women at this meeting. One of her major speeches centered on the horrific working conditions for women and children. In another she implored the attendees to address the issue of equal pay for equal work by women, an issue which is still important to women today.

Two years later, she spoke at the first Italian Pedagogical Conference in Turin where she discussed the concept of the blending of pedagogy and medicine with specific reference to children with disabilities, a topic which she would repeat for many years. To further this theme, she published an article entitled "Social Poverty and the New Discoveries in Science." Concurrently, she was working with Professor Bonfigli to found the National League for the Education and Care of the Mentally Retarded, which would become a formal organization in January 1899, six months after the conclusion of the Turin conference.

Montessori continued to research further in this field, and she traveled to the Bourneville Institute in Paris where she observed Seguin and Itard working with children with mental challenges. By the end of the same year Baccelli, Italy's minister of education, asked her to lecture to three teacher training schools in Rome in order to urge all school boards to provide schooling for children with special needs.

At the same time, she continued on the lecture circuit with a series of four presentations in Italy entitled, "The New Woman," in which she appealed to women to pursue scientific thinking using their brains, not their hearts, to argue. In her next talk at a feminist congress in London, Montessori revisited the theme of prohibiting children under fourteen from working in the mines.

Montessori was not all talk. Some of her accomplishments include: "sanitariums for women with tuberculosis, colonies in the Apennines for convalescing children, laboratories for poor mothers, centers for abandoned children, and institutions and separate classrooms for children with mental disabilities" (Povell, 2009, pp. 42–43). Her busy life was filled with her medical practice, her volunteer hospital service, and her work with the National League for Retarded Children; yet she found time to serve as a lecturer in hygiene and anthropology at a teacher training college for women. This experience would give her practical knowledge of the pedagogical curriculum which she would utilize in later years.

In 1900, she accepted an appointment as co-director with Montesano, at the Orthophrenic School, a teacher training demonstration site, to work with children with mental disabilities. Here, she developed her program of scientific observation, based on the work of Wundt and the hands-on and sensory methods of Seguin and Itard, to teach orphan children. Much of the literature has deemed that the children with whom she worked were "idiots." We cannot be certain that these children had mental retardation. They may have been sensorially deprived, under-fed, and under-stimulated, and perhaps some did have some mental problems. While taking courses in pedagogy at the University of Rome, Montessori worked with these children for over a year using sensory materials, and many were able to pass the Italian state national exams for entrance into the schools. In 1901, Giuseppe Montesano married Maria Aprile, and Montessori left the Orthophrenic School, ending one chapter in her life and moving on to the next where she continued to write and lecture and promote feminist causes. In 1906, she, along with other social feminists, petitioned a number of Italian cities for the right of women to vote.

The beginning of the new century witnessed many efforts worldwide to assist the poor and indigent. The United States and Great Britain saw the rise of settlement houses to educate and train this population for integration into their societies. Italy began a project of building tenement houses to provide better living conditions for the poor working class. Eduardo Talamo, an engineer and philanthropist, built a large housing project in the San Lorenzo district of Rome. He believed that all people, regardless of their economic status, should have clean living arrangements. Among the tenants were at least 50 children between the ages of three and seven who were not yet attending public schools, and, out of necessity, many of their mothers were working. Talamo feared that if these children were left unattended, they might damage the new building.

After speaking with Ernesto Nathan, the mayor of Rome and the husband of one of Montessori's friends, Talamo learned of the success Montessori had achieved at the Orthophrenic School with the orphan children, so he invited her to set up a school in the new tenement. She agreed and established the Casa dei Bambini, or Children's House, which would become the first full-day child care center in Italy, opening on January 6, 1907.

Theoretical Concepts Related to Early Childhood

Maria Montessori was excited to work with this population of children and to be able to apply the ideals and philosophy she had developed during her medical school lectures and internships. She came to this task with a fresh perspective on how children learn rather than a specific method, which would later evolve from her observations of the children.

In her inaugural address upon the opening of the first Casa, Montessori proclaimed:

> In quarters where poverty and vice ruled, a work of moral redemption is going on. The soul of the people is being set free. ... The little children too have a "House" of their own. The new generation goes forward to meet the new era, the time when misery shall no longer be deplored but destroyed.
>
> (Montessori, 1964, p. 48)

Her medical background, her understanding of the scientific method, and her belief that the environment was crucial in the development of the child, coalesced to produce a distinctive educational theory, which was a child-centered method with new responsibilities for both teacher and child.

Immersed in the literature of her time, and the methods of Sergi, Itard, Seguin, and multiple other sources, she came to the conclusion that the current systematized training of teachers should be rejected. Guided by this belief, she named a directress rather than a teacher of her first Casa dei Bambini. The role of the directress was to prepare an environment, to observe, and to have the confidence and patience that the inner life of the child would be released through his or her work. She held the belief that a teacher should honor the child's motto of "help me to help myself."

Researchers and educators around the world heard of Montessori's success in the Casa and large numbers of them arrived in Rome wanting to see these children for themselves. This unprecedented response led Montessori to set up teacher training courses in a number of European cities, and soon Montessori schools began to open in cities across Europe and the United States.

Although Montessori schools continued to thrive around the world, she did not rest but continued her research beyond the ideas of the initial psychologists and theorists which had been the foundation of her method. In particular, one area she explored was periods of growth. She was aware that growth does not occur in a linear fashion, but in stages, which she named "planes of development." She divided the first plane into ages birth to six with a sub-category of birth to three. The next plane was six to twelve, followed by twelve to eighteen and eighteen to twenty-four, the age of maturity. Grazzini writes that these are only a framework and yet are extremely significant because "it is Montessori's overall view of development: the development of the individual from birth (or even before birth) right through maturity." He continues, "[it is] a *holistic* view of the developing human being and it explains and justifies the constant Montessori idea of the importance of education as a *help to life*" (Grazzini, 1996, pp. 27–28). Educational reform, Montessori contended, must be grounded in the personality of the person at all stages of development.

Montessori described the period between birth and three as the unconscious absorbent mind in which the child takes in stimuli from his or her environment and explores objects, ideas, and language, and she considered this stage as one which had "an intense and specialised [British spelling] sensitiveness in consequence of which the things about him awaken so much interest and so much enthusiasm that they become incorporated in his very existence" (Montessori, 1967, p. 23). She concluded that the child absorbs these imprints into his or her everyday experiences of life.

In the following sub-plane, from three to six years old, the child, who is now in the period of the conscious absorbent mind, is fascinated with organizing and ordering all of his or her prior knowledge. Montessori trusted that the arrangement and progression of her prepared environment coupled with an observing adult would provide the foundation for this transformation to occur. Unlike general education, which proceeds in a linear fashion, "Montessori education alters with each plane in the child's development. In this way, each stage serves as a solid foundation upon which the next may be built" (Lillard, 1996, p. 21).

Montessori wrote, "The education of our day is rich in methods, aims and social ends, but one must still say that it takes no account of life itself" (Montessori, 1967, p. 8). She believed that one of the first steps in enabling children to discover and experience the world around them is to allow them to move about freely, as opposed to being trapped like butterflies on a board. She understood that movement was a major component of learning, unlike the existing schools of the beginning of the twentieth century. She wrote, "in our new conception the view is taken that movement has great importance in mental development itself, provided that the action which occurs is connected with the mental activity going on. ... Mind and movement are parts of the same entity" (cited in Lillard, 2005, p. 40).

Freely moving about has been mistaken for unruly behavior. Montessori explained the difference. She writes, "We call an individual disciplined when he is master of himself, and can, therefore, regulate his own conduct ... Since the child learns to *move* rather than to *sit still*, he prepares himself not for the school, but for life" (Montessori, 1964, pp. 86–87). This concept is referred to today as self-regulation.

Montessori modified the environment to fit the child rather than the reverse. Child-sized furniture was substituted for the over-sized nailed-down desks and benches that were typical of classrooms at the turn of the century. Montessori designed and manufactured all of the wooden furniture which she felt would be more durable; and although the idea of furniture which is made to fit the child is commonplace today, this was not the case when she introduced these for her classrooms.

Montessori prepared the environment with specially designed and sequenced learning materials. Her belief that children learned best in an ordered setting resulted in an organized classroom set up "both physically in terms of layout and conceptually in terms of how the use of materials progresses" (Lillard, 2005, p. 33). Lillard concludes that Montessori was right on track with today's research on order and its influence on children's learning.

Originally, the materials were stored in easy to open cabinets and were distributed by the teacher and replaced there by her. Shortly thereafter, a teacher recognized that the children wished to replace the materials by themselves. Then one day when the teacher appeared in the classroom a little late, she discovered that the children had already taken the materials and begun to work with them. The teacher considered this to be theft, but Montessori "interpreted the incident as a sign that the children now knew the objects so well that they could make their own choice" (Montessori, 1966, p. 147). Thus began the use of low, open shelves for easy access by the children.

Within these orderly surroundings, children are given the freedom to choose their own learning materials, as opposed to the traditional classroom where the teacher decides what the children will learn and when they will learn it. The children's ability to choose, within boundaries set by the directress who has shown them how to use a particular material, enables them to gain greater freedoms as they learn to control their inner and outer selves. Current research details how children who are involved in a particular area of interest tend to pursue in greater depth the curriculum areas they are studying as opposed to subjects prescribed by the teacher, the district, the state, or federal government (Lillard, 2005, pp. 114–151).

Montessori developed the materials in the three-to-six-year-old period for multiple purposes. She divided the materials for "physiological and psychological development" into three areas: motor education, sensory education, and language (Montessori, 1965, pp. 49–50). For example, buttoning, lacing, zippering, and snapping frames allow children to become autonomous in their dressing skills but also incorporate the use of fine motor skills required for beginning writing.

Learning by doing is an integral part of a Montessori education. Children are not instructed by the teacher or by textbooks read in unison with the whole class. Materials are provided in the curriculum areas of math, science, geography, language, and music, which are manipulated by the children in the process of their individual learning.

Although the space Montessori was allotted for her initial experimental class was limited, she provided as much of an outdoor area as possible to give the children the freedom to come and go as they wished, all day long. In this setting, using the scientific method of Wilhelm Wundt, now known as the father of modern psychology, she studied the children in their surroundings to determine "*the liberty of the pupils in their spontaneous manifestations*" (Montessori, 1964, p. 80). She visualized a triangle with equal sides: the teacher, the child, and the environment. The outdoor setting where children were able to plant and tend their own gardens gave meaningful context to their learning. They were able to assimilate their knowledge about plants and animals into their prior schemas, thus enhancing their individual knowledge bases.

The same process was applicable in the classroom in the practical life area. Washing tables, watering plants, and making and providing snacks and lunch for all the children have been criticized by some as unnecessary tasks for children. Lillard elaborates on the rationale behind these exercises:

> 1). to educate children's movements to be geared to a purpose; 2). to develop children's ability to concentrate on a task; 3). to help children learn to carry out a series of steps in sequence; 4). to help children learn to care for the environment.
>
> (Lillard, 2005, p. 48)

All of the materials were made to attract the children's interest and engage them in preparation for their daily living. The dressing frames assisted the children in becoming proficient in dressing themselves, eliminating the extra time required by working parents to help them during busy morning routines.

These exercises require deep concentration on the part of the children. Montessori termed their intense involvement in their work "normalization." Paula Lillard (1996) writes, "It is by work that children organize their personalities. ... Adults work to change the environment; children use the environment to change themselves" (p. 42).

The materials permit children to sustain attentiveness in an area of relevance to them. Montessori has written about one child who while working with the wooden cylinders did not notice other children dancing around her and reported that the child's focus was not broken at all by the tumult. This is in direct opposition to the traditional classroom that mandates silence while working. Current research has begun to incorporate a concept called mindfulness into early childhood classrooms and beyond. Lillard explains this idea as a "quality of focused attention on the present moment accompanied by a non-judgmental stance" (Lillard, 1996, p. 78).

Montessori introduced a lesson of silence into her classroom routine. One morning before entering a classroom, she witnessed a woman carrying a sleeping infant. She brought the child into the classroom and told the children she had brought them "a little teacher ... because none of you know how to be as quiet as she does." The children observed and "almost ceased to breathe" (Montessori, 1964, pp. 212–214). Thus, began the silence game, a time of focused attention.

To further develop these periods of intense absorption, Montessori introduced a three-hour cycle of extended learning time built into the program to allow children an uninterrupted stretch to work on a project or material of their choice. This time also permits interaction between peers in a three-year age grouping, facilitating the ability for children to learn from each other. Montessori required multi-age grouping of children into three-year age spans: 3–6 years old, 6–9 years old, and 9–12 years old. Many Montessori programs today have included children of six weeks to three years of age, necessitated by the exceptionally large number of two-parent working families, single-parent homes, homeless children, and many other social situations. These groupings encourage peer learning and imitative learning by the younger children from those slightly older. Children are permitted to observe others in the next multi-age group when they or the teacher find it appropriate for the next stage of learning. Although many activities are completed individually, working in pairs or small groups is definitely promoted.

Unlike traditional schools where the emphasis is on competition and external rewards for completing a task, Montessori believed in peers learning with and from each other. She recognized that children demonstrated greater satisfaction from internal motivation rather than from praise from the teacher. On numerous occasions she observed children demonstrate that they were more interested in completing their work satisfactorily rather than receiving verbal or material rewards from the teacher. Observation also led her to conclude that punishment was an ineffective method of assisting children in their learning. The manner in which she handled a disruptive child was to isolate him or her in a comfortable chair where he or she could observe the class at work. She found this calmed the child, and observation of how the other children proceeded with their work, she felt, was a lesson for the child.

As previously stated, Montessori's method is divided into three parts: motor education, sensory education, and language. She wrote, "The care and management of the environment itself afford the principal means of motor education, while sensory education and the education of language are provided for by my didactic materials" (Montessori, 1965, p. 50). Teacher-directed lessons, to introduce the materials and new concepts when the child is ready, are broken into discrete segments of limited amounts of time in order to hold the child's interest.

Materials such as the pink cubes, brown prisms, sound boxes and musical bells serve to educate and refine the senses. Each sense is isolated to highlight its significant feature in what she termed "auto-education" or self-correcting materials. She posited that development is informed by sensitive periods which appear at various stages, and once they are shaped they disappear and can never be as well refined in an adult.

In 1949, Montessori published *The Absorbent Mind*, in which she wrote of the innate structure of language in infants. This is the same year that Noam Chomsky, the world renowned psycholinguist, was beginning the study of morphophonemics (study of sounds) of the Hebrew language for his undergraduate thesis. It wasn't until the 1960s that Chomsky revealed a similar theory to Montessori's of the predisposition of infants to learn language at specific stages in the developmental process. His theory "rocked the world of psycholinguistics" (Lillard, 2005, p. 34). Today, this idea is accepted by most psychologists, educators, and psycholinguists. Both Montessori's and Chomsky's premises are in direct contrast to B. F. Skinner's belief that language is the result of reinforcement from the environment.

The old term "reading readiness" has been replaced by the idea of "emergent literacy" in the literature. Montessori believed that writing precedes reading in young children and the didactic materials which she prepared for the children led to what she termed "spontaneous writing." The knobs on the cylinders handled by the children with the pincer grip laid the groundwork for holding the pencil. Geometric shapes traced with the fingers and later with colored pencils led to refinement of manipulating the writing instruments. Tracing specially made sandpaper letters of the alphabet in script while naming the sound of the letter enabled the children to not only learn to write but to emerge into reading.

Many of Montessori's ideas and materials have found their way into current early childhood classrooms and have become so imbedded in the curriculum and syllabi that it is almost impossible to distinguish them from good early childhood methods. Unfortunately, mandated state and federal requirements, such as No Child Left Behind, replaced by the Every Student Succeeds Act on December 10, 2015, have focused on basic skills, annual testing, and Adequate Yearly Progress reports, leaving young children pressured to perform at levels which are inappropriate to their planes of development.

The next section will highlight some of Montessori's principles that early childhood educators should concentrate on when advocating for developmentally appropriate curricula for young children to their local, state, and federal officials.

Applying Montessori's Ideas to Early Childhood Today

Many of the outer trappings of Montessori schools have been adopted and adapted to early childhood classrooms today. However, the essence of Montessori's principles has been overlooked in the process. The Casa dei Bambini was the first full day child care center. Today, full day child care can be found in the United States and other countries around the world. Although Montessori specifically called it a house of children, many lay people and educators still term it "day care," rather than child care. Re-emphasizing Montessori's focus on the child would be one step in elevating the importance of the early years to the general public.

In 1896, 120 years ago, Montessori campaigned at the first feminist congress in Berlin for equal pay for equal work. Child care workers are paid the same and perhaps less than fast-food workers today. The majority of the staff at child care centers are women and it is far past time for them to be recognized and paid accordingly, as this would be another step in recognizing their value in working with our most important assets at the most significant plane of development (birth to six years old).

Montessori recommended two nutritious meals a day be fed to the child. She spends an entire chapter in *The Montessori Method* discussing what then were thought to be healthy foods. She had two further recommendations that could be applied to child care centers today: First, a place where sick children could be housed so that the women may go to work when their children needed to be isolated; and second, she advocated for a healthy meal to be given to the working mother at the end of the day so she does not need to prepare dinner after a hard day's work. Both of these suggestions would be advantageous to single parent homes and homes with two working parents or guardians.

Today's early childhood classrooms reflect much of the physical environment found in the first Casa dei Bambini: child-sized furniture, open shelves, replicas of the dressing frames such as Dressy Bessy and Dapper Dan dolls, and the latest Blizzard Penguin with buckling apparatus. The "science behind the genius," however, plays little or no part in the emergent literacy that Montessori so carefully planned: motor skills, large and small, the manipulation of the writing instrument, the sandpaper letters, and the repetition of the sounds necessary for writing and reading. Teachers need to be reminded of the essentials associated with early literacy. Piaget (himself a researcher in Montessori's teacher-training programs and president of the Swiss

Montessori Society), Vygotsky, and other constructivists understood the stages of development so carefully laid out by Montessori. State, federal, and local laws have brought inappropriate reading and writing programs into the early childhood setting and need to be carefully evaluated by teachers who understand the developmental needs and interests of very young children.

Since many child care centers serve children from six weeks old to six years old, Montessori's specific attention to expanding the infant's knowledge and understanding of the world during this period of unconscious absorption, and her concept of multi-age grouping, would work very effectively in these settings. Multi-age grouping would also be applicable in Head Start settings and private nursery schools, as children learning from each other has proven successful.

The outdoor environment in many schools is utilized for running and playing, important activities for the growing child, but careful design can include other areas supportive of children's growth and interests, such as a garden of their own to tend and from this to be able to consume the vegetables at lunch or snack time. Modern Montessori schools and good early childhood programs have extended the concept to observation and care of animals in outdoor environments.

Montessori began her work in a self-contained special education setting. Utilizing self-constructed sensory materials, she was able to reach all children and motivate them to progress to the level where they passed the Italian state national exams. These same materials, rather than the external stickers and candy that are being used as rewards today in special education classrooms, would be more effective in teaching children with special needs. Extended periods of time where the children would be engaged in meaningful self-chosen activities with self-correcting materials would enable them to reach a state of "normalization" or self-regulation. Lillard cites studies which are indicative of this premise (Lillard, 2005).

Montessori's view that mind and movement are inseparable should be incorporated into the ever-growing progression of first grade curriculum down into the kindergarten classroom since recently reported research reveals many more teachers believe children should enter kindergarten familiar with numbers and letters. They also believe children should be reading upon completion of kindergarten. In 1998, only 31% of teachers held this belief, contrasted to 80% in 2010 (Camera, 2016).

If children are to accomplish reading, writing, and arithmetic at so young an age, they should at least be utilizing materials specifically made for these purposes. Montessori's set of three mathematical materials—the pink cubes for teaching size, the brown prisms for thickness, and the green rods for length—can be manipulated as is or substituted by similar materials which can be touched and moved by the children. These items assist the children in understanding the concept of numbers. Sandpaper letters extend the representation to the actual written number. Her arithmetic frames and bead materials allow for movement and assimilation of numbers in base ten (Montessori, 1965).

The directress' role in the classroom can be compared to the contemporary adage that the teacher should be "the guide on the side as opposed to the sage on the stage." Early childhood teachers should realize that children need to have hands-on experiences in order to assimilate and accommodate new knowledge.

Observation and documentation of the children by the directress provides authentic assessment leading to differentiation of instruction rather than whole class teaching.

Yet, 29% of teachers indicated they used standardized tests to assess children's growth at least once a month (Camera, 2016).

Montessori said:

> It is important to understand that the child takes not only with the mind but with his hands and his activity. This is because the child grows up with an entire, a whole personality made up of character, sentiment, mind, knowledge, activity, all bound up together.
>
> (cited in Buckenmeyer, 1970, n. p.)

Teachers today should reframe their viewpoints to focus on the "whole child" and not just on the three R's.

Current educational research has begun to explore the concept of mindfulness practices. Mindfulness encompasses focused mental attention with a sense of non-judgment and self-awareness. Montessori's emphasis on intense and uninterrupted concentration supports this theory. Some schools have even introduced meditation to achieve these same goals (Davis, 2015).

Maria Montessori died on May 6, 1952, yet some of the outcomes of mindfulness training, which Montessori foresaw over a hundred years ago, such as persistence, less impulsiveness, flexible thinking coupled with metacognition, collecting data by means of all the senses, thinking independently, and learning from experience, are as relevant today as they were then.

All of these directly tie in with the latest catchphrase in educational circles: "executive functioning," which includes planning, organization, memory, time management, and flexible thinking. Harvard's Center on the Developing Child asserts that: "Providing the support that children need to build these skills at home, in early care and education programs, and in other settings they experience regularly is one of society's most important responsibilities" (Center on the Developing Child, 2015, pp. 1–2).These goals for early childhood are the heart of the Montessori Method.

The ideals of Maria Montessori have become staples of good early childhood education in America and around the world. Her passionate devotion to young children and their needs as individuals in their own right, and not as miniature adults who were to be seen and not heard, was the mainspring of her method, as was the inclusion of the family for social and educational progress. As Montessori concludes, "The experiment [Casa dei Bambini] has been tried and the result is remarkable" (Montessori, 1964, p. 59).

References

Babini, V., & Lama, L. (2000). *Una donna nuova: Il femminismo scientifico di Maria Montessori*. Milan, Italy: Franco Angeli.

Buckenmeyer, R.E. (1970). The philosophical principles of pre-primary education according to Dr. Maria Montessori. *The American Montessori Society Bulletin*, 8(3), n. p.

Camera, L. (2016). www.usnews.com/news/articles/2016/01/07/kindergarten-today-looks-like-first-grade-a-decade-ago, 1–4.

Center on the Developing Child, Harvard University. (2015). Executive function and self-regulation. http://developingchild.harvard.edu/science/key-concepts/executive-function/

Davis, L.C. (2015). http://theatlantic.com/education/archive/2015/08/mindfulness-education-school

Grazzini, C. (1996). The four planes of development. *The NAMTA Journal*, *21*(2), 27–61.

Lillard, A.S. (2005). *Montessori: The science behind the genius*. New York: Oxford University Press.

Lillard, P.P. (1996). *Montessori today: A comprehensive approach to education from birth to adulthood*. New York: Schocken Books.

Montessori, M. (1964). *The Montessori method*. New York: Schocken Books.

Montessori, M. (1965). *Dr. Montessori's own handbook*. New York: Schocken Books.

Montessori, M. (1966). *The secret of childhood*. Notre Dame, IN: Fides Publishers.

Montessori, M. (1967). *The absorbent mind*. Kalakshetra, India: Kalakshetra Publications.

Montessori, M. (1976). *The discovery of childhood*. New York: Ballantine.

Povell, P. (2009). *Montessori comes to America: The leadership of Maria Montessori and Nancy McCormick Rambusch*. Lanham, MD: University Press of America.

Rava, V. (1902). *Le laureate in Italia. Notizie statistiche*. Rome: Cecchini, pp. 634–654.

Suggested Websites

The American Montessori Society: www.amshq.org
The American Montessori Society Archives: www.amshq.org/archives
The American Montessori Society Publications: www.amshq.org/publications
Association Montessori Internationale: www.ami-global.org
Association Montessori Internationale America: www.amiusa.org
International Montessori Council—The Montessori Foundation: www.montessori.org
National Center for Montessori in the Public Sector: www.public-montessori.org
North American Montessori Teachers' Association: www.montessori-namta.org

3

THE ERIKSONS' PSYCHOSOCIAL DEVELOPMENTAL THEORY

Elizabeth Jones and Sandra Waite-Stupiansky

Erik and Joan Erikson spent over half a century analyzing the human life cycle. Although the theory is usually credited to Erik Erikson, much of it was co-constructed with Joan Erikson, his wife of over 60 years. Thus, we are calling it the *Eriksons' Psychosocial Developmental Theory*. Their thinking was motivated by time and place, by their heritage and culture, and by the social issues that defined the tensions in their lives. So that is where this chapter on the Eriksons' theory begins.

Who Were the Eriksons?

Erik and Joan Erikson were born at the beginning of the twentieth century, Erik in Germany, Joan in Canada. In their lifetimes, they explored possibilities through the arts, psychology, and cultural anthropology. They experienced marginality—being on the edge—in rules for gender behavior, in language, in moving from here to there and back again. They lived through two world wars and escaped the Holocaust in Europe.

Erik's mother, raised in a prominent Jewish family in Copenhagen, moved across the Danish border to give birth to Erik in Germany in 1902. She stayed there, marrying Theodor Homburger, a pediatrician in the Jewish community in Karlsruhe, who became Erik's stepfather. Erik was uninterested in school and did not go to university; he became an artist and a wanderer in Germany. In his mid-20s, he arrived in Vienna.

Joan Serson was born in 1903, and raised in Canada (her Canadian father was an Episcopal pastor, her mother was American). She had earned a B.A. and M.A. at major U.S. universities, studying German and modern dance. A liberated young woman, she biked around Europe with a knapsack, collecting data for a doctoral dissertation on dance. She arrived in Vienna in the 1920s.

Vienna at that time was a popular destination for young people interested in the arts, political activism, and modern thought. Sigmund Freud famously created psychoanalytic theory there, and Erik was attracted by its community of clinical practice, research, and never-ending academic dialogue. The relatively new science of psychology was being transformed by Freud's investigation of emotions and the unconscious, as it invited focus on ego development and individual emotions from childhood through adult life.

Erik's interest in the new profession of psychoanalysis was welcomed by Anna Freud, Sigmund's daughter, who became his training analyst and shared her interest in child analysis with him. She hired him as a teacher in a small school she had started. Throughout his career, much of his work as a therapist was with children and adolescents. With them, he explored play with materials as a therapeutic alternative to the adult dreams that were Sigmund Freud's route to the subconscious.

Vienna was also a place for music and dance and romance, a place for young adults to learn through play with possibilities and to confront the life cycle issues of identity and intimacy, issues which became basic in the Eriksons' theory. Joan and Erik met at a dance. They promptly fell in love, moved in together, got married in 1930, and had a son. They went on to have three more children.

They were married for over 60 years. In their long life together they encountered all four of the adult stages of their life cycle theory: Identity, Intimacy, Generativity, and Integrity. And the four childhood stages with which the theory begins were central to their work and their family life.

Vienna was also on Adolf Hitler's agenda for the persecution of Jews. When he extended his power from Germany into Austria, the Eriksons' lifetime of traveling as a family began. In 1933, they went by train to Denmark with Erik's maternal family. But unable to get residence approval, they moved on by ship to Ellis Island, New York. Joan had U.S./Canadian dual citizenship. Erik spoke only German. He got U.S. citizenship in 1939, which is when he changed his surname to Erikson, with Homburger as his middle name. He spent the rest of his life immersed in English.

Two looming social issues that shaped the many tensions in their lives were *gender* and *marginality*. Both contributed to Erik's long-term preoccupation with the developmental challenge of identity: Who am I? Who are we? His biographer (Friedman, 1998; 1999) characterizes him as "Identity's Architect."

Erik became a fully focused writer in his 40s. Joan contributed to Erik's work all along; she taught him English; she edited his writing; she challenged his thinking. But she did not become his acknowledged partner in theory-building until she was nearly in her 80s. Her name first appeared on an article in 1981 (Erikson with Erikson, 1981) and on their book entitled *Vital Involvement in Old Age: The Experiences of Old Age in Our Time* (Erikson, Erikson, & Kivnick, 1986). She published independently *Wisdom and the Senses: The Way of Creativity* (Erikson, 1988), and a revised version of her husband's 1982 book, *The Life Cycle Completed: A Review*, was published in 1997, after his death, as *The Life Cycle Completed: Extended Version with New Chapters on the Ninth Stage of Development* (Erikson with Erikson, 1997). Its new developmental stage (transcendence, which dancer Joan chose to spell transcen*dance*) is all hers.

Theory is constructed in response to current issues. Erik began his theory building about childhood when he was working with children. He focused on identity when he was studying adolescents and reflecting on his own complex life (Erikson, 1968). Sixty years ago, he was a pioneer in taking childhood seriously, recognizing childhood's critical role in developing critical thinkers, "technical and mental virtuosos" (Erikson, 1950/1963, p. 12).

Because of the Eriksons' influence, *individual quality of life* has become a focal point in education and psychology, not only material and social life but social/emotional life. The Eriksons' developmental theory is thus referred to as a psychosocial developmental theory. It not only addresses childhood, it includes the entire life cycle and focuses on the inherent tensions that must be balanced and rebalanced within each stage of development. The theory offers a predictable pattern in which to examine every person's life story. And, over the history of Erik's and Joan's writing,

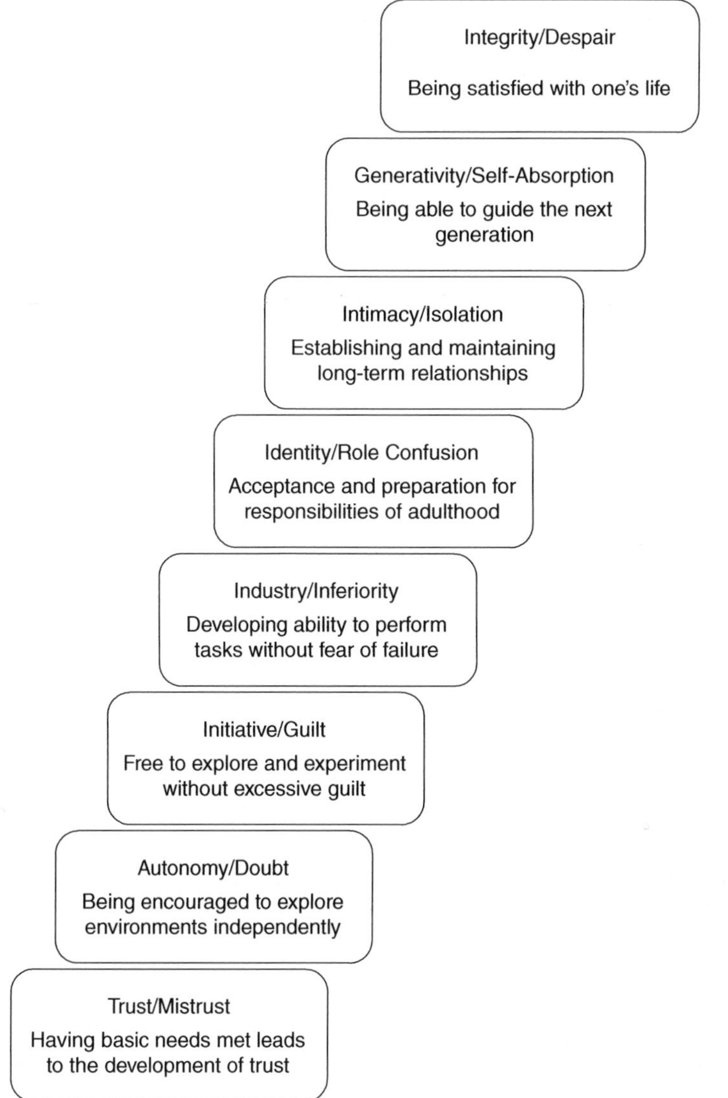

Figure 3.1 Erikson's Eight Stages of Psychosocial Development as represented in a series of progressive steps that begin in infancy and culminate in late adulthood.

a whole series of visual patterns emerged as well: diagrams re-visioned, elaborated, made still more challenging across the decades. Most famous is their model of the eight life stages, of which the first four will be the focus of this chapter.

The Eriksons' Psychosocial Developmental Theory

The theory is about stages in the human life cycle—the life of each human being, from birth to death. The psychosocial theory emphasizes the social context within which a human being resolves the tensions of each stage of development. The stages help educators predict the important issues in each child's life and help a child come to a healthy balance within that stage and any previously experienced stages which may need to be rebalanced in light of life's events. Every child is different because of the interactions and relationships in his or her life. Thus many of the implications discussed below reflect the relationships that children form with the people and the environment around them as they progress through the developmental stages forming important relationships within each stage.

The first four stages of development—infancy, toddlerhood, preschool, and school age—will be examined in detail with emphasis on how an early childhood classroom based on the Eriksons' principles would look and operate (Jones, 2011). The other stages, experienced in older years, are important, especially in light of the balancing and rebalancing that occur as one ages, but will not be elaborated upon here. A further note should be made that the "vs." used in the Eriksons' labels (e.g., Trust vs. Mistrust) was downplayed later in their writing because they recognized that a healthy tension includes both poles of the spectrum as a person finds the right balance between its two ends (Erikson & Erikson, 1997). For the purposes of this chapter, the "vs." has been replaced by a slash (e.g., Trust/Mistrust) to recognize the constant balancing and rebalancing that occurs throughout one's lifetime.

Infancy

Infancy (Trust/Mistrust) is the first stage of the Eriksons' psychosocial developmental theory. It is the occasion to build basic *trust* and to develop the strength of *hope*. During this stage, children learn to balance trust and mistrust in their environment and with their caregivers. Trust develops when children's needs are met consistently, predictably, and lovingly. Children then view the world as safe and dependable.

> *The hungry little baby is crying. A door opens. Here comes Mommy! The baby recognizes when Mommy's shirt gets unbuttoned, I get to suck milk. Yum.*

The crying is transformed to sucking. A few weeks later, Mom gets—and returns—a smile as well as a suck. Both are truly reinforcing of trust for both mother and baby. The sense of trust that a child develops during infancy sets the foundation for all relationships to come. The human infant is completely dependent on care from others, and trust is essential to survival; yet a little mistrust is necessary for survival as the infant learns that familiar adults are different from strangers. The latter will be greeted with a healthy dose of fear and mistrust until trust is earned.

As babies become crawlers, they begin to explore the larger world.

> Crawlers delight in moving out into their surroundings to discover what's there. Their encounters with other crawlers may result in two crawlers handling the same toy simultaneously, most often a gentle back-and-forth exchange, the tugs escalating at times, but never to the point of being divisive. Such an encounter is simply shared joint attention, a moment spent exploring the actions of another, rather than a conflict over possession.
>
> (Maguire-Fong, 2015, p. 159)

Then they become toddlers.

Toddlerhood

The second stage, Toddlerhood (Autonomy/Shame and Doubt) is the opportunity to practice autonomy and to develop strength of will. This is the stage when children want to do things for themselves. "I want it, Mommy. I want it NOW!" Words, especially "Mine" and "No," have been added to the baby's tools.

> With toddlers, conflicts over possession of toys are fraught with anger over possession. They start to claim explicit possession as they invest more feelings in objects. The utterance "Mine!" is one of the child's first expressive phrases and communicates clearly to others that "what I desire" is an extension of "me."
>
> (Maguire-Fong, 2015, p. 159)

Oral language is an essential connector in all human communities. It is acquired very early and used to assert what one wants. Furthermore, when opportunity presents itself, a newly mobile toddler, eager to practice his or her skills, is likely to run away from the mother's knee. Suddenly separated, he or she is equally likely to panic and look for safety. The mantra is: "I go away and I come back." Has he or she built the trust needed to do both?

As a child becomes mobile and able to control his or her body during toddlerhood, the sense of autonomy develops if children are given safe parameters within which to take risks, try new actions, and begin to master the environment. This stage brings a tension between the will of the child and the will of the constraints put upon him or her by the people and environment. Children often display frustration, which may take the form of temper tantrums and defiance, during this stage.

Preschool Age

The preschool stage (Initiative/Guilt) is the play age, the time to master *initiative* and to develop the strength of *purpose*.

> Three four-year-olds are converting several large boxes into a house in the play yard.
>
> VALERIE: That will be our 'frigerator, right? Get the blankets!
> JILL: Father, what are you doing?
> ROBERT: I'm getting back here.
> JILL, CRAWLING AROUND THE OUTSIDE OF THE HOUSE: Father, say "Get back in your bed."
> ROBERT: Get back in your bed!
> JILL DUTIFULLY CRAWLS BACK INTO THE BOX: Go to sleep, Father, it's night.
> VALERIE, TAKING OFF HER SHOES: Okay, Little Foot, here I come.
> JILL, WRAPPED IN A PINK BLANKET, CLOSES HER EYES FOR A SPLIT SECOND: Morning!
> VALERIE: Morning!
> JILL: Who wants to be the grandma? I want Valerie to be the grandma.

VALERIE: I don't want to play the grandmother.
JILL: Well, Robert wants to play the mother really bad, right?
ROBERT: Right! We could have two moms.
JILL: I'm Little Foot, I'm the baby.
ROBERT: I know. We could have a girl Little Foot and a boy Little Foot.
JILL: I'm gonna be the girl Little Foot and he's gonna be the boy Little Foot.
VALERIE: And I'm the mom. And you two live in the same little room and I live next door.

(Reynolds & Jones, 1997, p. 9)

As this vignette illustrates, during the years from three to five years of age, children are developing and practicing the skills and dispositions basic to membership in a human community, including use of complex language, constructive and dramatic play with materials and with people, and the beginnings of literacy, including reading pictures, symbols, signs, and names.

Play is prevalent in this stage as children seek to experiment, learn, and practice new things through pretense. Preschoolers constantly strive to practice the power of play, with others and by themselves. This is the stage when children show a strong sense of initiative and drive to try new experiences. They show their curiosity through asking questions, touching everything around them, taking new risks, and more. If their initiative is successful, they become more confident. If they often fail, guilt may develop: "I can't do anything right. There must be something wrong with me." As with the other stages, a little bit of guilt is healthy as it leads to a sense of conscience. Yet, a child who is overwhelmed by a sense of guilt is stymied in healthy development.

In each stage a child is intrinsically motivated, building on motor and brain development in the context of human relationships. Just as the urge for autonomy arises along with the ability to walk or run away in the previous stage, initiative builds on both those strengths; developed consciousness and communication skills make purposeful behavior possible. Pleasure in relationships sustains experimentation and creativity and the development of empathy.

School Age

School age (Industry/Inferiority) offers time for industry and starting to be productive, leading to the strength of competence.

Before they are five, children have moved from the simple survival of beginning infancy to mastery of layer after layer of body skills and language and all the facts of living together day to day. And so they are ready for the systematic practices that occur in formal schooling.

Tammy had written the word "brother." Her teacher said, "If you take away the 'br' what word do you have?" Tammy was a little puzzled, and Eva said "other." "How do you know?" Her teacher asked. "Well, if you take away the 'br' that's 'br' and that leaves 'other.'" "Eva, I didn't know you knew that?" "I didn't know it either," said Eva. This was followed by a period of list-making of words like shot, hot, lot, dot, got (changing the beginnings) and then another period of changing the endings. Eva was so excited (she who is usually so resistant to journal writing) that she made a whole series of

> *"twirling journals" on the transparent lids of coffee cans. She wrote around the lids in a circle. They fly like frisbees. This was all her idea.*

Early childhood educators developing teaching and learning strategies claim children six to eight years old as part of early childhood. Erikson extends *school age* through elementary school and what Sigmund Freud labeled as *latency*: the years during which oral, anal, and genital developmental phases of ego development have been resolved, and the huge physical and emotional challenges of adolescence have not yet arisen. It is a time-out period, these psychoanalysts imply; in it, a child has room to concentrate on becoming a responsible member of society. Preadolescence, with its complexities, is not part of early childhood. But if teachers of younger children can anticipate it with a solid foundation of individualized competence and confidence, society will be a safer and more productive place for all of us.

In all societies, children are expected to become responsible by the time they are six or seven years old. By now, children have obligations to meet and responsibility to rules they have to follow. Social knowledge is learned by watching and listening to adults and older children. Skills like writing and math are practiced most effectively when there is a sense of community that includes adults and peers.

Translating Theory to Early Childhood Education

Educators who use the Eriksons' theory in their practice consider the learning environment—physical, cognitive, social/interpersonal, cultural, and political—available to each person from birth, and the implications of each stage in the life cycle for all the stages that will follow it. Their theory is historical, offering a chronological framework for analyzing life from birth to death. The Eriksons' theory reminds teachers of young children that life is a cycle; it goes round and round in a spiral. It also reminds teachers that the focus is on the relationships children form with the adults around them, starting with their families and extending to other adults and children as their worlds widen.

In its implications for teaching and caregiving, this is a very complex theory. There are two contrasting kinds of theories. Some acknowledge (and embrace) complexity and uncertainty (there is even one called *chaos theory*); they rely on qualitative and narrative data. Others value order and predictability, and rely on quantitative analysis, recognizing numbers as much tidier than words. The Eriksons' psychosocial developmental theory is the former type. It recognizes the complexity of human development and always considers the social context within which development occurs.

Erik Erikson was a therapist, not a teacher. He didn't formulate his theory to answer the question, "How should we teach young children?" His focus was on mastery of life tasks, all through a life, in the context of emotional health and social relationships. Yet the implications for teachers of young children are a logical extension of the theory.

Implications for the Early Childhood Classroom

If one is a teacher, what are the criteria for constructing a learning environment for young children? How does one organize space and time and interactions? How does one interact with the children and form relationships with them? Why is the Erikson theory important for their practice? These are the questions educators must answer in the light of the Eriksons' theory if they are to implement a classroom based on the psychosocial developmental theory.

Infancy

Implications for this stage focus on the first year of life when the sense of trust is developing for all infants. Since the social environment is the key to an Eriksons-inspired classroom, the relationships formed in infancy lay the foundation for the trust (and appropriate levels of mistrust) the child will take forward with himself or herself throughout life and influence all future relationships. In group care, this translates into ensuring that children have stable, consistent, and responsive caregiving. The adults who work with the child every day should be consistent, ideally the same few persons, and have a small number of children so that the adults can respond to each child in their care in a timely and appropriate manner. Moving a child from classroom to classroom or shifting caregivers every several hours or days would run contrary to the child forming secure relationships with the adults. Since relationships are two-way, the adults need to have time and experience with the few children in their care so that they can know each child and his or her needs, interests, proclivities, and other factors that make humans individuals.

In order to form trust, the adults must be trustworthy. They need to be responsive, taking time to interact with each child throughout the day. As they change diapers, feed the child, and soothe the child to sleep, caregivers take each opportunity to sing, speak softly, and engage in simple games such as peek-a-boo and clapping to communicate their undivided attention.

Just as the relationships formed outside of the home are important, the paramount relationships for the child in the first year occur within the home and family. Educators in a psychosocial classroom honor these relationships and do everything in their power to preserve the bonds between the child and family members. This means supporting mothers, fathers, grandparents, and other family members so that they can be responsive and available to the child.

The physical environment, which is secondary to the social environment in this theory, is predictable and safe but allows for flexibility and individual accommodations. Play materials are in excellent shape and organized so that the children can access play items appropriate for their level. Caregivers watch, acknowledge, and respond.

> A large red ball rolls across the floor of the playroom. The 10-month-old who batted it in that direction is crawling rapidly after it, but it is scooped up by an artful walker several months older. The baby cries, indignantly. "Baw!" she demands loudly. The ball's new possessor sits down abruptly but holds on tightly. He tries to push the crawler away. The observing adult joins them on the floor, with a gentle hand on each. "You want the ball," she says clearly to the crawler. "And you want the ball," she says to the toddler. "What can we do, I wonder?" She reaches out with her foot to snag another ball—a yellow one—nearby on the floor. "Would someone like this ball?"
>
> (Jones & Cooper, 2006, p. 79)

As this vignette shows, the adults form a social and physical environment that needs to be positive, predictable, and responsive to each child's individual needs, developmental level, and personality. It should welcome each child from arrival until departure with warm smiles, kind words, attractive spaces, and adults who care for each child in a trustworthy way.

Toddlerhood

This is the stage, the second and third years of life, when children start to exert their will and passions in full force. Children become mobile as they start to walk; yet they are still rather unsure on their feet and may toddle, hence the name "toddler." Developing coordination requires endless practice. An encouraging environment offers objects to practice on, easily visible and accessible to the very small.

> On the edge of the low-walled sandbox are three dump trucks, one red, one blue, and one yellow. In the sand is an orderly array of four pails, two red with yellow handles, two yellow with red handles. Each pail is tipped on its side, with some sand in it. Each has a shovel matching its handle.
>
> Not only the dumpers and diggers, but also the animal lovers are welcomed. Three groups of plastic animals—six horses, four cows—are also waiting in the sand.
>
> (Jones & Cooper, 2006, p. 90)

There are fascinating items to play with. But the child is not alone; there are other children, too, so the teacher is challenged to become a skilled play watcher, alert to whether intervention is needed or whether children can devise their own solutions to problems. Here are two 15-month-olds with a recurring problem in which, whenever the boy found a toy he wanted, the girl arrived and ...

> the boy let go right away and the girl walked off with the toy. She was always taking things from him and he let her, though he looked disappointed every time. The teacher was confident that they would work it out sooner or later—and then one morning, it happened.
>
> The boy got there first and was enjoying walking around with a small ball. The girl arrived and immediately grabbed it away from him. The boy looked upset. He walked over and picked up a small basket—immediately the girl took it. Then he picked up a plastic block—same thing. When she came for the puzzle piece he had in his hand, he held it out to her. Then he went over and got a purse and gave it to the girl. Then came a small blanket, but by now she was so overloaded she could hardly hold another thing. He was headed for a doll when she dumped all the toys in a pile on the floor and walked away. The game was over ... without any adult intervention.
>
> (Gonzales-Mena, 2009, p. viii)

Caregivers find that having a sense of humor is valuable when working with toddlers. As they explore the new words they are learning, the power of pretending for the first time, and the limits of their environment, a sense of humor goes a long way to relieve tensions and maintain positive relationships. In the same vein, promoting a culture of forgiveness and being able to correct one's mistakes will prevent a child from slipping into an overwhelming sense of self-doubt and shame. A child is learning to dress, feed himself or herself, use the toilet, get along with peers, and so much more, and mistakes happen. It is how the adults respond to these mistakes that can lead to a sense of autonomy or a sense of doubt and shame.

Along with their newfound mobility, toddlers have another powerful tool at their disposal: words! They recognize the power of words when they use simple one-word phrases like "NO" or "MINE." They start to use words to communicate their wants and needs ("I hungry." "No like."). Responsive adults use these first words, expand on them, add new words, and communicate constantly with these new speakers. If children speak a different language than the teacher, learning some basic words to communicate in this language is essential to maintain healthy, respectful relationships. If the child uses sign language, teachers respond in sign themselves. Language is the powerful tool that burgeons during this stage, and children are receptive to learning it at a speed that will never be possible again in their lives. Language helps children build relationships with the adults and children in their lives in new and exciting ways.

Preschool

Erik Erikson called preschool the "play stage" because play predominates in the child's interests and activities. He also recognized the power of play as a therapeutic tool in his psychoanalytic work. He contended that through make-believe play a child explores who she or he can become. Preschoolers try on different roles, explore power hierarchies, and engage in slightly taboo behaviors when they engage in pretend play. Children develop a sense of purpose, which the Eriksons called initiative. Yet the sense of guilt lurks if children have too many restrictions or inhibitions placed upon them.

Preschool educators often marvel at the important role that relationships with peers start to have in the lives of three- and four-year-olds. Yet the relationship with the teacher remains of central importance, as it is adults who can invoke a healthy sense of guilt in a preschooler's mind by a simple verbal response, glance, or imposition of a consequence for a child's behavior.

Just as in the two previous stages, a relationship with an adult needs to be consistent and responsive to the child's individuality. A sense of co-construction of the rules of behavior as children learn the mores of right vs. wrong as established by their society can develop if the adults explain the reasons for rules and are consistent and reasonable in enforcing the consequences for mistakes the child makes along the way. When a child commits an infraction, the adult and child can work out a way for the child to make resolution and amends to his or her victim. Simply saying, "I'm sorry" may be enough in some cases, but helping the victim in a real way is even better. If a child knocks over another child's block structure, working together with both children to arrive at a mutually agreeable solution helps both victim and perpetrator learn the power of negotiation and compromise, and rectifies a temporarily damaged relationship. "Use your words" is a familiar phrase in most preschools. Words can be used to acknowledge feelings, good and bad—your feelings and my feelings and their feelings.

> In a responsive classroom, we study things *because they happen*. No lesson plan can predict the emergence of serendipitous opportunities for learning. The eruptions of feelings that happen unexpectedly in the best of classrooms can be deplored, ignored, or selectively transformed into curriculum. Feelings that are ignored generally reemerge in some mutation that disrupts learning. Living together in restricted space, day-to-day, is even more challenging than the three R's.
>
> (Jones, Evans, & Rencken, 2001, p. 155)

The three R's (reading, writing, and 'rithmetic) can also be learned in this context.

> Richard is sad about his mother's departure and has been crying for some minutes. The teacher invites him to join the children who are involved in a writing activity. "Here's some yellow paper. Write Mommy a note and tell her you miss her." Pointing to the container, she asks, "Would you like to choose a pen?" Then, "We'll give Mommy the note when she comes to pick you up this afternoon."
>
> Literacy gives power. Richard stops crying immediately, though he continues to look sad. He clutches the pen high above the point, making letters and letter-like forms. The teacher sits close to him.
>
> (Jones & Reynolds, 2011, p. 71)

Sharing representations in drawings, pictures, and words with children happens when the teacher takes on the basic role of *observer and scribe*. This focuses the teacher on children's strengths and challenges and interests; it provides a discussion topic with the children; it offers practice in reading pictures and words; it documents children's learning for parents.

> This group of 4-year-olds were gathered in the house area, using the telephones. Rosa was talking to the doctor: "Doctor, mi niña esta muy enferma."
>
> Juan, Joanie, Yolanda, Alex, and Diana had dressed up with clothes from the house area and sat in a row of chairs, one in back of the other. Yolanda was driving the "train." There were plastic crates that were hauled from the block area; Yolanda put all her belongings in the crates, and then all the other children on the train did, too.
>
> Their teacher, who likes to draw, made a picture of them. The next day she brought it to circle time. "Do you know what I saw yesterday?" she asked the children, "I saw Rosa talking to the doctor on the telephone. 'My baby is very sick,' she told the doctor. And I drew a picture of her. Do you see her?" She held up the picture and the children squeezed close to see. "Rosa," they said. "Con el telefono." Rosa, overwhelmed, put her hands over her face. Yolanda, who had been looking closely at the picture, burst out, "That's me! I driving!"
>
> "Yes, that's Yolanda," agreed the teacher. "Yolanda and Juan and Diana and Alex and Joanie went on the train. And here they are." There was great excitement. Our teacher drew our picture and there we are!

> At the end of circle time there was a rush for the crates and chairs. Reminding children of their interesting play encourages them to replay it, to understand and elaborate it more fully.
>
> (Jones & Reynolds, 2011, pp. 66–67)

Overall, the developmental preschool classroom provides a positive atmosphere where children and adults feel welcome, accepted, and safe to try new ideas and practice initiative, free from an overwhelming sense of guilt.

School Age

The kindergarten/primary age child experiences a tension between industry and inferiority, according to the Eriksons. Children in this stage become very productive, taking up hobbies, creating artwork, asking for homework, and the like. They start to compare themselves and their productions to those of others, which can lead to a sense of incompetence or inferiority if the comparisons are over-stressed or focused upon by the adults and peers around them. Children may appear to be rather "thin-skinned" when criticized by others and resort to tears or destruction of their products if they think others do not approve of them. If this happens too often, the child may develop a sense of inferiority rather than a sense of self-confidence and competence.

The early childhood classroom that allows for individual differences and varying competencies works best for children's developing sense of industry. Open-ended, hands-on activities that allow children to work at their own pace and at their own level without comparison with others correspond with the classroom based on psychosocial developmental theory. Nonjudgmental questions and comments by teachers that seek the child's judgment of his or her own work reinforce the child's sense of industry (e.g., "Can you tell me about your drawing?" rather than "I love your drawing.").

Divergent thinking is a skill to be practiced at school. It invites brainstorming, a different sort of learning that asks children to share the responsibility for solving problems that affect us all. It addresses their fears directly, going beyond basic trust and obedience to ask for imagination and reasoning. In a California classroom, in earthquake country,

> The teacher asked her 5- and 6-year olds, "Does anyone know anything about earthquakes?" She scribed their words and read them back to the class. "Is that a good idea? Let's make two lists—one of good ideas, one of not-so-good ideas."
>
> Children drew pictures and dictated stories, after the discussion. And then they all practiced earthquake drill in the different parts of their space, in the classroom and outdoors too. It went on all morning. One child, fearful that he wouldn't remember everything he was supposed to do, was smiling by the end of the morning, reassured by all that practice. It was clearly important to his teacher that every child learn this skill.
>
> Since that day, more questions have come up. "What if the ground is shaking too much?" "What if you're in the bathroom doing a poop?" Children know what the really important problems are!
>
> (Jones & Cooper, 2006, pp. 12–13)

The schedule and the physical arrangement of the classroom allow for children's choices. Decisions as to in what order to complete the tasks, which media to use, and whether to work alone or with others are built into the schedule without losing academic focus. Children's work may be collected for portfolios to share with parents, peers, and teachers, which are used by many professionals in the field. The selection of items for the portfolio should be orchestrated by the child, not selected solely by the teacher. Presentation of the portfolio should always include the child who can explain the process and thinking that went into the work.

Systematic instruction usually begins at this age, which can be difficult for some children to adapt to and lead to feelings of incompetence and inferiority. Allowances for individual attention spans, activity levels, areas of interest, and biological rhythms can help children adapt to the constraints of systematic instruction.

In summary, teachers using the Eriksons' psychosocial developmental theory will be striving for *developmentally appropriate practices* as defined by the National Association for the Education of Young Children (Copple & Bredekamp, 2009), with opportunities at each stage for each child to experience and work on the basic competence of that stage. An infant needs to experience adults as caring and trustworthy and to discover compensatory strategies in an adult's absence. A toddler needs safe ways to assert himself or herself, to say, "No," to run away, and welcome a hug on return. Preschoolers need lots and lots of practice in choosing and doing and negotiating and representing in words and images as they master play. Children aged six to eight need practice in taking responsibility and following through, which involves choice, not just obedience.

Implications for Policy

Early childhood educators are constantly being challenged, in their advocacy for children, by politicians, funders, parents, quantitative researchers: How does one *know* if the children are learning? Advocacy requires informing others with evidence that developmentally appropriate practices are healthy and effective for young children. Informed advocates need to gather quantifiable facts, success stories, testimonials, and the like. They need to build credible relationships with decision makers. They need to communicate their knowledge to parents, and keep learning from parents as well for they are effective collaborators in advocacy efforts.

Human life is full of internal feelings and external facts. Articulating feelings may be as important as articulating facts in one's advocacy work. It was only about a century ago that a few avant-garde thinkers, including Erik and Joan Erikson, went beyond the physical sciences to undertake the systematic study of persons and peoples, complex, unpredictable systems not readily quantifiable. They found that they needed, for deeper understanding, not numbers but persons' individual and collective *stories*: ethnographies, case histories, case studies. Their stories are still informing early childhood education today. Advocates for young children can continue this tradition as they add their own stories and those of the children with whom they work to the voices of history.

References

Copple, C. & S. Bredekamp. (2009). *Developmentally appropriate practice in early childhood programs serving children from birth to age 8* (3rd ed.). Washington, DC: N.A.E.Y.C.

Erikson, E.H. ([1950] 1963). *Childhood and society*. New York: Norton.

Erikson, E.H. (1968). *Identity, youth and crisis*. New York: Norton.

Erikson, E.H., & Erikson, J.M. (1981). On generativity and identity. *Harvard Educational Review*, 51: 249–269.

Erikson, E.H. (1982). *The life cycle completed: A review*. New York: Norton.

Erikson, E.H., & Erikson, J.M. (1997). *The life cycle completed: Extended version with new chapters on the ninth stage of development*. New York: Norton.

Erikson, E.H., Erikson, J.M., & Kivnick, H.Q. (1986). *Vital involvement in old age: The experiences of old age in our time*. New York: Norton.

Erikson, J.M. (1988). *Wisdom and the senses: The way of creativity*. New York: Norton.

Friedman, L.J. (1999). *Identity's architect: A biography of Erik H. Erikson*. New York: Scribner.

Friedman, L.J. (1998). Erik H. Erikson's critical themes and voices: The task of synthesis. In R.S. Wallerstein & L. Goldberger (Eds.), *Ideas and identities: The life and work of Erik Erikson*. Madison, CT: International Universities Press, pp. 353–377.

Gonzales-Mena, J. (2009). Foreword. In R.A. Hammond, *Respecting babies: A new look at Magda Gerber's RIE approach*. Washington, DC: Zero to Five.

Jones, E. (2011). Play across the life cycle: From initiative to integrity to transcendence. *Young Children*, 66(4), 84–91.

Jones, E., & Cooper, R. (2006). *Playing to get smart*. New York: Teachers College Press.

Jones, E. & Reynolds, G. (2011). *The play's the thing: Teachers' roles in children's play*. 2nd ed. New York: Teachers College Press.

Jones, E., Evans, K., & Rencken, K.S. (2001). *The lively kindergarten: Emergent curriculum in action*. Washington, DC: N.A.E.Y.C.

Maguire-Fong, M.J. (2015). *Teaching and learning with infants and toddlers: Where meaning-making begins*. New York: Teachers College Press.

Reynolds, G., & Jones, E. (1997). *Master players: learning from children at play*. New York: Teachers College Press.

Suggested Websites

www.psychology.about.com/od/psychosocialtheories/a/psychosocial.htm
www.en.wikipedia.org/wiki/Erik_Erikson
www.en.wikipedia.org/wiki/Joan_Erikson
www.erikerikson.org

4

THE IMPORTANCE OF URIE BRONFENBRENNER'S BIOECOLOGICAL THEORY FOR EARLY CHILDHOOD EDUCATION

Jonathan R. H. Tudge, Elisa A. Merçon-Vargas, Yue Liang, and Ayse Payir

If early childhood educators know and appropriately use just one theory that is relevant to early childhood education, Bronfenbrenner's is the theory for them. As all good teachers know, it is the typically occurring activities in which their children engage, including the interactions that they have with their teachers and their peers inside the classroom and with their friends and family outside the classroom, that are so important for their development. Of course, how those activities occur depends in part on the personal characteristics of all individuals involved: the children, their parents, their friends, and their teachers. Those activities also are heavily influenced by the contexts in which they occur, whether home, child care center, the park, their grandparents' home, or with a child minder or some other type of more informal care. The way in which the children's classroom is organized clearly has an impact on the ways in which the children can engage in activities and interactions. And what happens in one context also influences what goes on in other contexts. Children who arrive at school hungry will engage with their teachers and peers quite differently than will those who arrive well fed; children who come from homes in which parents have time, interest, and energy to invest in them will arrive in school much better prepared than those who do not; children whose language at home is the same as that of the classroom will find interactions much simpler than those for whom this is not the case; children who share the same racial/ethnic background as their peers and teachers will engage differently with them than will children who stand out as being different.

This, in brief, captures the essence of Bronfenbrenner's theory, about which we will go into more depth later. First, however: How did he arrive at this theoretical approach? Does it help to answer this question by understanding his personal background? The answer to the second question is "yes!" Providing some biographical details of his life will go some way to explaining why he developed his bioecological theory of human development.

Biographical Details

Urie Bronfenbrenner was born in 1917, in Russia, but his family moved to the United States just six years later, with his father working as a neuropathologist at an institution in upstate New York for persons with mental disabilities. As Bronfenbrenner (1995b) wrote, the experiences he had there, talking and walking with his father, made a long-lasting impression. He clearly remembered his father worrying about the self-fulfilling prophecy of his patients being labeled "morons" (the word in vogue at that time) inculcating the belief that there was nothing that could be done to allow them to live any sort of productive life. He also remembered that he first started thinking about the interdependence of the organism and its environment (something that would come to be at the center of his theory) thanks to those walks with his father, "a field naturalist at heart" (Bronfenbrenner, 1995b, p. 602).

After graduating in psychology and music from Cornell University, completing a master's degree and his doctorate at Harvard University, and at the University of Michigan, Bronfenbrenner joined the faculty in Child Development and Family Relations at Cornell, worked there virtually his entire career, and, having by then retired, died in 2005. During his academic career he wrote widely on various subjects: contemporary approaches to child rearing in the Soviet Union, early childhood education in the United States and other Western societies, ways of helping poor families educate their children and adolescents, family policy and the problem of taking a "deficit approach" to the situation of families in poverty; and, of course, he was one of the scholars who played a major role in the development of the Head Start program (for more details, see Tudge, 2013).

During most of this time he was also developing what started life being called the ecology of human development (during the 1970s and 1980s), was subsequently termed "ecological systems theory" (in the late 1980s and early 1990s), and ended being called "the bioecological theory of human development" (from the mid-1990s) (Rosa & Tudge, 2013). What is quite clear is that his theoretical approach was in no way divorced from his writing on other topics; rather, his thinking about children's development and ways of supporting families were both informed by his theory and served to help him develop it. Consistently, he incorporated an ecological approach into his study of children and families; just as in biology, ecology refers to the relation between organisms and the environments in which they live, so Bronfenbrenner felt that the only way to understand child or family development was to study it within its naturally occurring context.

The Ecological Model

In the final form of Bronfenbrenner's theory (Bronfenbrenner, 1994; 2001; Bronfenbrenner & Morris, 2006; Rosa & Tudge, 2013), person and context are thus two of the most important concepts. They are not the most important concepts, however; pride of place is given to what he called "proximal processes" in his process-person-context-time (PPCT) model. Proximal processes are the everyday activities and interactions in which developing individuals engage, and are so important that he named them the "engines of development" (Bronfenbrenner & Morris, 2006, p. 798). Time is the fourth element, and signifies that in order to study development, one must both collect data over time—during proximal processes themselves (examining the nature of the interactions) and longitudinally (focusing on their frequency and consistency)—and also examine the ways in which the passage of broader sweeps of time is likely to influence the ways in which we think about raising and/or educating our children. All four elements function interdependently rather than independently; that is, one cannot trace the effects of one without considering the others, but here we will describe each of them in turn.

Proximal Processes

Bronfenbrenner defined proximal processes in the same way in several of his publications from 1993 onwards:

> Especially in its early phases, and to a great extent throughout the life course, human development takes place through processes of progressively more complex reciprocal interaction between an active evolving biopsychological human organism and the persons, objects, and symbols in its immediate environment. To be effective, the interaction must occur on a fairly regular basis over extended periods of time. Such enduring forms of interaction in the immediate environment are referred to as *proximal processes*.
>
> (Bronfenbrenner, 1995a, p. 620)

He continued by noting that proximal processes are influenced simultaneously by characteristics of the person, the context, and time:

> The form, power, content, and direction of the proximal processes effecting development vary systematically as a joint function of the characteristics of the developing person; the environment, both immediate and more remote, in which the processes are taking place; and the nature of the developmental outcomes under consideration.
>
> (Bronfenbrenner, 1995a, p. 621)

Bronfenbrenner wrote about proximal processes almost exclusively in a positive manner, the "developmental outcomes" being either the promotion of competence or the reduction of what he termed "dysfunction" (that is, by helping individuals do better than would be expected given the situation that they find themselves in). In other words, a child who is expected to do well at school will become increasingly competent by engaging in plenty of positive and challenging activities and interactions with teachers and peers. By contrast, in the case of a child who is struggling with the demands of school, engagement in positive activities, and interactions with teachers and peers will reduce the likelihood of school failure. These proximal processes serve as a means to protect this child from the negative consequences of those early struggles.

Person Characteristics

As Bronfenbrenner noted above, how those regular activities and interactions occur depends, at least in part, on the "characteristics of the developing person." What are these characteristics? He wrote about three types, naming them "demand," "resource," and "force." We will first consider *demand characteristics*. Earlier in his career, Bronfenbrenner had used the phrase "personal stimulus" instead of demand, and in our opinion, the earlier term captured better what he meant by it. A teacher in child care center or school has her first look at some children who are entering her class for the first time. What does she see? (Here, and subsequently, we will treat the teacher as female, as most early childhood teachers are female, despite the fact that some males, the first author included, have worked or do work in early childhood classrooms.) She sees girls and boys, some taller, some shorter, some fatter, some thinner. She sees children of different skin colors, and one who has her head covered. Two children are speaking a language that she doesn't understand. One child quickly goes over to look at a book, another hangs back, a third is crying, and another seems surly. All these initial impressions (that is, personal-stimulus or demand characteristics) can influence the first interactions in which teachers and children engage, and could set the stage for subsequent interactions if these first ones go well or poorly.

At the same time, the teacher's demand characteristics, and those of the other children, are being picked up by the children as they enter the room. Does the teacher look kind, worried, harassed, or threatening to them? They each might be thinking: Does she look anything like my mom looks? Will I be able to understand her? Will I be able to make any friends here, because no one looks like I do? Different answers to these questions, whether expressed consciously or not, are likely to influence the children's first interactions with others in different ways.

By comparison, *resource characteristics* (previous experiences, current abilities, and so on) are not immediately apparent, although sometimes they are inferred from demand characteristics, e.g., using skin color or gender or other easily noted characteristics to make assumptions about resource characteristics. Assuming that the teacher is not prone to major prejudices, however, no matter what her initial reaction (based on demand characteristics) is to the new children in her class, in the course of observing them engaging in whatever activities are encouraged in the classroom and interacting with them, she will come to know something of their past experiences and current competencies. The child who immediately on entering the classroom went to the book corner is one, it turns out, who cannot read a word and at home only has a few picture books. The proximal processes relevant to books and reading will be quite different than they would have been if she were already reading fluently. The child who appeared to be surly turns out to be one who has had a great deal of experience with mathematical concepts. The teacher, having learned this, interacts in a way quite differently than she had anticipated. The same is true, of course, for the teacher's resource characteristics. The child who worried because the teacher does not look at all like his mother (a demand characteristic) discovers that she has had a lot of experience working with children of a different skin color than her own and she has learned ways of putting at ease all the children in her class. Proximal process that might initially have been difficult because of the child's wariness become warm-hearted and open because of the teacher's particular resource characteristics.

Finally, *force characteristics* are those having to do with things like temperament, motivation, and persistence. The child, mentioned earlier, who only has experience of picture books is, it turns out, desperate to learn how to read "real" books; that drive and determination to read will dramatically affect the proximal processes in which she engages both with books and with those who are helping her learn to read. By contrast, the child who has had a good deal of experience with mathematical concepts and has learned them easily finds that her expectations that everything will be easy to learn are dashed, and has little persistence to learn things that are at all challenging. Children's different degrees of motivation and persistence have profound influences on the relevant proximal processes in which they are engaged. Similarly, teachers' force characteristics can also dramatically affect the proximal processes in which they are engaged. One teacher might have a great deal of experience; another one might be in her first teaching position. If the first teacher's experiences have led to burnout or a belief that no matter what she does the children in her classroom are destined for failure, her motivation to try to ensure success could be far less than that of the second teacher who arrives with little experience but a burning desire to change children's lives for the better.

Context

As we have just shown, proximal processes are heavily influenced by person characteristics of the developing individuals of interest and of any people with whom they are interacting. But they are also heavily influenced by the context, or, as Bronfenbrenner wrote, "the environment, both immediate and more remote, in which the [proximal] processes are taking place" (1995a, p. 621). It is unfortunate, but Bronfenbrenner is most widely known as a theorist of context. Having used the metaphor of Russian nesting dolls to describe the individual embedded within multiple levels of context, his theory is typically described as being one that deals with the influence of context on the individual (Tudge, Mokrova, Hatfield, & Karnik, 2009). In fact, as we have shown, context is merely one of the elements of the PPCT model, a model in which proximal processes are of most importance.

Of the four levels of context about which Bronfenbrenner wrote, the *microsystem* is the most important, as proximal processes only occur within microsystems, "immediate" environments. These are environments in which the developing individuals of interest—young children, in the case of this chapter—have the opportunity for face-to-face contact with others and to be active with objects or symbols for significant portions of time. For early educators, obviously the child care or school classroom is the most important microsystem. How that environment is organized, the types of activities and interactions that are encouraged (and discouraged), how calm or chaotic things are, and so on, all are likely to influence the manner in which children engage in activities and interact both with their peers and their teachers, in other words, are likely to influence proximal processes. It is easy to see how this can be true by thinking about one classroom in which children are expected to sit at individual desks while their teacher talks and occasionally poses questions, and another classroom in which activity areas are set up, with children choosing which of the areas to be in, and the teacher going around to different areas to talk with small groups about what they are learning.

Children develop in more than one microsystem, of course, and Bronfenbrenner used the term *mesosystem* to describe the relations between two or more microsystems. The child's home is the obvious example of a microsystem, but if children spend a good deal of time also at their grandparents' house or with a peer group, these also would count as different microsystems. The home context is most important, assuming the child spends most time there, because how that environment is organized will influence the ease with which children make the transition to a new classroom in a child care center or school. Children coming from homes in which they are expected to carefully follow directions, obey their parents and other adults, and stay neat and clean would be most likely to find it easier fitting into the first classroom described above. By contrast, children who have become used to having to decide many things for themselves and to learn to exercise autonomy are more likely to fit into the second type of classroom. Mesosystem analysis helps us to understand why a child from the first type of home might find it difficult to engage in productive proximal processes in the second type of classroom, and vice versa. This is not to say that Bronfenbrenner thought that there needs to be a close fit between different microsystems in order for children to succeed; in fact, it is clearly helpful for children to learn that different types of environments require different types of behavior and afford the learning of new roles and new ways of acting and interacting.

The *exosystem*, in Bronfenbrenner's typology of contexts, is a setting in which the developing individuals of interest are not situated but which nonetheless has an important indirect effect. In the case of a child, an important exosystem would be a parent's work situation or what is happening in the teacher's home. Think of parents whose job requires them to carefully do all that their immediate supervisors ask them to do, and for whom success at work means being punctual, always looking neat and clean, and following the rules that others have laid down. Given that this type of job typically does not require much, if any, education beyond high school, such parents are likely to have viewed school success also in terms of doing what the teachers want. Given their views of what is necessary for success, whether at school or work, it is not at all surprising to find that they are likely to value obedience in their children as the way to achieve later success. By contrast, parents who during their education have been encouraged to think for themselves (typically in the course of higher education) and whose job also requires them to exercise self-direction, are more likely to value autonomy in their children (for empirical support for this view, see Kohn, 1995). The experiences that parents have had in their earlier education and are currently having at work (settings in which their children are not situated) are thus likely to have influential indirect effects on the ways in which they typically deal with their children at home—effects, in other words, on proximal processes.

Similarly, if a teacher is facing family problems at home or is getting insufficient sleep because her child is ill or not sleeping well, this will have an influence on the proximal processes in which she is involved with the children at school. If the teacher is the developing individual in whom we are interested, the home–school issues are related to the mesosystem. However, if our developing individuals of interest are the children in her class, the indirect effects on proximal processes related to what is happening in the teacher's home count as an exosystem effect.

The final aspect of context is the *macrosystem*, which Bronfenbrenner conceived of as akin to culture, whether considered as an entire society or a racial, ethnic, regional, or socioeconomic group within a society. A macrosystem includes people who share values, beliefs, practices, access to resources, and a sense of common identity. People living in the United States can be distinguished in these terms from those living in Russia; these two countries constitute two different macrosystems. Within the United States, however, if members of two racial/ethnic groups or two socioeconomic groups or two groups living in different regions can be differentiated in terms of their values, beliefs, practices, and sense of identity, they also count as different macrosystems. One should not be surprised to find, then, that members of these different within-U.S. macrosystems have different child-rearing values, beliefs, and practices.

If middle-class parents are more likely than their working-class counterparts to value the ability of children to make their own decisions—and working-class parents more likely to value following the rules that others have laid down—for the reasons mentioned earlier, and they spend more time in the company of other parents from the same socioeconomic background, it should not be surprising to find that these ideas become more solidified. If their own parents were also from a middle-class background, and this is their experience of being raised, again they may be more likely to have taken on these same values. Then, to the extent to which parental practices (proximal processes, in other words) are in line with their values, middle-class parenting practices should be different from those found among working-class parents. In other words, parents' values are not simply the product of their own personal characteristics, but reflective, in part, of the macrosystems of which they are a part. In this sense, the choice of child care center or type of school is not simply a personal choice but stems, at least in part, from the values and beliefs shared by the cultural group of which the parents are a part.

Access to resources, one of the important components of macrosystems, also is clearly important in this choice. Some child care centers, situated in affluent areas, are able to charge high prices, and thus may have better quality materials and equipment, smaller class sizes, better paid—and thus probably better trained—educators than do child care centers situated in poorer areas. Similarly, school districts in affluent suburbs typically can provide so much more for their children than school districts in run-down areas of cities or in impoverished rural areas. The macrosystem thus influences proximal processes in many ways, including the ways in which parents interact with their children and, through the choices they make with regard to child care and schooling, how children are likely to interact with teachers and peers in school.

Time

This is the fourth and final aspect of the PPCT model, and can be thought of in two different ways. The first is that cultural values, beliefs, and practices are not static, but change over time. Whether children are expected to go to school at all, the age at which they should go and how long they should stay in school, and the ways in which they should be treated while in school have all changed dramatically over the past several centuries, and changed considerably from one generation to the next. These types of changes clearly have implications for proximal processes, or what is expected to go on in child care or school.

The second way has to do with what is occurring, over time, within any given proximal process, for example, when a teacher and child are interacting, is the former's attention completely on the child or is her attention divided between this child and the others in the room? Proximal processes, Bronfenbrenner argued, will be far more effective in the first than the second case. Second, how often does this teacher interact with this child? If the proximal processes are to be effective they must occur regularly and with increasing complexity; a single interaction once a month is unlikely to be helpful.

Bronfenbrenner was also clear that if one wants to study development, one has to do so over time. Cross-sectional studies, while adequate to show that children differ in cognitive abilities or socioemotional understanding at different ages, can never answer the developmental question of how development occurs. Just as teachers see how their children develop over the course of the school year, so researchers need to conduct longitudinal research to understand development.

Putting Bronfenbrenner's Theory into Practice in the Classroom

It would help teachers to think about the proximal processes in which they and the children in their class typically engage. That is, how do the children spend their time, being occupied in what types of activities and interactions? How does the teacher spend her time? To what extent are the children's activities or interactions with other objects and symbols (for example, with blocks or books), with other children, or with the teacher? What is the evidence that the children's activities and interactions become "progressively more complex" (Bronfenbrenner, 1995a, p. 641) over time? To the extent to which they are becoming increasingly complex, Bronfenbrenner would argue that they are likely to be beneficial for children's development.

As we pointed out earlier, person characteristics modify those proximal processes. Let us first consider the teacher's role. We might assume that teachers reading this text have an interest in applying this theory as a way to help foster children's development. Their willingness to try a new approach is a highly relevant person characteristic. But obviously there is more. All classrooms have a range of objects that are designed to be helpful for the children's learning, relative to their ages. What can teachers do to encourage increasing complexity as the children interact with those objects, with other children, and with the teacher herself? For example, a child should be encouraged to do more than simply build the same structure with blocks, but can be encouraged to think how to make it taller, stronger, incorporate bridges, and so forth. To the extent to which teachers are motivated to encourage challenges and persistent enough to ensure that it will happen, they are more likely to achieve enhanced development on the children's part. Each of the teachers' three main types of person characteristics is important here. There are the teacher's demand characteristics: those that the children first notice when they enter the classroom for the first time. There are her resource characteristics, such as the extent of experience she has teaching this age group. And there are her force characteristics, such as her motivation to establish positive and developmentally appropriate activities and interactions between her and her children, and among the children themselves.

But the teacher is only one of the persons whose characteristics are relevant to proximal processes. What about the children, and what can teachers do given the wide range of person characteristics that they possess? Given that wide range, a teaching strategy that essentially treats all children in any given classroom as the same (whole-class instruction) is unlikely to be as effective, at least in terms of maximizing proximal processes, as a strategy that takes account of individual differences. Think of the child who is shy (a force characteristic) and finds it difficult to integrate into a small group: How can teachers help that person engage in activities and interactions in developmentally effective ways? What about the child who seems far more capable than or at a different stage from (a resource characteristic) the rest of the class: How can teachers ensure that this one is intellectually stimulated and not bored? Another one comes from an ethnic background quite different from the rest of the class and, thanks to skin color or type of clothing, does not look the same as the others (a demand characteristic). What will teachers do to make this child feel welcomed by the group, and thus be able to engage with it in helpful and appropriate ways? Another child seems to be very bright (a resource characteristic), but is completely unmotivated to engage in any task that is in any way challenging (a force characteristic). How can teachers interact with this child so as to encourage a different, and more developmentally helpful, approach?

How do teachers deal with the context? One answer to that is quite straightforward, as they have some power to set up their own classroom as they think best. The manner in which the classroom has been set up (for example, the placement of chairs and tables, the choice of objects with which the children play or work, where artwork is displayed, and so on) influences how the children will engage with the materials, with the teacher, and with each other. In other words, teachers have a good deal of control of the microsystem in which proximal processes occur.

However, as Bronfenbrenner made clear, development never occurs simply in one microsystem, no matter how important it is. In the case of the children, their home background is another important microsystem, and how proximal processes proceed within the classroom is highly influenced by proximal processes that occur at home. By the same token, of course, what is going on in the teacher's home microsystem also influences the ways in which she engages in proximal processes within the classroom microsystem. Some children come to school from homes in which they are accustomed to engage and interact with one or more adults around activities such as reading or playing games together. Others interact far less in the course of these activities but spend more of their time engaged with the television, video games, or a variety of "smart" technology. What the teacher should expect from these two groups of children will be, initially at least, quite different; and the ways in which she engages and interacts with them will also need to be different. In any case, knowing about the children's home microsystem can only help teachers ease children's transition to the classroom microsystem.

Similarly, it may be that in the classroom there are children from different social-class backgrounds. Building on the work of Melvin Kohn (1979, 1995; see also Tudge, Hogan, Snezhkova, Kulakova, & Etz, 2000; Tudge et al., 2013), we might expect that children from middle-class backgrounds have been more often encouraged to decide things for themselves (where possible) whereas their peers from working-class backgrounds will have been more often encouraged to follow the rules that adults establish. Depending on how the classroom is set up, the transition from home to school will be easier for one of those groups of children than for the other. The more teachers want the children to think for themselves, the harder it will be for those who are accustomed to being told what to do. By contrast, the tighter the control exercised over the children in the classroom, the more difficult it will be for those who are less accustomed to being restricted. In both cases there are implications for how proximal processes proceed in the classroom. But knowing about the children's background can help teachers understand the difficulties that some, or all, of the children are experiencing, and plan activities and interactions in a way designed to smooth the transition. As time goes on, those proximal processes will become more complex; as teachers and children become accustomed to each other and the ways in which they are expected to engage with the teachers and with their peers, teachers can have increased expectations of them and, as Bronfenbrenner argued, development will follow.

The same is of course as true of ethnic/racial differences as of social-class differences. It is equally or more important for the teacher to understand something about the home experiences of children who come from a different ethnic or racial group than that of her own. It is not simply skin color, appearance, or style of dress (i.e., demand characteristics) that influence, initially at least, proximal processes, but the values, beliefs, and practices commonly held by groups of different racial or ethnic backgrounds.

As noted earlier, both social class and racial/ethnic group are examples of what Bronfenbrenner termed the macrosystem, which is the level of context in which values, beliefs, practices, access to resources, and a sense of identity are most relevant. However, the macrosystem only exerts its influence within microsystems, via proximal processes. As Kohn (1995) argued, there is good reason to believe that working-class parents typically stress obedience to adults as the best way to ensure their children's success; whereas middle-class parents see the exercise of autonomy and self-direction as more relevant to success. These beliefs may be widespread within these two social classes, but the effect of these beliefs can only occur by parents typically encouraging obedience or autonomy with their children. To the extent to which either of these practices typically occurs in the home we are, of course, considering proximal processes.

The other thing to remember about macrosystems is that they are always undergoing change. All one has to do is think about values and beliefs about early childhood education and how they have changed, even within the same society. How people thought about formal settings for young children 50, 100, or 200 years ago, and how they thought children should be educated are so very different. Similarly, the values, beliefs, and practices that distinguish one cultural group from another (even within the same society) change over time. Although Bronfenbrenner wrote about time in a number of ways, as pointed out earlier, macrosystem change over time (macro-time) must always be considered, calling into question the unfortunate habit of using a child's membership in one or other cultural group as the reason to try to explain his or her behavior.

Putting Bronfenbrenner's Theory into Practice in Research

The theory may appear to be far too complex to use either in research or in the classroom. The PPCT model, after all, specifies that proximal processes are simultaneously influenced by three types of person characteristics (demand, resource, and force) for each of the individuals involved in the proximal process of interest, four levels of context (micro-, meso-, exo-, and macrosystem), and time. Perhaps this is one reason why so many researchers seem content to think of the theory as something much simpler, one that deals just with contextual influence on development.

However, as we have made clear in some of our writing about Bronfenbrenner's theory (see, for example, Tudge et al., 2009; Tudge et al., 2016), there is absolutely no requirement to include all types of person characteristics and all levels of context in any study. The one essential component to include in any research based on his theory is proximal processes. That is, the study must focus on the typically occurring everyday activities in which the developing individual of interest is involved. Because the theory specifies that proximal processes are influenced by person characteristics, the study has to include at least individuals who differ on at least one (but not necessarily more than one) of the characteristics viewed as most relevant. Similarly, as the theory states that proximal processes are also influenced by context, the study has to include variation in at least one level of context. So long as data are gathered over time (by studying what is going on during proximal processes and by gathering data at least at two points in time), the minimum requirement for including time in the model will have been satisfied. It is also helpful, however, to specify the historical time within which the research is being conducted. Data gathered during a period of rapid economic growth or during peacetime may very well not be replicable should a similar study be conducted during a period of worsening recession or in the middle of a war. It is in fact possible to loosen these minimum requirements a little more. If a study were only conducted in a single type of context (just in school, or only with children from a working-class background, for example) and thus could not show how context influenced proximal processes, it would be sufficient to acknowledge the lacuna and point out that another study would need to be done in a different context in order to compare contextual influences on those proximal processes.

Conclusion

Early childhood educators might think that a theory of human development may be important in terms of research, but is not particularly relevant to their practical work with young children. Bronfenbrenner, however, was fond of quoting Kurt Lewin: "There is nothing more practical than a good theory" (Lewin, 1952, p. 169). That quote is exemplified by Bronfenbrenner's theory that allows teachers to think more clearly about the different, often interrelated, factors that influence how they work and succeed with the children in their class. A word of caution is in order, as most brief discussions of his theory describe it as a theory that only deals with different layers of context and how they each influence development. As we have shown in this chapter, that is far from the case.

Teachers know well that it is the school-related activities in which their students engage and the interactions that they have with their teachers and their peers (proximal processes, in other words) that are so important for their development, particularly in the early years of schooling. How these activities and interactions unfold is obviously dependent partly on the personal characteristics of the individuals (students and teachers alike) involved and partly by the context, of the classroom, the home, and the broader socioeconomic and racial/ethnic background of the family. Helping children learn is facilitated when teachers are mindful of the interplay among these factors. By contrast, when educators attend solely to the children's personal qualities, or to how they have set up their classroom, or only to their home backgrounds, the children's education and development will be hampered. The insights provided by Urie Bronfenbrenner's bioecological theory, as we hope to have shown in this chapter, can help teachers ensure that their students flourish.

References

Bronfenbrenner, U. (1994). Ecological models of human development. In T. Husen & T.N. Postlethwaite (Eds.), *International Encyclopedia of Education* (2nd ed., vol. 3, pp. 1643–1647). Oxford: Pergamon Press.

Bronfenbrenner, U. (1995a). Developmental ecology through space and time: A future perspective. In P. Moen, G.H. Elder, Jr., & K. Lüscher (Eds.), *Examining lives in context: Perspectives on the ecology of human development* (pp. 619–647). Washington, DC: American Psychological Association.

Bronfenbrenner, U. (1995b). The bioecological model from a life course perspective: Reflections of a participant observer. In P. Moen, G.H. Elder, Jr., & K. Lüscher (Eds.), *Examining lives in context: Perspectives on the ecology of human development* (pp. 599–618). Washington, DC: American Psychological Association.

Bronfenbrenner, U. (2001). The bioecological theory of human development. In N.J. Smelser & P.B. Baltes (Eds.), *International encyclopedia of the social and behavioral sciences* (vol. 10, pp. 6963–6970). New York: Elsevier.

Bronfenbrenner, U., & Morris, P.A. (2006). The bioecological model of human development. In W. Damon & R.M. Lerner (Series eds.) & R.M. Lerner (Vol. ed.), *Handbook of child psychology: Vol. 1. Theoretical models of human development* (6th ed., pp. 793–828). New York: John Wiley.

Kohn, M.L. (1979). The effects of social class on parental values and practices. In D. Reiss & H. Hoffman (Eds.), *The American family: Dying or developing?* (pp. 45–68). New York: Plenum Press.

Kohn, M.L. (1995). Social structure and personality through time and space. In P. Moen, G. H. Elder, Jr., & K. Lüscher (Eds.), *Examining lives in context: Perspectives on the ecology of human development* (pp. 141–168). Washington, DC: American Psychological Association.

Lewin, K. (1952). *Field theory in social science: Selected theoretical papers by Kurt Lewin.* London: Tavistock Press.

Rosa, E.M. & Tudge, J.R.H. (2013). Urie Bronfenbrenner's theory of human development: Its evolution from ecology to bioecology. *Journal of Family Theory and Review*, *5*, 243–258. doi: 10.1111/jftr.12022

Tudge, J.R.H. (2013). Urie Bronfenbrenner. In Heather Montgomery (Ed.), *Oxford bibliographies on line: Childhood studies.* New York: Oxford University Press. doi: 10.1093/OBO/9780199791231-0112

Tudge, J.R.H., Hogan, D.M., Snezhkova, I.A., Kulakova, N.N., & Etz, K. (2000). Parents' childrearing values and beliefs in the United States and Russia: The impact of culture and social class. *Infant and Child Development*, *9*, 105–121. doi: 10.1002/1522-7219(200006)9:2<105::AID-ICD222>3.0.CO;2-Y

Tudge, J.R.H., Lopes, R.S., Piccinini, C.A., Sperb, T.M., Chipenda-Dansokho, S., Marin, A.H., ... Freitas, L.B.L. (2013). Parents' child-rearing values in southern Brazil: Mutual influences of social class and children's development. *Journal of Family Issues*, *34*, 1379–1400. doi: 10.1177/0192513X12453820

Tudge, J.R.H., Mokrova, I., Hatfield, B.E., & Karnik, R. (2009). The uses and misuses of Bronfenbrenner's bioecological theory of human development. *Journal of Family Theory and Review*, *1*, 198–210. doi: 10.1111/j.1756-2589.2009.00026.x

Tudge, J.R.H., Payir, A., Merçon-Vargas, E.A., Cao, H., Liang, Y., Li, J., & O'Brien, L.T. (2016). Still misused after all these years? A re-evaluation of the uses of Bronfenbrenner's bioecological theory of human development. *Journal of Family Theory and Review*, *8*, 427–445. doi: 10.1111/jftr.12165

Suggested Websites

It is worth noting that the vast majority of internet sites do little more than describe the theory as comprising various levels of context (from microsystem to chronosystem), and so are not particularly helpful or up to date.

www.psychologicalscience.org/index.php/uncategorized/in-appreciation-urie-bronfenbrenner.html.

www.bctr.cornell.edu/about-us/urie-bronfenbrenner/

www.education.com/reference/article/bronfenbrenner-urie-1917-2005/

www.nytimes.com/2005/09/27/nyregion/urie-bronfenbrenner-88-an-authority-on-child-development-dies.html?_r=0

5

THE VYGOTSKIAN AND POST-VYGOTSKIAN APPROACH

Focusing on "the Future Child"

Elena Bodrova and Deborah J. Leong

Often called "the Mozart of Psychology," Lev Vygotsky is one of the most influential thinkers of the twentieth century. Born on the outskirts of czarist Russia in what is now the independent nation of Belarus, Lev Vygotsky never received formal training in psychology and instead earned a degree in law. At the same time he completed coursework for degrees in philosophy and history. After graduation, Vygotsky returned to his native Gomel, where he began teaching classes on varying subjects to students ranging from young children to in-service teachers. Intensive self-study in psychology combined with teaching experience solidified Vygotsky's interest in human development, which, in turn, led to his brilliant presentation at the Second Psychoneurological Congress, followed by his appointment to the Moscow Institute of Experimental Psychology in 1924.

During his short life of 37 years (1896–1934), Vygotsky was able to influence profoundly multiple disciplines from literary criticism to neuroscience to special education, and to raise a cohort of talented students who built on the insights of their mentor to develop a comprehensive approach to human development known as "cultural-historical psychology." The ideological pressure exerted on the social sciences by communist leaders in the late 1930s led to an almost complete ban on the Vygotskian approach in the USSR that was only lifted during the "thaw" of late 1950s and early 1960s. Most of Vygotsky's foundational works are now available in translation; however, the practical applications of his theory to education carried out by second- and third-generations of post-Vygotskians are not yet fully accessible to the Western audience.

The Vygotskian approach best fits the category of "developmental," with one significant caveat: Vygotskians view child development as driven by a complex interplay of biological maturation, societal expectations, and the child's own active participation in culturally determined activities and social interactions. Child development thus may follow different trajectories depending on the social context. With this disclaimer, the theories of Vygotsky and his students should be viewed in the social context of their time, which includes existing as well as emerging practices of child rearing and education at that time. Awareness of similarities and differences in these practices now and then is important when considering the applicability of Vygotskian ideas to today's early childhood education in the West and elsewhere. To help readers better understand the Vygotskian-based theories of early childhood education we will begin with defining some terms and providing a brief overview of an educational system that served young children in the times of Vygotsky and his students.

The Definition of Early Childhood: Same and Different

First of all, it is important to see how the terms "early childhood" and "early childhood education" are used in the writings of Vygotsky and his students when they first began writing in the early 1900s. In Western literature these terms are not used consistently, with the most broad definitions issuing from the National Association for the Education of Young Children (Copple & Bredekamp, 2009) and the Organization for Economic Co-operation and Development (OECD, 2001), who have defined early childhood as the period from birth to 8 years of age; and from the World Health Organization (Irwin, Siddiqi, & Hertzman, 2007) which includes the prenatal period in its definition of early childhood. At the same time, most publications on curricula and pedagogy in early childhood classrooms focus on children from the age of three until their entry into elementary school. This inconsistency of terms related to early education is closely mirrored in Russia and in the Soviet Union where a substantial body of Vygotskian and post-Vygotskian work was conducted. In Vygotsky's day, children entered school at age 8; the entry age was subsequently lowered to 7 with an option to enroll children at age 6 to give them one extra year of primary education. As a result of lowering the school entry age, the 6- and 7-year-old children who were described by Vygotsky and his post-Vygotskians as "senior preschoolers" would today be considered to be primary grade students, with whom the instructional practices of early childhood education are no longer used.

As for the relationship between the cultural-historical approach and early childhood education, Vygotsky and his students applied their theories primarily in the context of center-based or classroom-based education, with the amount of research focusing on other contexts such as family being significantly smaller. This can be attributed in part to the collectivist ideology imposed by the Soviet government on the social sciences and in part to the increasing number of children of working mothers enrolled in center-based programs. The greatest number of children served by preschool programs were between the ages of 3 and 6, while a smaller number of infants and toddlers attended nurseries that were also center-based and staffed with certified early childhood teachers.

For the purposes of this chapter, we will use the term "early childhood" to describe Vygotskian and post-Vygotskian ideas mainly as they apply to children aged 3 to 6, and will include a short description of Vygotskian views of infants, toddlers, and the students of primary grades.

The Cultural-Historical Paradigm as the Basis for the Vygotskian Approach to Early Childhood Education

The Cultural-Historical View of Development

To understand how Vygotskians view early childhood education, it is important to understand their approach to education in general and the *cultural-historical* definition of development as its foundation. Vygotsky's approach which was named by Vygotskians themselves as the cultural-historical approach, but here the terms *history* and *culture* have meanings somewhat different from the conventional ones. Vygotsky proposed that to truly understand psychological processes that are unique to humans, one has to study the history of the development of these processes as they unfold through an individual person's history or *ontogeny* and the history of humankind or *phylogeny*. Fully developed psychological processes are hard to study due to the fact that they usually exist in an internalized and "folded" form where many of the component processes are not easily visible. Processes under development, on the other hand, still have an extensive external, and therefore accessible to observation, component, which may provide researchers with an insight into the nature of this particular process (Vygotsky, 1978). The word *historical* in the phrase *cultural-historical approach* refers to the study of the formation of mental processes and represents Vygotsky's special interest in the development of children at the age when their mental processes are still taking shape.

The definition of *culture* also differs from that commonly assigned to it. Vygotsky focused mainly on one component of culture: the various signs and symbols that serve as *cultural tools* and their role in human development (Vygotsky, 1997). Another place *culture* appears in the cultural-historical approach is when Vygotskians look at the specific *socio-cultural contexts* of learning and development to see how these contexts shape development in an individual or in a particular group.

The Concepts of Cultural Tools and Higher Mental Functions

The concept of *cultural tools* is one of the central concepts in Vygotsky's theory. Building on the idea that humans are "tool making animals," Vygotsky extended it to new kinds of tools: cultural tools. Similar to the way physical tools extend one's physical abilities by acting as an extension of the body, cultural tools extend one's mental abilities by acting as an extension of the mind (Vygotsky, 1978). The use of these tools made it possible for humans to engage in increasingly more complex behaviors, thus starting humankind on a path of cultural evolution that largely replaced the biological one. In post-Vygotskian literature, cultural tools are often referred to as *mental tools* or *tools of the mind*, so in the future we will be using these terms interchangeably.

In his own writings, Vygotsky focused primarily on language-based mental tools, from gestures to oral speech to drawing and written speech, and the ways the use of these tools transforms human thinking. Subsequent generations of post-Vygotskians applied the idea of cultural tools to other mental processes and demonstrated how mastery of a variety of tools, including non-linguistic ones, can transform other mental processes including perception, attention, and memory. Examples of non-linguistic mental tools include *sensory standards*, which reflect "socially elaborated patterns of sensory characteristics of objects" (Venger, 1988, p. 148) such as colors, shapes, musical tones, and so on.

Defining mental tools as cultural, Vygotsky underscored the cultural-specific nature of these tools as well as the fact that children are not born knowing how to use existing tools and need to learn them from adult members of their society. Therefore, for Vygotsky, one of the major goals of education, formal as well as informal, is to help children acquire the tools of their culture (Karpov, 2005). Teaching children how to use mental tools results in children mastering their own behavior, gaining independence, and reaching a higher level of development. As children are taught and practice an increasing number of mental tools, it not only transforms their external behaviors but shapes their very minds, leading to the emergence of a new category of mental functions—*higher mental functions*.

Vygotsky's theory of lower and higher mental functions was developed as an ambitious attempt to create a new, revolutionary psychology, the psychology that would synthesize (in the Hegelian sense) the objectivist psychology that focused on observable behaviors common to humans and animals alike, and the subjectivist psychology concerned with the uniquely human experiences. Vygotsky's contemporaries described lower mental functions as features manifested in reflex, perceptual, and motor behaviors that are easy to observe and measure. Higher mental functions, on the other hand, were thought to be more complex processes to which objective methods of study were not applicable and which could only be accessed through a person's self-report. Vygotsky, however, did not consider lower and higher mental functions to be completely independent of each other, but instead proposed a theory in which these two sets of functions interact (Vygotsky, 1997). Vygotsky describes *lower mental functions* as common to humans and higher animals, innate, and depending primarily on maturation to develop. In the beginning, lower mental functions in humans are culturally independent; however, they may be later transformed and re-structured as a result of the development of higher mental functions. Examples of lower mental functions include sensations, spontaneous attention, associative memory, and sensorimotor intelligence. Sensation refers to using any of the senses and is determined by the anatomy and physiology of a sensory system in a particular species; reactive attention refers to attention that is drawn to strong or a novel environmental stimuli; associative memory is the ability to connect two stimuli together in memory after repeated presentation of the two together; and sensorimotor intelligence in the Vygotskian framework describes problem solving in situations that involve physical or motor manipulations and trial and error. Unique to humans, *higher mental functions* are cognitive processes children acquire through learning. The main difference between lower and higher mental functions is that the latter involve the use of mental tools. For example, learning words standing for different colors allows children to develop mediated perception, which would result in their differentiating between more or fewer shades depending on the size of their color vocabulary. In a similar way, children's mastery of mental tools transforms other lower mental functions, leading to the development of focused attention, deliberate memory, and logical thinking. All higher mental functions are acquired in a culturally specific way that affects their development via a system of mental tools and a corresponding system of practices associated with the use of these tools. According to Vygotsky, all higher mental functions share the following three characteristics: they all are *deliberate*, *mediated*, and *internalized* (Vygotsky, 1997). By characterizing higher mental functions as deliberate, Vygotsky means that they are intentionally controlled by that person and not by the environment. The behaviors guided by higher mental functions can be directed or focused on specific aspects of the environment, such as ideas, perceptions, and images, while ignoring other inputs. In Vygotsky's own words (Vygotsky, 1978), as children develop higher mental functions they begin to "master [their] attention" (p. 26) and "control [their] own behavior" (p. 28). These deliberate behaviors become possible because they do not depend on the environment in an immediate and direct fashion but instead are *mediated* by the use of tools. By the time higher mental functions are fully developed, most of the tools used are not external but internal (such as mnemonics) and so are the processes involved in using these tools. For example, counting that starts in young children as a physical action involving the use of tangible objects (e.g., counters or fingers) eventually evolves into a cognitive process that does not depend on external actions or objects. Vygotsky describes this process as *internalization*, emphasizing that when external behaviors "turn inward" they maintain the same focus, and function as their external precursors (Vygotsky, 1978, p. 57).

Describing the history of higher mental functions, Vygotsky points out that these functions do not appear in children in their fully developed form. Instead, they undergo a long process of development in the course of which a fundamental reorganization of lower mental functions occurs (Vygotsky, 1994). As children start utilizing higher mental functions more frequently, their lower mental functions do not disappear completely, but get transformed and integrated with the higher mental functions:

> In the thinking of the adolescent, not only completely new complex synthetic forms that the three-year-old does not know arise, but even those elementary, primitive forms that the child of three has acquired are restructured on new bases during the transitional age.
>
> (Vygotsky, 1998, p. 37)

Vygotsky described the mechanism of the development of higher mental functions in ontogeny as their gradual transformation from being shared by a child with other people to something that belongs to this child only. Vygotsky called this transition from shared to individual *the general law of cultural development*, emphasizing that

> [e]very function in the child's cultural development appears twice: first, on the social level, and later, on the individual level; first between people (inter-psychological), and then inside the child (intra-psychological). This applies equally to voluntary attention, to logical memory, and to the formation of concepts.
>
> (Vygotsky, 1978, p. 57)

Vygotsky's view of higher mental functions differs significantly from other developmental theories because while acknowledging other people's influences on a person's individual development, these theories hold that all mental processes still ultimately reside in the individual's mind. In contrast, for Vygotsky, not only *what* a child knows but also *how* this child thinks, remembers, or attends is shaped by the child's current and prior interactions with parents, teachers, and peers.

The Vygotskian View of Child Development

One of the hallmarks of the Vygotskian approach to education is that he and his students did not see the classroom as merely a place to apply their theories of learning and development. Instead, they saw schools as "laboratories" to study child development as it is being shaped by the social context. This approach extended to the programs designed to serve children with special needs as well as those designed to replace parental care, such as orphanages and boarding schools. Integrating research done in all these varying contexts allowed Vygotsky and his students to generate a rich theory describing child development in a social context.

Early childhood for Vygotsky is more than just a chronological concept. Being qualitatively different from middle childhood, it consists of three distinct periods or "age periods," each age period being built on the foundation of the previous one (Karpov, 2005). Infancy describes the period from birth to approximately 12 months of age; toddlerhood (or "early age" in Vygotskian terms) lasts from 12 to 36 months, and preschool age lasts until the time of school entry and includes what in the West is counted as the kindergarten year. One can see some similarities between this Vygotskian view and the stage theory of Jean Piaget; however, Vygotskian "age periods" are as much social formations as they are biological constructs. Each age period from infancy and toddlerhood to preschool and primary school age is defined in terms of the systemic changes that take place in the structure of a child's mental processes and in terms of a child's major developmental accomplishments that emerge as a result of a child growing up in a unique "social situation of development" that Vygotsky viewed as both the "engine" and the "basic source" of development. This idea determines Vygotsky's approach to the transition from one age period to the next one, since the social situation of development

> represents the initial moment for all dynamic changes that occur in development during the given period. It determines wholly and completely the forms and the path along which the child will acquire ever newer personality characteristics, drawing them from the social reality as from the basic source of development, the path along which the social becomes the individual.
>
> (Vygotsky, 1998, p. 198)

While Vygotsky did not complete his theory of child development in his lifetime, his writings indicate that he viewed development as a succession of stable periods followed by what he called "critical periods." During these critical periods, qualitative changes happen and the entire system of mental functions undergoes major restructuring that results in the emergence of cognitive and social-emotional "neo-formations" or developmental accomplishments. During stable periods no neo-formations appear, but children still continue to develop their existing competencies. During these stable periods, growth occurs as a quantitative change in the number of things the child can remember and process.

On the outside, the critical periods (or "crises" in Vygotsky's words) are accompanied by changes in child behavior that are often perceived by adults as negative: children who used to be easy and compliant start acting in an "oppositional-defiant" way. Vygotsky explained these sudden changes as the indication that a child's new emerging needs enter into conflict with the constraints imposed on this child by his or her current social situation of development. Overcoming this gap propels the child to the next developmental level. Vygotsky and his students identified the typical ages associated with these crises as 1, 3, and 7. These turning points corresponding to the transitions from infancy to toddlerhood, from toddlerhood to preschool age, and from preschool to school age. While Vygotskians did not consider that all two-year-olds went through a "terrible" period, they had "terrible ones" and "terrible threes" instead!

In the work of post-Vygotskians, his original view of stable and critical periods was refined and expanded to form a theory that contains well-defined developmental stages as well as the explanation of the mechanisms underlying children's transitions from one stage to the next (Karpov, 2005). One of the major contributions made by the post-Vygotskians to his theory of child development is the elaboration of his notion of the social situation of development, resulting in the idea of *leading activity*. Leading activity was defined as a type of interaction between children at a certain developmental stage and the social environment; an interaction that is the most beneficial for their development. Children's engagement in leading activity leads to the emergence of the neo-formations (developmental accomplishments) of this age period and prepares children for the next age period (Elkonin, 1972; Leontiev, 1981). *Developmental accomplishments*, in turn, were defined as competencies and skills that are not only new to a specific age period, but are also critical for the child's ability to engage in a leading activity of the following period (Karpov, 2005). For example, the ability to use objects in a pretend way that signals the emergence of symbolic thinking appears by the end of toddlerhood and lays the foundation for the development of make-believe play, which is a leading activity of the preschool age.

Vygotskians on Make-believe Play and Its Role in Child Development

One cannot describe Vygotsky's approach to early childhood education without mentioning his views on play. Not only is play considered the leading activity of preschool and kindergarten years, but Vygotskian-based approaches to supporting play also serve as an example of the practical application of the main tenets of the cultural historical theory. While Vygotskians share the belief in the importance of play with many other theorists of child development, their definition of play and their view on the role of adults in supporting children's play is unique. First of all, in their definition of play as the leading activity,Vygotskians focus on a specific kind of play—what is commonly referred to as pretend, socio-dramatic or make-believe play—leaving out many other kinds of activity such as movement, games, object manipulation, and exploration that were (and still are) referred to as "play" by most educators and non-educators alike. In addition, the characteristics of play in the writings of Vygotsky and his students imply that they describe what was later called a "fully developed" form of play (Elkonin, 2005) and not play in its emergent state as it exists in toddlers and younger preschoolers.

This "fully developed" play, according to Vygotsky, has three major features: children create an imaginary situation, take on and act out roles, and follow a set of rules determined by specific roles (Vygotsky, 1978). Each of these features plays an important role in children's development understood as the development of their higher mental functions. Role-playing in an imaginary situation requires children to carry on two types of actions: external and internal. In play, these internal actions, "operations with meanings" (Vygotsky, 1967 p. 15), are still dependent on the external operations on the objects. However, the very emergence of the internal actions signals the beginning of a child's transition from the earlier forms of thought processes—sensory-motor and visual-representational—to more advanced symbolic thought. Thus, make-believe play lays the foundation for two higher mental functions: thinking and imagination.

> Imagination is a new formation that is not present in the consciousness of the very young child, is totally absent in animals, and represents a specifically human form of conscious activity. Like all functions of consciousness, it originally arises from action. The old adage that children's play is imagination in action can be reversed: we can say that imagination in adolescents and schoolchildren is play without action.
>
> (Vygotsky, 1967, p. 8)

Thus, contrary to a widely held belief that in order to play children need imagination, Vygotskians consider imagination an outgrowth of play that emerges when children no longer need toys and props serving as physical "pivots" that help assign a new meaning to an existing object.

According to Vygotsky, another way make-believe play contributes to the development of higher mental functions is by promoting intentional, deliberate behaviors. Here again, the Vygotskian view of play differs from other theories where play is seen as an activity where children are totally free of any constraints. Moreover, Vygotsky's student Daniel Elkonin, who elaborated on his teacher's ideas to develop a cultural-historical play theory, called play "the school of deliberate behavior" (Elkonin, 1978, p. 287).

This feature of play becomes possible because of the inherent relationship that exists between the roles children play, the pretend props they use, and the rules they need to follow when playing these roles and using these props. For preschoolers, play becomes the first activity where children are driven not by the need for instant gratification, prevalent at this age, but instead by the need to suppress their immediate impulses:

> The role the child plays, and her relationship to the object if the object has changed its meaning, will always stem from the rules, i.e., the imaginary situation will always contain rules. In play the child is free. But this is an illusory freedom.
>
> (Vygotsky 1967, p. 10)

Finally, one more defining principle of the Vygotskian theory of play is its social and cultural nature. As children across cultures differ in their social situations of development, so does the function of play in their development. While in pre-industrial cultures the function of play was mostly to prepare children for engagement in well-defined "grown up" activities, modern play is non-pragmatic in that it does not prepare the child for specific skills or activities, but prepares the child's mind for the learning tasks of today as well as future tasks that humans cannot yet imagine (Elkonin, 1978; 2005). The Vygotskian view of play through this "cultural-historical" lens means that play cannot be viewed as something that spontaneously emerges in an individual child. Instead, play is something that is co-constructed by a child in interactions with other people. The nature and the extent of these interactions are determined by social context. While multi-age play groups with older children functioning as play mentors used to be a common feature of the culture of childhood in many Western countries, today these kinds of interactions are less and less common, which results in fewer children reaching the level of "fully developed" play by the end of their kindergarten year (Miller & Almon, 2009; Russ & Dillon, 2011; Smirnova & Gudareva, 2004). With more children spending their preschool and kindergarten years in center settings with peers of the same age, teaching children how to play becomes the responsibility of an adult.

The Vygotskian Theory of Teaching and Learning

Unlike other developmental theories that hold that children can learn only those skills and concepts for which they are ready, Vygotskians suggest that this readiness itself can be determined and promoted through the processes of teaching and learning. While it is true that some learning cannot occur until the developmental prerequisites are in place, such as in the case of children not being able to write until their motor skills allow them to have sufficient control of a writing instrument, the opposite is also true: certain developments in cognitive, social, or language areas cannot simply emerge as a result of maturation but rather depend on what a child learns. Arguing with the proponents of "following the child's lead," he writes:

> The old point of view ... assumed that it was necessary to adapt rearing to development (in the sense of time, rate, form of thinking and perception proper to the child, etc.). It did not pose the question dynamically. The new point of view ... takes the child in the dynamics of his development and growth and asks where must the teaching bring the child.
>
> (Vygotsky, 1997, p. 224)

Vygotsky's idea of the Zone of Proximal Development, or ZPD, reflects both the complexity of the relationship between learning and development and the dynamics of the transitions from shared forms of higher mental functions to their individual forms:

> what we call the Zone of Proximal Development ... is a distance between the actual developmental level determined by individual problem solving and the level of development as determined through problem solving under guidance or in collaboration with more capable peers.
>
> (Vygotsky, 1978, p. 86)

The word *zone* is used because Vygotsky conceived children's development at any given time as a continuum of skills and competencies at different levels of mastery. By using the word *proximal*, he pointed out that the zone is limited to those skills and competencies that will develop in the near future or are "on the edge of emergence" and not *all* possible skills and competencies that will eventually emerge. Thus a child's ZPD is defined by its lower boundary indicating this child's level of independent performance, and its upper boundary representing this child's assisted performance. The closer a skill or a competence is to the level of independent performance, the less assistance is needed for this skill to emerge. When even with the greatest amount of assistance a child fails to master a skill or a concept, it is a sign that this particular skill or concept currently lies outside this child's ZPD.

These skills and competencies contained within the ZPD do not determine children's current level of development but rather their learning potential. In the absence of guidance or collaboration with more competent others, this potential might not be realized and consequently a higher developmental level will never be attained. A child's ZPD changes as the child learns. A task that requires assistance today will be performed independently tomorrow. Then, as the child tackles more difficult tasks, a new level of assisted performance emerges. This cycle is repeated over and over again, as the child acquires increasingly more complex skills and competencies.

The idea of development being in part contingent on teaching and learning led Vygotsky to propose a different approach to assessing children. The assessment methodology used in Vygotsky's time (and that is still used today) prohibited testers from providing any help to a child. As a result, assessments of a child's cognition or language skills did not discriminate between the child's low level of performance being a result of developmental delay or educational deprivation. Vygotsky suggested incorporating adult assistance in the form of hints, prompts, or rephrasing the test questions into the very procedure of assessment. This modification allows for assessing not only children's existing skills and competencies but also the ones that have not yet surfaced due to the lack of educational opportunities but nonetheless have a potential to develop (Vygotsky, 1956). Vygotsky's insight later led to the emergence of a new methodology of assessment called "dynamic assessment" that is currently used in psychology and education (Haywood & Lidz, 2006).

In addition to influencing assessment practices, the Vygotskian concept of ZPD also expands the idea of what is developmentally appropriate to include concepts the child can learn with assistance. Vygotsky argues that the most effective teaching is aimed at the higher level of a child's ZPD, which means that teachers should provide activities just beyond what children can do on their own but within what they can do with assistance. While this idea soon became popular among educators, its practical implementation in the classroom met with some challenges. First, addressing each child's individual ZPD to maximize the effects of instruction did not seem feasible, given the endless variability between the ZPDs of individual children plus various ranges and levels of ZPDs within a single classroom. The second challenge was presented by the fact that for many children the ability to perform "under guidance or in collaboration" did not seem to eventually translate into their ability to perform independently at the same level. As a result of these challenges facing the use of ZPD in a classroom, most research on the interactions within the child's zone is limited to one-on-one interactions examined in a laboratory setting or in a family context

At the same time, the work of several generations of post-Vygotskians, as well as our own experience in implementing Vygotskian theory in early childhood classrooms (Bodrova & Leong, 2007; 2012), demonstrates that these two problems can be successfully solved, and one can design instructional practices in such a way that they will target each child's individual ZPD. First of all, the notion of assistance within ZPD needs to be expanded beyond an adult or a more experienced peer to include various social contexts (such as working in a pair, mentoring a less experienced peer, or engaging in a specifically designed group activity), various aids and instruments, and behaviors that children can use to self-assist (such as using private speech, writing, or drawing). With this expanded view of assistance, the idea of having the entire class functioning at the highest levels of performance no longer sounds unrealistic. For children of preschool and kindergarten age, Vygotskians consider fully developed make-believe play to be the most beneficial context, allowing all children to function at the highest levels of their respective ZPD, regardless of the range or the size of these ZPDs.

As for helping children make the transition from assisted to independent performance, the idea of scaffolding (Wood, Bruner, & Ross, 1976) proves very helpful. Although not used by Vygotsky himself, this concept helps us understand how aiming instruction within a child's ZPD can promote this child's learning and development. For most children, the transition from assisted to independent is a gradual process that involves moving from using a great deal of assistance to slowly taking over until eventually no assistance is needed. From other-assistance to self-assistance and finally to independence, designing appropriate scaffolding means planning to start withdrawing support from the very moment this support is first provided. Children who use assistance other than direct teacher support (e.g., using private speech to direct their attention or drawing a picture to support their memory) are already one step closer to becoming completely independent; children who act independently are now ready to be presented with a more difficult task and provided new assistance. By orchestrating the quantity and quality of assistance to fit each child's individual needs and strengths, it is possible to maximize each child's learning potential.

Vygotsky's idea of effective teaching being aimed at a child's ZPD was further extended by his students, notably by Alexander Zaporozhets, who founded the All-Soviet Research Institute for Preschool Education and for 20 years served as its director. Emphasizing the need to teach skills and competencies within rather than outside young children's ZPD, Zaporozhets condemned the practice of *acceleration of development*, something that intends to prematurely turn a toddler into a preschooler and a preschooler into a first-grader (Zaporozhets, 1986). An alternative to this unnecessary acceleration is *amplification of development*: using the child's ZPD to its fullest by making sure that all skills and competencies that have potential to emerge do emerge at the appropriate time

Applications of the Vygotskian Theory in the Early Childhood Classroom

The educational philosophy of teaching young children based on the Vygotskian theory can be summarized in the following principles:

- Early childhood has its own unique value and cannot be viewed as merely "preparing" children for school or for the adult life.
- Teachers focus on promoting the development of higher mental functions and on children's acquisition of mental tools (linguistic and non-linguistic) and not on children's mastery of discrete skills and concepts.
- School readiness is viewed in terms of supporting the emergence of developmental accomplishments that will ensure children's ability to make the transition to the leading activity of the primary grades—learning how to learn. The most important developmental accomplishments of early childhood include self-regulation, imagination, and ability to operate with symbols. Specific content knowledge and skills (e.g., writing or counting) are taught to promote these developmental accomplishments and are not considered as ends in themselves.

- Teachers promote and foster development by engaging children in the activities that are the leading activities for their age (such as emotional interactions for infants, joint object-oriented play for toddlers, and make-believe play for preschoolers and kindergartners).
- Teachers scaffold children's learning and development by first designing and then following a plan for providing and withdrawing appropriate amounts of assistance at appropriate times.
- Teachers constantly revise and adjust their practices to make sure that they target the zone of proximal development of their students. They assess individual and group ZPDs using dynamic assessment.

Conclusion

The Vygotskian approach combines a developmental perspective with a theory of teaching and learning, so both researchers and practitioners working in this tradition focus on the child "to be" or "the future child" rather than on the "present child," or what she or he is like at this moment. As Leontiev stated in his discussion with Urie Bronfenbrenner, "American researchers are constantly seeking to discover how the child came to be what he is; we in the USSR are striving to discover not how the child came to be what he is, but how he can become what he not yet is" (as cited in Wertsch, 1988, p. 67).

References

Bodrova, E., & Leong, D.J. (2007). *Tools of the mind* (2nd ed.). Columbus, OH: Merrill/ Prentice Hall.

Bodrova, E., & Leong, D.J. (2012). Scaffolding self-regulated learning in young children: Lessons from Tools of the Mind. In S. Sheridan, R. Pianta, L. Justice, & W. Barnett (Eds.) *Handbook of early education* (pp. 352–369). New York: Guilford Press.

Copple, C., & Bredekamp, S. (Eds.) (2009). *Developmentally appropriate practice in early childhood programs: Serving children from birth through age 8*. Washington, DC: National Association for the Education of Young Children.

Elkonin, D. (1972). Toward the problem of stages in the mental development of the child. *Soviet Psychology*, *10*, 225–251.

Elkonin, D.B. (1978). *Psikhologiyaigry* [Psychology of play]. Moscow: Pedagogika.

Elkonin, D.B. (2005). Chapter 1: The subject of our research: The developed form of play. *Journal of Russian and East European Psychology*, *43*(1), 22–48.

Haywood, H.C., & Lidz, C.S. (2006). *Dynamic assessment in practice: Clinical and educational applications*. Cambridge: Cambridge University Press.

Irwin, L.G., Siddiqi, A., & Hertzman, C. (2007, March). *Early child development: A powerful equalizer. Final report for the WHO's Commission on Social Determinants of Health*. Geneva, Switzerland: World Health Organization, Commission on Social Determinants of Health.

Karpov, Yu.V. (2005). *The Neo-Vygotskian approach to child development*. New York: Cambridge University Press.

Leontiev, A.N. (1981). *Problems of the development of the mind*. Moscow: Progress Publishers (original work published in 1959).

Miller, E., & Almon, J. (2009). *Crisis in the kindergarten: Why children need play in school*. College Park, MD: Alliance for Childhood.

Organization for Economic Co-operation and Development. (2001). *Starting strong: early childhood education and care*. Paris: OECD.
Russ, S.W., & Dillon, J.A. (2011). Changes in children's pretend play over two decades. *Creativity Research Journal*, *23*, 330–338.
Smirnova, E.O., & Gudareva, O.V. (2004). Igraiproizvol'nost u sovremennykhdoshkol'nikov [Play and intentionality in modern preschoolers]. *Vopprosy Psychologii*, *1*, 91–103.
Venger, L.A. (1988). The origin and development of cognitive abilities in preschool children. *International Journal of Behavioral Development*, *11*(2), 147–153.
Vygotsky, L.S. (1956). *Izbrannye Psychologicheskije Trudy* [Selected psychological studies]. Moscow: RSFSR Academy of Pedagogical Sciences.
Vygotsky, L.S. (1967). Play and its role in the mental development of the child. *Soviet Psychology*, *5*(3), 6–18. (Original work published 1966).
Vygotsky, L. (1978). *Mind in society: The development of higher mental processes*. Cambridge, MA: Harvard University Press.
Vygotsky, L. (1994). The problem of the cultural development of the child. In R.V.D. Veer & J. Valsiner (Eds.), *The Vygotsky reader* (pp. 57–72). Cambridge, MA: Blackwell.
Vygotsky, L. (1997). *The history of the development of higher mental functions* (M.J. Hall, Trans.) (Vol. 4). New York: Plenum Press.
Vygotsky, L. (1998). *Child psychology* (Vol. 5). New York: Plenum Press.
Wertsch, J.V. (1988). *Vygotsky and the social formation of mind*. Cambridge, MA: Harvard University Press.
Wood, D., Bruner, J.C., & Ross, G. (1976). The role of tutoring in problem solving. *Journal of Child Psychology and Psychiatry*, *17*, 89–100.
Zaporozhets, A. (1986). *Izbrannye psychologicheskie trudy* [Selected works]. Moscow: Pedagogika.

Suggested Websites

Classroom Applications: www.toolsofthemind.org
Vygotsky's Works: www.marxists.org/archive/vygotsky
The Vygotsky Project: http://webpages.charter.net/schmolze1/vygotsky/
Lev Vygotsky – Cultural Historical Theory: http://education.stateuniversity.com/pages/2539/Vygotsky-Lev-1896-1934.html
Lev Vygotsky: www.newworldencyclopedia.org/entry/Lev_Vygotsky
Lev Vygotsky: www.encyclopedia.com/topic/Lev_Semenovich_Vygotsky.aspx

Part II

INFANT/TODDLER THEORIES

6

THE EDUCARING APPROACH OF MAGDA GERBER

Ruth Anne Hammond

Biographical History of Magda Gerber

Magda Gerber often began or ended her lectures with the query, "Why shouldn't infants get the very, very best that our society can offer?" (Gerber, 1998, p. 189). Indeed, her many questions, and the answers she offered, have inspired a dedicated and still growing following in the infant–family field, even though she passed away in 2007 after a lengthy career as an educator, consultant, and mentor to countless parents and professionals. Born in Hungary and educated at the Sorbonne, having originally studied linguistics, she found her way to her profession in the same way that many early childhood professionals do, by first becoming a mother. Raising her family in Budapest between the two world wars, she chanced to meet the famously innovative pediatrician, Emmi Pikler, because her own family doctor was out of town. Gerber's little daughter, Mayo, suggested she call her friend's mother (a doctor) to fill in. This meeting ultimately led to Gerber becoming an expert in and advocate for the respectful care of infants in her own right. With Pikler, Gerber studied and taught the positive results of allowing infants to develop their movement skills without adult intervention or manipulation, as well as the foundational impact of secure versus insecure attachment with their primary caregivers.

Though Pikler's work originated in her medical practice, which was largely preventative, with typical families as a pediatrician, she was invited by the Hungarian government to create a residential nursery home for infants without families to care for them in the aftermath of World War II. So in 1946, Pikler opened the National Methodological Institute for Infant Care and Education, casually called Lóczy (for the name of the street on which the house stands), which was at once a full-time home for up to 40 infants aged 0–3, and a research and training institution. Lóczy was Magda Gerber's second training ground, after her own family "laboratory." At this writing, the organization, which, after Pikler's death, was renamed The Emmi Pikler National Methodological Institute for Residential Nurseries, is still conducting research, training parents and professionals, and providing child care for working parents, under the directorship of clinical psychologist Anna Tardos, who is Pikler's daughter. Tardos was, all those decades ago, the little kindergarten friend of Mayo Gerber, who suggested her mother phone Dr. Pikler in the first place! The families stayed connected through the traumas of the war. With the upheaval of the Hungarian revolution, Gerber and her family left for America in 1957, while Pikler and hers stayed in Hungary. However, the two women stayed friends and colleagues for life.

Upon immigrating, and after a relatively short stay in Boston, where she worked as a translator at Harvard University, Gerber settled in Los Angeles with her husband Imre and their three children: Mayo Erika, Daisy, and Bence. Having had what she described as the great privilege of learning about infant care and development under the mentorship of Dr. Pikler, and having become well versed in the other leading developmental theories of her time, including those of Freud, Erikson, Bowlby, Winnicott, and Piaget in her early childhood studies, Gerber was well equipped. After devoting a good deal of time becoming grounded and comfortable in her understanding of mainstream American family culture, she set out to find a way to support parents and child care providers in her new homeland in rearing confident, competent, and authentic children (Beatty & Stranger, 1984).

Gerber began her American teaching career in Los Angeles first at Children's Hospital as a therapist for children with cerebral palsy, then at the Dubnoff School for children with autism. In both settings, her emphasis in working with the children was on respect for their innate capacities for growth and self-actualization. Later, beginning in 1973, she began facilitating infant–parent groups for a diverse range of families, both typical and with risk factors, in the Palo Alto Health Council Demonstration Infant Program (DIP) which she conducted with pediatric neurologist Tom Forrest (Gerber, Greenwald, & Weaver, 2013). In 1978 they co-founded the not-for-profit corporation Resources for Infant Educarers (known as RIE), based in Los Angeles, of which Gerber was the founding director. She coined the term "educarer" to emphasize that education is first transmitted through the quality of the caregiving an infant receives (Hammond, 2009). It was in the context of RIE that Gerber's teaching career flourished, and her influence began to spread. Her teaching style was unique, in that she offered her adult students the same respect for each individual's personal learning space as she offered to infants.

In addition to her work with RIE, Gerber designed a course, which she taught for over 20 years at Pacific Oaks College, called Authentic Infant/Competent Child, which was a sought-after class by generations of graduate and undergraduate students of human development who went on to share her perspective (or approach) in all manner of early childhood and human services settings. She spoke all over the country and abroad at conferences for early childhood professionals (notably the N.A.E.Y.C.'s national and local events) and deeply influenced the values commonly known as developmentally appropriate practice (DAP) (Copple & Bredekamp, 2009) in infant and toddler care programs. She personally taught and trained hundreds, if not thousands, of child care professionals and parents in the course of her career, which spanned nearly half a century, and her writing still speaks eloquently of her admiration and respect for infants and the very young. She has inspired a counter-cultural approach to their care, which is spreading throughout North America, Asia, Australia, New Zealand, and Europe. This effort is spearheaded by the growing numbers of RIE Associates certified by Resources for Infant Educarers, as well as countless others (Hammond & Greenwald, 2007) who continue to teach her very special way of seeing infants and toddlers, which is increasingly known as the Educaring Approach, though sometimes still referred to as the RIE philosophy. Gerber concentrated her efforts on these early stages because, she said, "Children who can speak can tell you if they don't like something" (Beatty

& Stranger, 1984) and because at the time she began teaching, few others were advocating for the rights of infants.

Basic Guiding Principles of the Educaring Approach

Based upon the belief that infants come into the world as fully worthy and complete, if immature, individuals, Educaring is based upon respect. Gerber states, "We not only respect babies, we demonstrate our respect every time we interact with them. Respecting a child means treating even the youngest infant as a unique human being, not as an object" (Gerber, 1998, p. 1). The goal of this attitude and resultant treatment is to foster in children a sense of safety and security, which in turn fosters the desire to cooperate with significant others, as well as genuine confidence in their own competence and autonomy. The abiding intention is to allow children to be authentic, to be themselves without needing to perform in order to receive love. To this end, Gerber developed some basic principles which function as guiding precepts for parents, caregivers, and child care administrators (Gerber & Johnson, 1998).

Trust in the Child

With respect as the basic orientation of all the principles, and recognizing that each principle is supported by the others, the first is "Basic trust in the child to be an initiator, an explorer and a self-learner" (Gerber & Johnson, 1998, p. 4). In this, Erikson's ages and stages of socio-emotional development are referred to (Erikson, 1950) and also somewhat inverted. While helping the child develop trust in the world and also himself or herself, as Erikson conceived, it is also important for adults to trust that there are some essential capacities in the child that adults must have faith in and allow to unfold without unnecessary prompting or anxiety. The inner intentions of even newborns, based upon genetic and epigenetic foundations, motivate them to gradually gain control of their bodies as they grow; to seek intimacy with their parents through visual, vocal, and tactile means; and to explore their ever widening environment with all it has to offer. Trusting children means giving them time and attention laced with large quantities of curiosity to find out what they are interested in, what they are seeking, and how they relate to the world. Even if a baby turns out to have special needs, this attitude of trusting the child will provide the temporal, physical, and psychic space for the child to grow into her or his authentic self (Pinto, 2013).

Involve the Child in All Caregiving Activities

Assuming that the child is motivated to connect, the adult invites the baby to be involved in all the caregiving events he or she experiences every day as an active participant, instead of as a passive recipient. Through these many body/mind interactions between the adult and child, the adult gets to know the preferences of the child and contributes to the child's feeling of being known and loved, which in turn leads to knowing and loving the adult. This is the beginning of authentic relationships and communication. To achieve this kind of reciprocity, which requires contingent responsiveness on the part of the adult, the adult is called upon to take the perspective of the baby. What is it like to have another, much larger, person manipulating one's body? What sort of pace can keep the baby engaged in the process? What cues must the adult offer to help the baby learn to anticipate the steps involved in a diaper change or getting bathed? How does the adult use words and gestures to lead the baby to understanding? These are the lessons Gerber so eloquently framed in her writing and teaching, and that are so beautifully depicted in *Paying Attention to Each Other: Infant and Adult During the Bath* (Tardos & Appell, 1992).

The biggest caveat during bodily care is to *slow down* and focus fully on the child and the activity being undertaken. Only once this has been accomplished is it possible for the adult to attend to what the baby seems to be experiencing and feeling, and take into consideration the baby's interests and preferences. If we touch and manipulate and handle the baby's body at the same pace we would an adult's body, the child will feel out of control and have no choice but to give up and check out or to resist and cry. This dissociation from the sensory and social experiences inherent in care would set the stage for less than optimal self awareness and relational attunement, and is counter to the best interests of the child. Even if the care involves something unpleasant for the child, like dealing with diaper rash, it is beneficial to explain what is happening and respond to the child's discomfort calmly without rushing. Even when parents would say, "When my child cries because she doesn't want the diaper change, I go fast so she can go back to her play sooner," Gerber (1984) would still want them not to rush. Slowing down during care is one powerful way adults can promote the healthy attention span children need later in school and in life. Habits of attention start early.

When the baby's attention does wander from the task (which it inevitably will, as there are so many things to be interested in!) the sensitive adult will momentarily pause in her actions in order to share joint attention, then gradually guide the child back, if possible, or return to the care with acknowledgment of the child's interest. The child is not required to participate, but rather invited. If the adult genuinely values the child's initiative in helping with the task, this will further motivate reciprocal action and attunement. It may seem as though slowing down in this way is impossible in a busy family or child care setting, but practitioners often say that, in fact, it saves time by lessening the child's resistance. No one really enjoys having things hurriedly done "to" them, which naturally creates resistance. Reciprocity is what sets the stage for real cooperation (not just passive compliance), and cooperative children are more pleasurable companions for adults, and more likely to take on responsibility as they mature.

Caregiving events constitute what Gerber referred to as "Wants Something Time," (Gerber, 1998, pp. 76–77), one kind of quality time together, in which the adult has an agenda, must get something done, and uses the task to build a respectful relationship with the child. The other type of quality time together, which Gerber conceived as "Wants Nothing Time," (p. 75) leads to the next principle.

Time for Uninterrupted Play and Free Movement

If babies and young children are not sleepy or hungry, and are feeling well and safe, their instinctual impulses lead to exploration of their world. They will explore a parent's face, they will explore whatever is in reach, and, at first, most particularly, they will play at finding out how to control their own bodies. The Educaring approach accommodates the infant's need for exploration by suggesting that babies be allowed to follow their desires in a prepared environment that is safe, interesting, and supportive. (More on this will be discussed later.) Based upon Pikler's research of the natural stages of psychomotor development (Gerber et al., 2013), Educarers are inclined to put babies on their backs (which is their most stable position until they learn to roll over) on a firm surface, in the least amount of flexible clothing weather will permit. This gives them time to get to know their own hands, arms, legs, feet and whole bodies, all the while building up their coordination, including the all-important hand–eye coordination. This free movement time in the early weeks supports their learning, before they are even offered objects to grasp and manipulate. Pikler's research shows that infants who are allowed to move freely and are not helped to reach milestones such as sitting, standing or walking, follow a natural progression toward being upright that is graceful, integrated and safe (Pikler, 2007). Babies who are allowed this freedom are aware of their own limits and are less likely to put themselves in jeopardy, presuming that the environment is safe but appropriately challenging. Not helping children climb, for instance, allows them to know *in their bodies* how high up they are, since *they* have climbed; most such children stay within the reasonable limits of safety, avoiding accidents and requiring less anxiety on the part of adults (Gerber, 1988). Being patient and allowing the child to develop "in one's own time and own way" (Gerber, 1988) also prepares the adult to respect the child's learning process and authentic way of being throughout life.

Simple toys are placed near the baby (not in his or her hand) only after the baby has gained voluntary control of the grasping reflex. This respect for the child's self-initiated, self-directed exploration in an appropriate environment allows both adult and child to have times when they are independently autonomous, within the parameters of their relationship. Yes, the child is dependent on the adult for safety and nurture of all sorts, but does not need constant care or stimulation by the adult. By allowing the child time for uninterrupted exploration (which leads to play with objects after the first few weeks) the adult communicates trust in the child's own unique learning process that would be disrupted should the adult feel it necessary to teach or motivate. The motivation is built in; and it is a wise adult who can observe without interrupting an independently active baby with joy and wonder. This is another essential way adults first begin to foster the ability to concentrate and pay attention to learning. Early play is when babies learn how to learn. "As you develop the art and skill of observing your baby, you will also see that every experience, day in and day out, is a learning experience for him" (Gerber, 1998, p. 36).

This attitude of honoring the child's inner drive to explore transmits basic trust to the child, which comes through especially during what Gerber (1998) called "Wants Nothing Time" (p. 75). During this time, which is only some of the time the child is autonomously active, maybe for 15 or 20 minutes a couple of times a day, the adult observes with full attention, with no agenda for what the baby should be doing or learning. "We fully accept the infant's beingness just by our own receptive beingness ... This free play in the parent's [or other caring adult's] presence teaches the child to depend on his own inner security" (Gerber, 1998, pp. 75–76) during those times when the adult is not focusing on the baby. This inner security, of course, is supported by the love and gentle need-fulfillment the child receives from the adult. The autonomous (some say independent) play proceeds most productively and pleasurably when the child is assured that his or her needs will be kindly and promptly met. This is the circular nature of sensitive Educaring in a nutshell!

Program Guidelines for Educaring Environments

The "physically safe, cognitively challenging and emotionally nurturing" environment that Gerber espoused (Gerber & Johnson, 1998, p. 4) includes the physical space, the objects in it, the visual and auditory surroundings, and also the presence of other people, especially a trusted adult to offer care and comfort as needed. Safety in the physical sense, to Gerber, means that if one, hypothetically, got locked out of the house or center for some hours, the baby or toddler would not get hurt in the adult's absence, even though he or she would be scared and upset. Having a child-proofed, designated area that is gated off from anything unsafe for the baby allows both child and adult to be autonomously active during times when they are apart. A safe, interesting play space, which is appropriate to the developmental level of the child, will set the stage for independent play while the adult takes care of other things, or other children. Gerber writes, "We believe that babies derive security not only from being near their parents [or caregivers] but also from being allowed to explore their environment freely on their own" (Gerber, 1998, p. 15). At first the space can be the crib, then a playpen, and later the floor. Eventually, to keep the child's interest, the challenge of climbing equipment such as bolsters, platforms, ramps, steps and cubes can be introduced (Greenwald, in Gerber et al., 2013), as well as the presence of peers.

Play with Peers

In the Educaring model, children are given the opportunity to play in small groups with other children of the same developmental stage, whether in playgroups or child care. Keeping the age range narrow means that the set up can be appropriate for their specific stage of gross and fine motor development, as well as equalizing power dynamics between the children. Ideally, no child is so much bigger, stronger, or so much more active that she or he can overwhelm the others during free play. We know that ideal situations can be hard to come by, and families are usually, by definition, mixed age groupings, which makes for a more complex facilitation. However, when one caregiver is responsible for a few children, the primary way she or he can safely give full attention to the child being diapered is to have like-aged (or staged) infants or toddlers who can generally hold their own in a group. This is why Pikler programs, RIE Parent–Infant Guidance classes, and RIE-guided child care programs are organized into small, like-aged groups.

Peaceful Surroundings

The overarching concept behind what Gerber espoused was always to take the perspective of the babies or young children when planning on their behalf. The organization of time, the way the room or rooms are arranged to separate play spaces from caregiving spaces, and the quality of the overall sensory environment that adults and children will be immersed in for many hours per day, can all contribute to or detract from the quality of life for both children and adults. Maintaining the comfortable feeling of home for a child who is in child care for many hours a day, with the added stimulation of a number of unrelated adults and peers, means being ever mindful of how much stimulation the children are getting. Therefore, Gerber taught against having too much noise, including constant background music, televisions or radios playing, and adults talking to each other needlessly without regard to the child's needs. Babies and toddlers need to have a quiet space in which to learn to concentrate on their own inner sensations and outer explorations. Likewise, she thought, too many bright colors on the walls and items like mobiles hanging over their faces also interferes with learning and the development of a calm, peaceful way of being. She also felt it was important to give babies and young children ample time outdoors, in a natural environment where trees, grass, and the singing of birds create the sensory surroundings. Ultimately, an Educaring environment provides children just the amount of stimulation that inspires them to tune in and pay attention, instead of having to tune out, and to be able to protect themselves from too much sensory input, information or "noise," and thereby reducing chaos so that they can make sense of the world in manageable doses.

Varied, Simple, and Open-ended Objects

Adults decide what objects to make available to the child, and the child then decides what to do with them. In the child's safe space, nothing should be off limits. Objects should be simple, not a complex jumble of colors, shapes and textures all in one. Certainly they should not require batteries, or "do" anything, because, Gerber said (1998, p. 101), active toys make passive children, passive toys make active children. It is the child's actions, not the objects' actions, that stimulate the child to more and more exploration. The safest very first object offered to a baby who is just beginning to control his or her grasp is a cotton cloth napkin, set near enough that the baby can reach and touch it. If the baby cannot yet control letting go, no harm will befall as the baby begins to learn to manipulate this first friendly "toy." Gerber recommended objects that stimulate movement, like balls of all kinds (the ones with holes are especially useful to the younger babies), wooden rings, and all kinds of items that are safe for chewing. Lately, RIE facilitators have introduced silicone coasters, muffin cups, and bowls into the play space. Containers of all kinds, like colanders, light stainless steel bowls and cups, are also endlessly useful, as are smaller vessels to put in them, like plastic hair curlers and other interesting sets of items. The RIE DVD, *See How They Play* (Hammond, Memel, Pinto, & Solomon, 2013) offers examples of how some RIE environments look and how infants and toddlers use them.

Organized and Comfortable Places for Caregiving

Having the caregiving space or spaces as well thought out as the play space will support the full focus of the adult on the child during care routines. A comfortable armchair for the adult to sit in while feeding the baby is essential. Only if the adult is at ease, with arms well supported, can the baby also be comfortable. Educaring practitioners would never prop a bottle so that a baby has to feed himself or herself, as this disassociates the caring of the adult from the food. It is the warmth and kindness of the feeding adult that truly nourishes the child, much more than the bottle. Babies who are propped sometimes develop an inappropriate attachment to the bottle; RIE values the attachment with the adult. When solids are being fed to a child who cannot yet sit up on his or her own, the adult holds the child on the lap during feeding. This, again, promotes a foundational association in the child's experience between nourishment, closeness and well-being. As the child gains motor skills, the feeding environment will need to be adapted. Gerber suggested the use of a low stool so the child's feet are flat on the floor at a low table, once the child can find his or her own way there to sit independently (Greenwald in Gerber et al., 2013). This physical autonomy supports the child's competence and self-confidence, while the continued focused attention of the adult during feeding of the increasingly independent child is not lost. Once the child can sit comfortably, milk and other liquids are offered in a small, wide-mouthed glass.

Care areas are gated off from the free play areas so that if the adult is feeding or diapering one baby, the others are not able to interrupt by climbing onto the caregiver, or tugging at his or her legs. This practice allows each baby to get the focused attention and intimacy he or she needs, and they learn to wait for their turn. For diapering, dressing, bathing, and feeding, the areas should be well organized, with all necessary items easy for the adult to reach, but not where they will overly distract the baby. The adult should have all items ready before taking the child into the area, so that the interaction is all the adult needs to worry about during the routine. The changing table should allow for the child's free movement. Ideally it should be at least 30 inches wide and deep, so the adult can be face to face with the baby, and have 18-inch railings on three sides, so that as the baby develops he or she can move to his or her knees during diapering and dressing. As the infant becomes the toddler, a platform or area with a bar for holding on will allow the child to stand up during diapering. For Educarers, freedom of movement is equally as valued during care routines as during play. This requires the adult to adapt to the child's preferences; it requires cooperation from both sides, not just passive acceptance by the child. This can be challenging for the adult, but worth the effort (Gerber, 1984).

Primary Caregiving and Continuity of Care to Support Security

Early care programs that fully embrace the Educaring approach, with its underpinning of attachment theory (Bowlby, 1988), provide not only small group size but primary caregiving, in which each caregiver is the key person for nurturing a sub-group of three or four infants, and also continuity of care, wherein the adult stays with the same group of infants until they are around 36 months of age. RIE Parent–Infant Guidance classes are designed so that the group of six to eight infants and their parents stay with the same facilitator for weekly 1½- to 2-hour classes until the class ends, when the youngest in the group turns two, or sometimes longer.

The emotional security this fosters allows the children to focus more of their attention on exploration, learning and peer interactions, and making friends. This practice, first formulated in the 1940s by Pikler to meet the needs of infants living in an institution, was introduced to the child care community in the U.S. by Gerber, and through her teaching, and has since been adopted as essential elements of quality child care by N.A.E.Y.C. (Copple & Bredekamp, 2009), WestEd/PITC (Butterfield & Gilford, 1992), and Early Head Start. With regard to primary care, Gerber says, "If I am a baby I would have difficulty always having to adapt to a different style; one is fast the other is slow ... one uses cold water to wash my bottom, one uses warm. You know, for me, if I am a baby I have to adapt to so much novelty that ... I want to still be able to predict a little bit" (Butterfield & Gilford, 1992). She goes on to say, concerning group size, "Babies, even very young babies, come to know each other. ... If you have a large group, and many big bodies ... and many small bodies ... and lots of noise, it's utter confusion" (Butterfield & Gilford, 1992). This way of looking at the world from the infant's point of view is what made Gerber's teaching so fresh and inspiring.

In the unique model Gerber designed for families in her RIE center, infants and toddlers are gathered weekly in RIE Parent–Infant Guidance Classes in small like-aged groups to provide a calm, facilitated forum for play and socialization for the infants, as well as peer support for the parents. This format provides parents and trainees the chance to learn the Educaring approach through direct experience over time, as the children grow and change led by certified RIE Associates and RIE Practicum students. Ideally, infants stay in the same group for two years, getting deeply acquainted with every adult and child, thereby being able to form predictions about human behavior and interaction over time. This stability is one of the hallmarks of Gerber's value system; she often said in her classes, "Babies thrive on boring sameness" (Personal communication, November 9, 1986) because predictability is what creates security and provides a basis for the appreciation of novelty and surprise. Without this grounding, everything can seem random, identifiable patterns do not emerge, and life seems chaotic.

Sensitive Observation and Selective Intervention

The pace at which events unroll throughout the day should account for the ebb and flow of the children's energy, their need for exuberant activity as well as rest and down time, and sufficient opportunities for emotional refueling with their primary caregivers in intimate interactions, especially during care routines. This requires full commitment from the administration as well as the caregivers. Making sure that the caregivers have time to observe each child deeply and sensitively in order to come to understand and attune with him or her is one of Gerber's most important caveats. Educarers take time as often as possible to sit and watch the children in play, without trying to judge or assess, but to learn what interests the child. Likewise, if a child is in distress, the Educarer may not jump in to "fix" the situation right away. She or he may move in and take time to see if the child can solve the problem on his or her own. By waiting and watching, the adult learns about the child and the child learns that not every feeling of distress requires adult help. Of course, when all indications are that the child does need help, the Educarer is right there with a well-informed intervention. "Selective Intervention" is how Gerber described what sensitive observation leads to. She says, "Selective Intervention means knowing when *not* to intervene, and this is more difficult than intervening indiscriminately" (Gerber, 1998, p. 68).

Clear and Consistent Limits

Authenticity and Emotional Honesty

Gerber believed that even the youngest baby would benefit from being spoken to as an intelligent individual. Perhaps the pitch, the tone of voice and the musicality of how one speaks to infants does not sound like speaking with adults, but she advocated using honest and informative language with young children so that they would have the information to help them understand what is going on around them, within them, and even to them. She says,

> To talk to your baby from the first hour of her life is not only pleasant and soothing to the baby, it can be a relief for you ... to say how you feel and what you want. It is also the beginning of a lifetime of communication. ... Just tell the baby how you feel and what you think; do not censor your feelings or thoughts.
>
> (Gerber, 1998, p. 33)

By this she encouraged authenticity on the part of the adult, as a way to allow the child to feel that what he or she intuits is matched by the overt communication. She felt it was better for adults to admit to a child when they were baffled by their child's needs, or frustrated with his or her behavior. In Gerber's paradigm, it is healthy to say, "I am feeling so bad that you are crying, and I can't seem to help you feel better. I am trying my best." In the DVD, *Seeing Infants with New Eyes*, she says, "If you want your child to be authentic, you have to work on your own authenticity" (Beatty & Stranger, 1984). She felt that if the adult can be self-aware enough to be honest with the child in a regulated way, the child will have a good model to work from in her or his own formation.

Reciprocally, the adult is able to allow the child to express all of his or her feelings authentically as well. It may be that the adult must limit some behaviors, but the child, Gerber felt, should be free to have and fully process all his or her feelings, without having to repress or pretend in order to make the adult happy. The child should not have to perform. This is similar to the concept of "holding" developed by D. W. Winnicott (1972; 1986) in which the mother, or other primary adult, is able to tolerate and even somehow digest on his or her behalf all the positive and negative feelings of the child, paving the way for integration of the full spectrum of feelings and desires into a coherent sense of self. This avenue leading to authenticity is one of the key principles of Educaring.

Providing Boundaries and Guidance

Allowing for all of children's feelings does not mean that Gerber was against setting limits on their behavior. She believed that children derive security knowing that they are operating within safe boundaries set by the adult, or adults, in charge. She was very clear that her approach was not permissive. She also appreciated that part of the developmental tasks of toddlers is to test limits. With no limits, what is there to test? Gerber (1998) writes:

> We need to remember that limits function as traffic signals, keeping things flowing smoothly between family members. Within this framework are those things a child is expected to do (non-negotiable areas), what she is allowed to do (negotiable areas), what is tolerated ("I don't really like that, but I can understand why you need to do it") and what is forbidden (I don't want you to do that"). These are the parameters of discipline.
>
> (p. 113)

Educarers feel entitled to create what Gerber (1998) called "House Rules" (p. 111); they do not shy away from their role as the ones in charge. They are comfortable wielding power in a conscious and benevolent way so as to create a structure to the child's life and environment that will allow self-discipline to emerge. A house rule is consistently expected. RIE Parent–Infant Guidance facilitators model this process for parents with a few very simple rules in class: (1) Children do not wear shoes in the playroom, or socks either, for safety's sake and for the benefits of going barefoot, which are numerous, especially for those just learning to move; (2) Adults sit low and mostly observe the children's play; (3) When joining snack time, children must leave toys behind, let their hands be washed, wear a bib, and be sitting down before food or a beverage will be offered. However, they do not have to come to snack, so they do have a choice within the structure. If they want to continue playing with toys, or if they object to having their hands washed, they can skip snack. Over time, it is remarkable to see the toddlers learning these "manners" in a way that makes the process a pleasure for themselves and all the adults who are either serving or observing. The consistency with which adults apply the rules allows children to predict how the routine goes, so that they can relax their vigilance. They know they are free to pursue their own agendas without concern that they may be unwittingly making the adult(s) unhappy. No one likes being in the situation of walking on eggshells, toddlers included. Too many rules, or rules that seem to come out of nowhere, create stress rather than self-regulation.

Appropriate limits allow children to adjust to fit into their families, their culture, their situation, and to become well liked in all their important circles. Gerber always gave children (and adults) the reasons behind rules and requests, so that they could internalize and understand them more coherently. She did not expect children always to like what was being asked of them, but she was willing to accept their protests and tears, without backing down. She would rather Educarers be direct than manipulative in their communications with toddlers. If a child is reaching for grandmother's fragile knick-knack, for instance, she would have the adult say something like, "I don't want you to touch this; it is too easily broken, and Grammy likes it and wants it to stay whole. When you are older you can hold it." If children get leisurely periods of free, uninterrupted play in an appropriate environment, it is easier for them to tolerate times when they cannot do whatever they want. This was one of her essential messages to parents who might mistakenly think that the value of allowing children to move and play freely means that it is bad to ever thwart their explorations or creativity. Children, like all people, cannot *always* do as they like.

Gerber also recommended encouraging desired behavior with appreciation or praise, like "It's good to see how gently you are touching Benjamin" (Gerber & Johnson, 1998, p. 196). These messages must be grounded in authenticity, and not delivered as rote reinforcers. Being honest in sharing one's true feelings about their actions, whether positive ("Oh, thank you for throwing your trash away!") or negative ("I don't like it when you hit me; it hurts. Please stop.") lets them construct an understanding of the social world and how they fit into it.

When toddlers are playing in groups, it is to be assumed that there will be conflicts for the adults to monitor. By knowing the children well through careful observation, Educarers are able to create a sense of safety so that they can intervene very selectively and effectively. By trusting the children to tolerate a certain amount of stress or discomfort (but not an overwhelming amount), they allow children to make mistakes and work to solve their own problems. Babies playing on the floor together are interested in each other and tend to explore as though the other were an object, at least at first. The Educarer intervenes gently, to model gentleness, and keeps the children safe without discouraging exploration and togetherness. This sets the stage for many peaceful exchanges as they grow to know one another over time (Gerber & Wright, 1978).

Toddlers, like babies, are not expected to share, but are allowed to experiment and engage in struggles with peers (Gerber, 1998). When problems seem too big for the solutions children are capable of, the Educarer moves in with a protective gesture, a word of caution or a gentle reminder of the rules. There are even times when the adult has to physically separate children, but this is rather a last resort.

The Educarer's language to accompany his or her actions and gestures is carefully chosen to clarify behavioral expectations without communicating negative judgments of the child's feelings. If the interaction does not include violence, but does include emotional upset, the Educarer will use descriptive, but not prescriptive, language: "I see you both want that truck. You are pulling and pulling. Toby is crying." By waiting, he or she is communicating to the children that this struggle has got his or her attention but is not an emergency, and that they can manage. However, there are instances when the adult must take a more active role. For example, if a child is about to hit another child, the Educarer will move in close and, if possible, prevent the blow from landing, saying something like, "I won't let you hit your playmate. That would hurt him." Then, if it is evident why the child was motivated to hit, more words can be useful, such as, "It seems like you are asking for more space," or "Even though you are angry he took your ball, I don't want you to hit. I wonder if you can find another ball?" Offering a description of what happened, some guidelines, and, without being directive, a possible solution, helps to widen the child's awareness of the consequences of the thwarted action and the potential for peaceful resolution without inhibiting the child's sense of owning his or her own feelings and desires. "I don't want you to hit," is a very different message from, "We don't hit," as the latter excludes the child and undermines his or her basic trust in self, especially if he or she *does* hit sometimes. It is the adult who sets the rule by stating her or his position on the matter, and when necessary, backs it up with action to enforce the rule. Toddlers need the physical presence of the adult in such situations; talking from across the room is rarely helpful. Sometimes, just moving in physically when it looks like a conflict is escalating will provide a sense of safety for both children so that the escalation does not occur. This is what "selective intervention" means. Gerber always recommended giving the least amount of help necessary to help the child through the impasse. When she spoke of such scaffolding, she would often refer to the work of Lev Vygotsky (1978), who wrote about ways in which the participation of adults or more mature children facilitates the young child's problem-solving.

An Integrated Approach

Although Gerber developed her approach prior to the explosion of neuroscientific advances in understanding the biology and resulting psychology of infant development which came along just as she was in the process of retiring, her work has been validated by recent research (Hammond in Gerber et al., 2013). The work of scientists Allan Schore (1994; 2012), Jaak Panksepp (1998; Panksepp & Biven, 2012), Daniel

Siegel (2012) and many others, have explicated the ways in which early relationships and experiences affect the development of the infant brain and long-term mental health. Gerber, and her mentor Emmi Pikler, knew from their own observations and practice how early experiences are likely to shape infants' development; it took some decades for "hard" science to catch up. Neuroimaging has made the case stronger for the constructivism of Piaget, Vygotsky, and the attachment theory of Bowlby, on which much of Gerber's work is founded. She articulated sound practical applications of what was just over the horizon for the interpersonal neurobiology community.

The physical, emotional, cognitive, and interpersonal aspects of development are all taken into account in the principles and practice of Gerber's Educaring approach. It supports the whole child, providing an integral framework to help adults nurture the child's autonomy and freedom, as well as his or her ability to take moral responsibility within an ever widening matrix of relationships with family, friends, and others, with whom he or she will help create the future.

Even though there are seven often-quoted principles of Educaring which have been touched upon herein (Gerber & Johnson, 1998), they should be seen as guiding principles, not directives. Providing infants and young children the conditions which will support the development of balance between the seemingly dual impulses of the need to feel personally powerful as well as deeply connected (agency *and* communion) does not require following a list of rules, but rather flexibly forming a respectful, open-minded, fully present way of being with children while relying on one's own inner truth as well as some learned intentions. It calls on adults to see infants as whole, if immature, people who are worthy of the same consideration – maybe even more – than we would offer other adults. Magda Gerber has provided a sort of philosophical flagpole to keep in sight while navigating the profound challenge of educating while we care and caring while we educate (Gerber, 1998), somehow in the process lessening the pressure to be perfect. By trusting nature, allowing for honest trial and error, and promoting genuine curiosity through sensitive observation, Educaring serves the needs of children and their caring adults, facilitating for both generations a deeply fulfilling and authentic life together.

References

Beatty, T., & Stranger, C. (1984). *Seeing infants with new eyes* (Video/DVD). Available from Resources for Infant Educarers. www.rie.org

Bowlby, J. (1988). *A secure base: Parent–child attachment and healthy human development.* London: Routledge.

Butterfield, G. (Producer, Editor, Writer), & Gilford, S. (Writer, Director) (1992). *Together in care: Meeting the intimacy needs of infants and toddlers in group care.* Sacramento, CA: California Department of Education.

Copple, C., & Bredekamp, S. (Eds.) (2009). *Developmentally appropriate practice in early childhood programs serving children birth through age 8* (3rd ed.). Washington, DC: N.A.E.Y.C.

Erikson, E. (1950). *Childhood and society.* New York: W.W. Norton.

Gerber, M. (1984). Off again, on again. *Baby Magazine*, pp. 58–59.

Gerber, M. (1988). *See how they move* (Video/DVD). Los Angeles, CA: Resources for Infant Educarers.

Gerber, M. (1998). *Dear parent: Caring for infants with respect.* Los Angeles, CA: Resources for Infant Educarers.

Gerber, M., with D. Greenwald & J. Weaver (Eds.) (2013). *The RIE manual for parents and professionals*. Los Angeles, CA: Resources for Infant Educarers.

Gerber, M., & Johnson, A. (1998). *Your self-confident baby*. New York: Wiley.

Gerber, M. (Writer), & Wright, P. (Writer/Director) (1978). *On their own/with our help*. (Video/DVD). Available from Resources for Infant Educarers, www.rie.org. Los Angeles, CA: Resources for Infant Educarers.

Hammond, R.A. (2009). *Respecting babies: A new look at Magda Gerber's RIE approach*. Washington, DC: Zero to Three.

Hammond, R.A. (2013). Educaring, interpersonal neuroscience, and selective intervention. In M. Gerber, D. Greenwald, & J. Weaver (Eds.), *The RIE manual for parents and professionals* (pp. 177–186). Los Angeles, CA: Resources for Infant Educarers.

Hammond, R.A., & Greenwald, D. (2007). In memoriam: Magda Gerber. *The Zero to Three Bulletin*, July.

Hammond, R.A., Memel, E., Pinto, C., & Solomon, J. (2013). *See how they play* (DVD). Available from Resources for Infant Educarers, www.rie.org. Los Angeles: Resources for Infant Educarers.

Panksepp, J. (1998). *Affective neuroscience: The foundations of human and animal emotions*. New York: Oxford University Press.

Panksepp, J., & Biven, L. (2012). *The archaeology of mind: Neuroevolutionary origins of human emotions*. New York: W.W. Norton.

Pikler, E. (2007). Give me time: Gross motor development under the conditions at Lóczy. In A. Tardos (Ed.) *Bringing up and providing care of infants and toddlers in an institution* (pp. 135–150). Budapest: Association Pikler-Lóczy.

Pinto, C. (2013). Supporting competence in a child with special needs: One child's story. In M. Gerber, D. Greenwald, & J. Weaver (Eds.), *The RIE manual for parents and professionals* (pp. 190–194). Los Angeles, CA: Resources for Infant Educarers.

Schore, A.N. (1994). *Affect regulation and the origin of the self: The neurobiology of emotional development*. Hillsdale, NJ: Lawrence Erlbaum Associates.

Schore, A.N. (2012). *The science of the art of psychotherapy*. New York: W.W. Norton.

Siegel, D. (2012). *The developing mind: How relationships and the brain interact to shape who we are* (2nd ed.). New York: Guilford Press.

Tardos, A. (Writer/Director), & Appell, G. (Writer/Director) (1992). *Paying attention to each other: Infant and adult during the bath* (DVD). Available from http://pikler.org/store.html

Vygotsky, L. (1978). *Mind in society: The development of higher psychological processes*. Cambridge, MA: Harvard University Press.

Winnicott, D.W. (1972, 1986). *Holding and interpretation: Fragment of an analysis*. New York: Grove Press.

Suggested Web Resources

www.rie.org

www.pikler.org

www.pitc.org

www.naeyc.org

www.YouTube.com. Real life illustrations of Educaring principles: *Ruby Reaches for a Toy* by Amy Jane; *Rolling—Feldenkrais with Baby Liv* by Irene Lyon.

www.facebook.com/RIEorg/

7

T. B. BRAZELTON'S DEVELOPMENTAL APPROACH TO LEARNING

Joshua Sparrow

Development begets development, and learning begets learning. Nature is economical. It does not jettison early experience, but retains it as the foundation for subsequent development and learning. Development proceeds nonlinearly toward growing complexity and coherence. This chapter briefly describes some of the central phenomena of early development described by T. B. Brazelton and colleagues. Parents, educators, and others engaged in children's learning and development can observe and elicit these phenomena even in subsequent development, when they can help children to build on this foundation in the service of the acquisition of new skills and capacities.

Social Justice and Scientific Revolutions

Brazelton was born in 1918 to an affluent Euro-American family and raised in Waco, Texas. Like most young children, he couldn't understand the social, economic, and racial hierarchies of the adult world around him. His care was delegated to an African American woman, alongside a child of her own, with whom he was not allowed to play. Mexican Americans performed the house and yard work, invisibly, as they were expected to do. In his autobiography, *Learning to Listen*, he explains that very early in life he experienced this social arrangement as an outsider, questioning what seemed illogical and wrong, and took on the mantle of maverick for change (Brazelton, 2013).

Young children, like scientists, are curious, and they question. Children do not begin with received wisdom, and scientists do not assume it is true. Instead, just as young children incessantly ask why, scientists advance knowledge by asking about the limits of our understanding, about what we remain unable to explain, and about what once seemed to make sense but no longer does. Also like young children, scientists are often gifted observers, in part because they too are naturally curious (Fraiberg, 1996). Young children's relative lack of unexamined assumptions, and scientists' healthy skepticism about them, bestow on both an openness to the surprising and unexpected, and prepare them for discovery.

After his pediatric training, Brazelton quickly concluded that although he had learned much about disease, he knew nothing about children. Perhaps there is a similar risk today for some educators, who may learn far more about curricula and content, classroom management, standards and competencies, teaching tools and techniques, than about how children develop and learn. Hoping to remedy the limitations of his education through his subsequent child psychiatry training, he encountered the wear and tear of a scientific stance that never really made sense (Kuhn, 2012).

In the 1950s, the problems of children with autism spectrum disorder, like those that he worked with, were thought to be the result of "refrigerator mothers" (Kanner, 1943). In those days, psychoanalytic theory often blamed adult mental illness on poor parenting. This belief was based on the erroneous assumption that infants and young children were blank slates whose development was singly determined by their parents' inscriptions. Few psychoanalysts studied very young infants. Not even Margaret Mahler, who proposed infant stages of development such as "symbiosis" and "hatching," had actually observed infants under six months of age. Brazelton and another pioneering infant development researcher, the late Daniel Stern, recounted a visit with Mahler to discuss her theories of infant development, during which she acknowledged that she had never studied infants less than six months old.

Individual Differences

As Brazelton carefully observed children with autism spectrum disorders, he noticed neurobehavioral similarities among them that just did not seem explainable by maternal behavior. These children's common characteristics and their differences from other children made him curious about when and how individual differences come about.

This led him to his revolutionary studies of newborn behavior, and to his discovery that it is purposeful and that there are individual differences in newborn behavior at birth (Brazelton, 1962; 1973; 1983). As he observed newborns across the globe, he also observed behavioral differences at birth from one group to another. He theorized that these were in part due to genetic differences, and in part due to *in utero* influences that varied with contexts and cultures that shape women's experience of pregnancy, and in turn, fetal development (Sparrow, 2013). Brazelton's observations of newborn behavior helped create the impetus for investigating infant brain development with brain imaging. His study of individual differences anticipated subsequent research on epigenetic programming demonstrating that *in utero* and early experience can alter the expression of genes (Meaney, 2001; Weaver et al., 2004; Szyf, McGowan, Turecki, & Meaney, 2010). Yet individuals acting alone rarely bring about scientific revolutions. Instead, it is the growing recognition of the inadequacy of the existing scientific paradigm that stimulates a generation of scientists to search for a new one (Kuhn, 2012).

At about the same time, Stella Chess and Alexander Thomas were developing their theory of temperament, for which they were studying older children (Thomas & Chess, 1968). Components of temperament include level of activity, attention span, distractibility, persistence, response to novelty and environmental stimulation, and flexibility. Understanding each child's individual differences—in temperament, and in learning styles—gives parents, educators, and children themselves critical insights into how to most effectively individualize the structuring of time, space, activities and interactions to optimize learning and development. Efforts to understand a child's temperament and way of approaching the world can begin at the very beginning of life.

Prior to scientific observations of the newborn, medical orthodoxy assumed that infants were born blind, deaf, insensate, and persisted in a neuro-vegetative state for the first several months of life, and that learning would only come much later. Conveniently, perhaps, this led to the belief that infant care was limited to the requirements of nutrition, hygiene, and safety. Brazelton was not, of course, the only scientist whose studies helped replace an aging scientific paradigm with a new one that could better account for the discoveries awaiting those who carefully observed newborns and very young infants (Kuhn, 2012). While Kathryn Barnard, Betty Caldwell, Frances Horowitz, John Kennel, Marshall Klaus, Margaret McGraw, Lynn Murray, Heinz Prechtl, Judith Rosenblith, Daniel Stern, Colwyn Trevarthen, Ed Tronick, Peter Wolfe, and many others were also turning their attention to this new scientific frontier, the limitations of the assumptions of the time were becoming increasingly evident.

Newborns Shape Caregiver Behavior

Brazelton's discovery of individual differences at birth led him to reject prevailing beliefs about parents' caregiving as unilaterally determining child wellbeing, or dysfunction. Newborn individual differences, he realized, are, in part, an expression of fetal experience, a kind of adaptation to and preparation for the unique and specific context into which each baby is born (Salisbury, Yanni, LaGasse, & Lester, 2004). Newborn behaviors express newborns' individual needs and potential, shaping the specific caregiving behaviors best suited to them (LeVine, 2004, 2010). From birth, children's behavior is purposeful, meaningful and has evolved as a form of communication with caregivers. For parents and educators, the challenge is to learn to watch and listen carefully, to understand how each child conveys meaning, what each child needs us to know, and how each child needs to change our behaviors as we learn to care for and learn with them.

State Regulation, Self-regulation

Among the purposeful newborn behaviors that will contribute to the foundation of future learning and development are those that indicate states of arousal, and those that aid in the regulation of these states. In the newborn, six states have been identified and are readily observed and distinguished: deep sleep, light sleep, drowsy, alert, fussing, and crying (Brazelton, 1973). Each state represents the infant's efforts to balance the challenges and opportunities offered by the environment with the infant's individual internal needs and capacities.

For the newborn, state regulation is carried out in several ways, and their manifestations may vary from one infant to another:

- *Self-soothing*, e.g., sucking a finger, or stroking a soft blanket;
- *Responses to soothing* provided by caregivers, for example holding, rocking, or singing; and

- *Habituation*, i.e., "filtering out" noxious, taxing or uninformative stimuli, to allow the infant to conserve energy that would otherwise be used to perceive, process, and store these stimuli in memory.

As children grow, their capacity for state regulation strengthens, and can be carefully reinforced and expanded by educators in the service of learning. Similarly, educators can help promote children's self-regulation, i.e., the capacity to manage the full range of emotions stirred up in each moment, as it emerges and builds on state regulation.

Changes in states, or state regulation, allow for the moment-to-moment adjustments necessary to maintain this balance between ever changing infant needs and potential, and environmental demands and opportunities. For example, when the infant is hungry, a shift to the intensely aroused state of crying helps procure needed sustenance. When a newborn can mobilize an alert state, interaction with caregivers and learning about the environment can begin. As children mature, they will need to gain increasing control over their states of arousal. They will need to learn, for example, to sustain alert states for prolonged periods when their environments have abundant learning opportunities to offer them, and to soothe themselves into sleep states, which are not only restful and restorative, but also promote attention, learning, and memory.

Behavior Is State Dependent

Throughout life, behavior and learning are dependent on state. It is obvious, of course, that one cannot benefit from the learning opportunities that the environment presents when one is in a state of sleep, and that the execution of complex actions may be less precise or successful when in a state of drowsiness, fussing or crying and their corollaries in older children and adults. Children's capacity to learn, and the behaviors they can mobilize or suppress in service of their learning, depend on their state of arousal, and their experience of their emotions, which in turn is affected both by their shifting internal needs (e.g., hunger, boredom, frustration, saturation) and capacities (curiosity, focus, persistence) as well as by the classroom environment and interactions with teachers and peers.

Prior to Brazelton, the neurological examination of newborns was conducted without regard for their state of arousal, and typically provoked a crying state throughout, leading to erroneous conclusions about the newborn's capacity for purposeful behaviors. Brazelton's Newborn Behavior Assessment Scale not only accounts for the effect of the newborn's shifting states behavior, but also requires the examiner to facilitate the newborn's efforts to initiate and sustain the state best suited for the behaviors to be assessed, e.g., the alert state when assessing the newborn's capacity for social interaction (Brazelton, 1973). Similarly, the teacher and the physical environment of the classroom can systematically facilitate arousal and emotional states best suited for different kinds of learning. The daily sequence of scheduled activities can be designed to take account of the changing needs of the child over the course of the day for different kinds and levels of stimulation, as well as protection from stimulation, rest, and "recharging." Although the classroom and schedule may be less immediately adjustable, the teacher's interactions with children that facilitate their learning can be guided by their moment-to-moment behavioral cues indicating their arousal and emotional states.

The Capacity to Register Protest

Crying can be understood as the critical capacity to register legitimate protest against noxious external conditions or intolerable internal phenomena: thoughts, feelings, sensations. When older children cry or express negative feelings with other nonverbal behaviors, it may be helpful for parents and teachers to examine these as protests against conditions, internal or external, that interfere with the child's wellbeing and learning. Even older children and adolescents (and for that, adults) may not always be able to express their legitimate protest with language. Carefully considering children's challenging behaviors as harboring an important strength, the capacity to register protest, and responding accordingly with a focus on supporting self-regulation, may help reduce and eventually stop them. Some of these behaviors can be seen as developmental advances that build on the fundamental functions of the earliest cries. This is not a recommendation to accept or encourage all such behaviors, but to aim for more than merely extinguishing behaviors that challenge. Looking for the meaningful communication within them, and responding to them as opportunities to advance self-regulatory capacities, may help teachers to reduce the rate of preschool expulsion, and the behavioral problems and academic failure that too often follow it. To do so, the child can be helped to understand that the protest itself is important and deserving of recognition, and that other expressions of it may be more effective, and less costly to the child and others.

Elevating the capacity to register protest to the status of a normative and essential developmental ability that can be identified and cultivated may also help draw attention to those children who do not clearly express their distress, and suffer in silence. Because they do not draw attention to themselves, these children often do not receive the attention they need. Children across this continuum may need help from their teachers to learn to regulate their states of arousal and emotions. This will allow them to develop individual strategies for balancing their moment-to-moment inner experience with the opportunities and challenges presented by their environments, a balance necessary for success in school and life. Just like those who display their distress disruptively, these children may need help in identifying and articulating their challenges. They may also need to learn how to make them known to and evoke caring responses in their teachers and others who can help them.

Attachment and the Capacity for Endearment

When the infant is well rested and fed, the alert state allows the infant to engage with caregivers, learn from them while shaping their behavior, and elicit and emit attachment behaviors that will help ensure, at a minimum, survival and adequate care. Attachment is a process that persists throughout life and involves both biologically related and unrelated individuals in caregiving relationships, including educators and children.

Older children emit attachment signals in the classroom that may also be thought of as the capacity for endearment. This capacity varies from individual to individual, and may also vary at different points in an individual's life. A robust capacity for endearment clearly confers advantages to children in classroom settings, since it is likely to elicit more attention, caregiving, and other resources from teachers, even from those who strive to spread these as equitably as possible.

Informal Assessment of the Capacity for Endearment

At the end of the first day of school each year, teachers may find it illuminating to reflect on all of the children they have just met in their new class. They are likely to first call to mind the most obstreperous children, the ones who are easiest to identify as most likely to challenge them in the weeks and months to come. A close second, though, may be those children who are the most effective in endearing themselves, the ones who right away create pleasure in interacting with them and convey the promise of rewarding work ahead. Last, along with those whose names may not come to mind at all, are those children who may be less attractive, less endearing, less skillful in eliciting a teacher's attention, deliberation, and emotional investment. Many teachers find this exercise useful in helping them to face these differences in their reactions, differences that their best intentions may make difficult to acknowledge.

If this last group of children is identified at the beginning of each year, teachers can carefully monitor the distribution of their efforts, err on the side of providing more to these children, and help them learn to engage others more effectively. Their capacity to endear may be bolstered through the experience of an attentive teacher who helps them become aware of and articulate their needs and desires, as these are rewarded with satisfying and reinforcing responses. As they learn to ask effectively for help and experience their teachers' interest in them, they may be more likely to be successful academically and in their interactions with peers.

Sensory Threshold, Sensory Processing, and Learning Differences

Development depends on learning, and both depend on interactions with the environment. These interactions depend in large part on the senses' perceptions of specific environmental phenomena and features, and on the motor system's capacity to avoid or approach and engage with them. Higher level cognitive functions, of course, process, organize, store memories of and eventually contextualize and attach language to sensory perceptions, and guide motoric responses for focused exploration or elaborate avoidance. In addition, the six senses (sight, hearing, touch, smell, taste, but also the vestibular and proprioceptive sensing of the body's position and movement) interact with each other and with the motor system to flesh out full-bodied three-dimensional cognitions of the material world.

To do so, given the potentially overwhelming onslaught of incoming information at any given moment, the sensory system is neurologically wired to attend, focus, and respond selectively to some kinds of input, for example, the human voice, face, and movements, and to screen out noxious stimuli, or repetitive stimuli that do not provide useful information (see habituation, above). Over time, circuits in the brain develop and mature that allow for the association of the different sensory experiences triggered by an event or object, so that each of the different sensations contributes to a fuller apprehension of it. Consider, for example, the combined sensations of smelling, tasting, touching, and sinking one's teeth into a warm, juicy hamburger that has been tucked, along with a few sour pickles, mustard, and a slice of cheese, into a soft sesame seed bun held in both hands between fingers and thumbs.

From the beginning of life, infants' sensory experiences, and their individually unique responsiveness to sensory stimuli, interact with their regulation of their states of arousal. For example, some infants may be either highly or minimally responsive to lights, colors, high- or low-pitched sounds, rocking, and other stimuli. When over stimulated or insufficiently stimulated, an infant may retreat into sleep, or surge into a crying state. When a level of stimulation is presented that corresponds to a particular infant's sensory sensitivity, the infant may shift from drowsiness or fussing into a sustained alert state in order to fully apprehend and engage with this environmental input. The term 'sensory threshold' refers to these unique individual differences in responses to varying amounts, intensities and combinations of sensory stimulation. Some differences in children's approach to and styles of learning may be understood on the basis of individual differences in sensory threshold, sensory hypo- and hyper-sensitivities, and variations in the associative processes that allow for the integration and interpretation of information garnered by several or all of the different senses.

Learning in Relationships

Social Orientation

Among the purposeful behaviors that Brazelton observed in newborns is their responsiveness to human sensory input, their preferential orientation to the human voice and face, especially to voices that they have been listening to prior to birth. The fetal auditory apparatus is functional at least as early as the beginning of the last trimester of pregnancy. The expectant mother's voice reaches the fetus most directly, and in nuclear families, the father's voice may be the one most frequently heard by the fetus through the abdominal wall. When a newborn turns the head to a parent's voice for the first time, opens their eyes, and locks their gaze onto the parent's, these behaviors also serve the purpose of drawing parents deeply into the attachment process, filling them with the abrupt and stunning realization of their own singular importance, for as long they live, to this fragile new being.

The expectations of pregnancy, the drama of birth, and the neuro-hormonal mechanisms of the attachment process make the newborn period a time of heightened parental openness to communicative infant behaviors. Yet parents remain responsive to their children's communications specifically directed to them as they grow older, and there is often an emotional dimension to teachers' experiences of children's bids for connection to them, one that may be best understood as also a potent form of attachment. Children's capacity to engage adults' emotional investment in their survival and wellbeing is not limited to biological relatives. Those who are not biologically related may nonetheless be drawn into attachment processes, perhaps even those that are neuro-hormonally mediated.

Mutual Regulation

During the first several weeks that follow birth, infant and parent learn about each other from their repeated interactions. By two or three months of age, if not earlier, infants display the capacity not only to follow and respond to adult caregivers' verbal and nonverbal expressions, but also to initiate conversations with their own cooing, babbling, facial expressions, and body language (Brazelton, Koslowski, Main, Lewis, & Rosenblum, 1974; Gianino & Tronick, 1988). Infant and parent each contribute to the process, mutually regulating each other's experience of and participation in these conversations, as well as each other's states of arousal necessary to initiate, sustain, and end these interactions. For example, a bit too much talk or tickling from the parent may lead the infant to disengage, or to shift from an alert state to a fussy or crying one. This response, in turn, if registered by the parent, may lead to a subtle modulation of activity that helps the infant to recover and re-engage. Or, if the baby turns away in order to reduce the amount of stimulation to a level that he or she can handle at this point, the parent may become silent, only to be drawn out a few moments later by the infant, now refreshed, who is ready to initiate the next conversational turn.

These brief sequences of matching and mismatching states, connection and disconnection, of error and repair, occur every 3–5 seconds and help infants and young children experience their caregivers as reliable, predictable, responsive, and as a result, trustworthy. This is one of the earliest instances of learning within relationships that depends on the occurrence of and reckoning with "mistakes." The resulting reparations help to develop coping capacities, a sense of agency, mastery and control, while learning conversational rules and conventions (Tronick, 1989; Tronick, Cohn, and Shea, 1986).

In studies using the Still Face Paradigm, in which an adult caregiver is asked to interact with the baby as she or he usually would, to then turn away, and then to turn back to the baby with a stony, unresponsive face, even two- and three-month-olds recognize the difference. They become distressed, and if they have had enough past successes in engaging their parents, they will recover, persistently display a rich behavioral repertoire of vocalizations, facial expressions and body language, periodically stopping and becoming distressed again as long as their caregivers do not respond (Tronick, Als, Adamson, Wise, & Brazelton, 1978). Infants who have not benefited from such prior successes and responses, for example in the context of parental depression, are likely to give up more quickly, as they have not learned to expect to be effective in drawing in their caregivers. They may display far fewer engaging behaviors, as they have lacked the opportunity to test out a broader range and experience their effects on and reinforcement by their parents.

Throughout life, of course, humans are highly attentive to and dependent on these kinds of nonverbal exchanges that allow them to situate themselves in the interpersonal spaces they share with others, including the classroom and the teacher–child and student–student relationships that inhabit them (Trevarthen, 1979). As in the Still Face experiments, limited or unclear nonverbal information conveyed in these classroom relationships is likely to provoke distress, uncertainty, and confusion. Then, a wide range of socially oriented behaviors driven by the child's need to know the teacher's or classmates' thoughts, feelings and reactions to him or her can be expected, unless the deprivation of interactive information exchange is so chronic and severe that such communicative behaviors have not been developed. In the latter case, a turning inward—and in extreme situations such as inadequately staffed orphanages, self-injurious—behavior may occur.

Systems Theory: Contexts and Interactions for Children's Development and Learning

Just as infants and adult caregivers interact together in service of their development and learning, children and educators co-construct learning environments, experiences, and accomplishments (Sameroff, 1975). The "empty vessel" theory of education, which supposes that children's brains simply need to be filled with parent- and teacher-provided information, has long been challenged by child-centered, active learning, and social constructivist models, among others. To one extent or another, these models all rely on a systems theory of the child in context, in interaction with the classroom, peers, and teachers. Yet the implications of such systems-theory based approaches to learning and development have not been fully understood and applied in many classrooms, schools, and the larger contexts that influence them. For this to be realized in educational institutions and policies, far greater integration of families within educational institutions, and of the other institutions (e.g., those providing health and mental health services) and entities that contribute to child and family learning and development, is needed (Bronfenbrenner, 1979; 2004; Bryck, Sebring, Allensworth, Luppescu, & Easton, 2010; Sparrow, in press).

Touchpoints: Disorganization and Reorganization in Development

Because infants and young children develop in family systems as well as institutional ones, the process of development affects and is affected by all members of these systems. The Touchpoints model (Brazelton & Sparrow, 2006; Brazelton & Sparrow, 2001) posits that development proceeds through predictable periods of temporary disorganization in the service of reorganization and the emergence of new skills and capacities. In infants, toddlers, and young children, temporary disruptions in sleep, feeding, self-regulation, and behavioral control are common examples, with resulting increases in crying, clinging, and seeking of physical contact (Plooij, 2010). These periods of regression (Heimann, 2010) are disorganizing not only for the child, but for the whole family, and other caregivers, including teachers.

Strong relationships within the family system, as well as those that connect the family system to supportive educational and health caregivers and systems, can help prevent developmental derailment and guide the child, family, and other caregivers through these developmental crises. Family-facing organizations such as early childhood care and education institutions, pediatric healthcare, child protective and welfare services, family resource centers, home visiting agencies, early childhood libraries and museums, and others can provide anticipatory guidance and ongoing support for family relationships through these stressful periods of heightened risk and vulnerability. These expectable developmental crises are also times of opportunity when parents and teachers can deepen their understanding of the child, and strengthen their relationship with each other in support of the child's development, and that of parents and teachers as well (Sparrow & Brazelton, 2011).

These touchpoints in a child's development add to the demands on family and teacher resources; for example, when the child's disrupted sleep awakens the whole family, or irritability requires more soothing, cuddling, and patience. They can also undermine parents' and teachers' sense of competence and mastery as the transient decline in one area of the child's functioning makes the adult caregivers doubt their own caregiving. During these periods, parents and teachers often feel defensive, competitive, and are likely to deflect the self-blame they may feel onto each other. Educational institutions may reinforce teachers' tendency to blame parents and consider themselves as more expert than they when parents are not fully engaged as equal partners (National Center for Parent, Family and Community Engagement, 2010). Brazelton has termed this predictable and widespread phenomenon, "gatekeeping."

Adults in conflict can face their disagreements with greater openness and readiness to compromise when gatekeeping can be anticipated, or brought to the surface and reframed as the natural result of the passion they share for the child's wellbeing.

Strengths-based Relationships through Shared Observation and Co-constructed Meaning

Parental effectiveness builds on parental sense of competence, and this can be enhanced through respectful, strengths-based parent–teacher relationships. To build partnerships with families strong enough to survive and support children through these touchpoints of development, teachers can elicit parents' expertise about their individual children, and help restore their sense of competence. Rather than starting with their own interpretations of a child's behavior, early education professionals can invite parents to listen and watch the child with them. They can express genuine curiosity about what parents notice, and what meanings they make of the child's behavior. As parents and teachers join together to co-construct their understanding of a child's behavior, the perspectives of each will enrich this understanding. This is especially true if the perspectives are widely divergent and these divergences can be welcomed with interest and respect. This process can also strengthen their relationships with each other, and these strong relationships will help advance a child's learning and development (Owen, Ware, & Barfoot, 2000).

Parent Advocacy, Leadership and Networks

When early care and education professionals and institutions see parents as partners in children's learning, rather than distractions, interferences, or adversaries, they are more likely to see parental advocacy and leadership skills as assets rather than threats. Education and care organizations can facilitate the emergence and development of these skills by creating opportunities for parents to participate in governance and other institutional roles, and by providing concrete supports for parents to connect with each other and expand their social capital (Putnam, Feldstein, & Cohen, 2004; National Center for Parent, Family and Community Engagement, 2013).

Conclusion

How do children learn? How do children show us who they are, what they need and are capable of? Through attachment, state regulation, and mutual regulation, children and adult caregivers learn about themselves, each other, their individual differences, and the relational processes that they co-create that will shape their developmental disorganization and reorganization.

What can children teach us? What do they know that we once knew, and have forgotten? Are there truths of childhood that children have the power to revive in us? Can we rediscover children's ways of knowing and being that can guide us over the course of our lives? These are questions that parents and teachers can share with each other as they work together to be with the children in their lives and to learn with them as they learn and grow. Each brings expertise about the individual child, but can also share the answers that can only come from the child, with quiet listening and careful observation.

References

Brazelton, T.B. (1962). Observations of the neonate. *Journal of the American Academy of Child Psychiatry*, *1*, 38–58.

Brazelton, T.B. (1973). *Neonatal Behavioral Assessment Scale* (1st ed.). London: Spastics International Medical Publications.

Brazelton, T.B. (1983). *Infants and mothers*. New York: Delta.

Brazelton, T.B. (2013). *Learning to listen*. Cambridge, MA: Da Capo Press.

Brazelton, T.B., & Sparrow, J.D. (2001). *Touchpoints three to six: Your child's emotional and behavioral development*. Cambridge, MA: Da Capo Press.

Brazelton, T.B., & Sparrow, J.D. (2006). *Touchpoints 0–3: Your child's emotional and behavioral development* (2nd ed.). Cambridge, MA: Da Capo Press.

Brazelton, T.B., Koslowski, B., Main, M., Lewis, M., & Rosenblum, L.A. (1974). The origins of reciprocity: The early mother–infant interaction. In M. Lewis & L. Rosenblum (Eds.), *The effect of the infant on its caregiver* (pp. 49–76). New York: Wiley.

Bronfenbrenner, U. (1979). *The ecology of human development: Experiments by nature and design*. Cambridge, MA: Harvard University Press.

Bronfenbrenner, U. (Ed.) (2004). *Making human beings human: Bioecological perspectives on human development*. The Sage Program on Applied Developmental Science. Thousand Oaks, CA: Sage.

Bryck, A.S., Sebring, P.B., Allensworth, E., Luppescu, S., & Easton, J.Q. (2010). *Organizing schools for improvement: Lessons from Chicago*. Chicago: University of Chicago Press.

Fraiberg, S. (1996). *The magic years*. New York: Scribner.

Gianino, A., & Tronick, E.Z. (1988). The mutual regulation model: The infant's self and interactive regulation, coping, and defensive capacities. In T. Field, P. McCabe, & N. Schneiderman (Eds.), *Stress and coping across development* (pp. 47–68). Hillsdale, NJ: Lawrence Erlbaum.

Heimann, M. (2010). Regression and reorganization in relational models of development. In B.M. Lester & J.D. Sparrow (Eds.), *Nurturing young children and their families: Building on the legacy of T.B. Brazelton* (pp. 95–106). Oxford: Wiley-Blackwell Scientific.

Kanner, L. (1943). Autistic disturbances of affective contact. *Nerv Child*, *2*, 217–250. Reprinted in Kanner, L. (1968), Autistic disturbances of affective contact. *Acta Paediatricia*, *35*(4), 100–136.

Kuhn, T.S. (2012). *The structure of scientific revolutions* (4th ed.). Chicago: University of Chicago Press.

LeVine, R.A. (2004). Challenging expert knowledge: Findings from an African study of infant care and development. In U.P. Gielen & J.L. Roopnarine (Eds.), *Childhood and adolescence: Cross-cultural perspective and applications* (pp. 149–165). Westport, CT: Praeger.

LeVine, R.A. (2010). Protective environments in Africa and elsewhere. In B.M. Lester & J.D. Sparrow (Eds.), *Nurturing young children and their families: Building on the legacy of T.B. Brazelton* (pp. 132–139). Oxford: Wiley-Blackwell Scientific.

Meaney, M.J. (2001). Maternal care, gene expression, and the transmission of individual differences in stress reactivity across generations. *Annual Review of Neuroscience*, *24*, 1161–1192.

National Center of Parent, Family and Community Engagement (2010). *The Head Start Parent, Family and Community Engagement Framework for early childhood care and education programs*. Office of Head Start, Administration for Children and Families. Washington, DC: United States Department of Health and Human Services.

National Center of Parent, Family and Community Engagement (2013). *Family connections to peers and community: Research to practice brief*. Office of Head Start, Administration for Children and Families. Washington, DC: United States Department of Health and Human Services.

Owen, M.T., Ware, A.M., & Barfoot, B. (2000). Caregiver–mother partnership behavior and the quality of caregiver–child and mother–child interactions. *Early Childhood Research Quarterly*, *15*(3), 413–428.

Plooij, F.X. (2010). The four whys of age-linked regression periods in infancy. In B.M. Lester & J.D. Sparrow (Eds.), *Nurturing young children and their families: Building on the legacy of T.B. Brazelton* (pp. 107–119). Oxford: Wiley-Blackwell Scientific.

Putnam, R.D., Feldstein, L., & Cohen, D.J. (2004). *Better together: Restoring the American community*. New York: Simon and Schuster.

Salisbury, A., Yanni, P., LaGasse, L., & Lester, B.M. (2004). Maternal–fetal psychobiology: A very early look at emotional development. In J. Nadel & D. Muir (Eds.), *Emotional development: Recent research advances* (pp. 95–125). Oxford: Oxford University Press.

Sameroff, A.J. (1975). Transactional models in early social relations. *Human Development*, 18(1–2), 65–79.

Sparrow, J.D. (2013). Newborn behavior, parent–infant interaction, and developmental change processes: Research roots of developmental, relational and systems-theory based practice. *Journal of Child and Adolescent Psychiatric Nursing*, *26*(3), 180–185. doi: 10.1111/jcap.12047

Sparrow, J.D. (In press). Communities raising children together: Collaborative consultation with a place-based initiative in Harlem. In J. Delafield-Butt, A.W. Dunlop, & C. Trevarthen (Eds.), *The child's curriculum: Working with the natural values of young children so the child may lead the way*. Oxford: Oxford University Press.

Sparrow, J.D., & Brazelton, T.B. (2011). Touchpoints for anticipatory guidance in well childcare visits in the first three years. In B. Zuckerman, S. Parker, & M. Augustyn (Eds.), *Zuckerman and Parker's handbook of developmental and behavioral pediatrics* (3rd ed.). Philadelphia, PA: Lippincott, Williams and Wilkins.

Szyf, M., McGowan, P.O., Turecki, G., & Meaney, M. (2010). The social environment and the epigenome. In C.M. Worthman, P.M. Plotsky, D.S. Schechter, & C.A. Cummings (Eds.), *Formative experiences: The interaction of caregiving, culture, and developmental psychobiology* (pp. 53–81). Cambridge: Cambridge University Press.

Thomas, A., & Chess, S. (1968). *Temperament and behavior disorders in children*. New York: New York University Press.

Trevarthen, C. (1979). Communication and cooperation in early infancy: A description of primary intersubjectivity. In M. Bullowa (Ed.), *Before speech: The beginning of human communication* (pp. 321– 347). New York: Cambridge University Press.

Tronick, E.Z. (1989). Emotions and emotional communication in infants. *American Psychologist*, 44(2), 112–119.

Tronick, E.Z., Als, H., Adamson, L., Wise, S., & Brazelton, T.B. (1978). Infants' response to entrapment between contradictory messages in face-to-face interaction. *Journal of the American Academy of Child and Adolescent Psychiatry*, *17*, 1–13.

Tronick, E.Z., Cohn, J., & Shea, E. (1986). The transfer of affect between mothers and infants. In T.B. Brazelton & M.W. Yogman (Eds.), *Affective development in infancy* (pp. 11–25). Norwood, NJ: Ablex.

Weaver, I.C., Cervoni, N., Champagne, F.A., D'Alessio, A.C., Sharma, S., Seckl, J.R. ... Meaney, M.J. (2004). Epigenetic programming by maternal behavior. *Nature Neuroscience*, 7, 847–854. doi:10.1038/nn1276

Selected Websites

www.brazelton-institute.com
www.brazeltontouchpoints.org
www.childcarecollection.com
www.eclkc.ohs.acf.hhs.gov/hslc/tta-system/family
www.naeyc.org

Part III

BEHAVIORIST THEORIES

8

THE WORK OF B. F. SKINNER

Effective Practices within Early Childhood Settings

Kathleen M. Feeley

"That's not the way children learn, that is how animals learn." "She won't demonstrate those skills when you stop rewarding her." "That just creates robots." "It is just a way to teach rote behaviors, the children don't actually learn." "Children should be inherently motivated to learn." It is very likely that, if in the field of early childhood education, one will have encountered one or more of these or similar comments with regard to a behavioral approach to teaching young children. They may be encountered within the college classroom, spoken by scholars charged with preparing professionals for careers in early intervention, or printed in textbooks and articles assigned as readings within the very same programs. So too are they likely to be encountered within the field: in childcare centers, preschool programs serving children with and without disabilities, and among professionals who provide in-home early intervention.

These comments, however, are in response to procedures that have been empirically demonstrated for over 66 years, have influenced the development of countless numbers of children, and have had a profound impact on the lives of children with disabilities and their caregivers. Who is responsible for introducing these procedures? It was one of the most influential, yet controversial psychologists of the twentieth century: Burrhus Frederick (B. F.) Skinner.

Skinner's Early Years

B. F. Skinner was born on March 20, 1904, in Susquahanna, Pennsylvania (Pierce & Cheney, 2013). He and his younger brother (who passed away at the age of 16 years) were raised in a middle-class family, with his father working as a lawyer for the Erie Railroad and in his own practice (O'Donohue & Ferguson, 2001). Skinner was interested in creating things and spent a great deal of his youth on mechanical inventions (Pierce & Cheney, 2013). He attended Hamilton College in Clinton, New York, and graduated in 1926 with a degree in English. At that time, Skinner became interested in behaviorism, which was just in its beginning stages, leading him to attend Harvard University in 1928. While at Harvard, he earned both his master's degree and his Ph.D. by 1930, and befriended Fred Keller, with whom he maintained a lifelong friendship (O'Donohue & Ferguson, 2001).

Skinner's early work stemmed from the findings of Ivan Petrovich Pavlov, a Russian scientist who, while examining the salivary reflex in digestion, made important discoveries about behavior. As Pavlov worked with dogs in his laboratory, he noticed they began to salivate, referred to as an *unconditioned* response (i.e., a behavior that had not been unlearned) in the presence of food, referred to as an *unconditioned* stimulus (i.e., one that elicited an automatic response), noting that a specific stimulus elicited a specific response. He also noted that the dogs began to salivate at the sight of the experimenter's lab coat, before having access to the food. This led him to test the hypothesis that an arbitrary stimulus may result in the same behavior, and thus, the lab coat was replaced with a ringing sound. The dogs did salivate in response to the ringing sound, which was the discovery of *conditioned reflexes*, which means that through conditioning (i.e., learning), an organism will emit reflexive behaviors.This is referred to as *respondent* or *classical* conditioning.

Pavlov was followed by Johan Boadus Watson, who posited that psychologists should study only observable behavior and who was quite outspoken against the study of phenomena that could not be observed (e.g., the mind). His most notable work was with a young boy who readily reached for a white rat, but was then conditioned (i.e., taught) to fear it, pairing the rat (the conditioned stimulus) with a loud noise (the unconditioned stimulus) (Watson & Raynor, 1920). Within only a few pairings, the child emitted the same startled response in the presence of not only the white rat, but in the presence of other furry things as well. Edward Thorndike was also quite influential at the time. He discovered trial and error learning in cats (Thorndike, 1898). Specifically, he observed cats working to get out of a box, and when they inadvertently emitted a response that resulted in opening the door of the box, they repeated that behavior in future opportunities; thus demonstrating that new behaviors were established as a result of the consequences that followed them (exiting the box), which was later termed *operant conditioning*. This stood apart from the respondent (or classical) conditioning of Pavlov and Watson, in which the same behavior occurs in the presence of various stimuli. Thorndike was actually teaching new behaviors.

These early behaviorists had a major impact on the work of Skinner. Early on in his career, he spoke of how the reflexes that Pavlov observed could be studied as behaviors, but the learning that Thorndike observed was due to a functional relationship between the behaviors and the consequences. He set out to demonstrate that the behavior of organisms could be studied by examining stimuli that occur *before* and *after* each behavior. Pavlov demonstrated that a reflex can be elicited by a variety of stimuli; thus, the presence of meat, the experimenter's lab coat, or the sound of the bell elicited the *same response*. In the operant model, the stimulus refers to an antecedent that sets the occasion for the behavior based on a history of reinforcement (referred to as a *discriminative stimulus*). Thus *new behaviors* are learned. This is the major difference between respondent conditioning and operant conditioning. In respondent conditioning, no new behaviors are established; the same response is paired with a range of stimuli. However, in operant conditioning, new behaviors are established because of contingencies in place. Thus, the stimulus functions as a cue that if the behavior occurs, reinforcement will be delivered. This is the very foundation of how learning occurs: specific behaviors that occur in the presence of specific stimuli are followed by reinforcement and, thus, continue to occur.

Early in his career, Skinner discovered several important behavioral principles in his animal laboratories. He used operant conditioning (i.e., systematically delivering reinforcers to establish a response) to teach a rat to pull a string to gain access to a marble that it lifted and then dropped down a tube, which resulted in access to food (Skinner, 1938). The marble actually functioned as a token, which could be exchanged for access to the *primary* reinforcer (in this case, the food). This would later be referred to as *token economy* or *token reinforcement*. His work teaching animals behaviors lead him to work for a project funded in part by the United States Office of Scientific Research and Development, from 1940 through 1944. While there, Skinner utilized operant conditioning to train pigeons to guide simulated bombs to destinations during World War II (Morris, Smith, & Altus, 2005). It was at this time that Skinner and his colleagues discovered another important principle, that of *shaping* behavior. They systematically reinforced a pigeon for approximations of swiping at a ball, with the terminal (final desired) response being swiping the ball in order to knock down pins (i.e., bowling). Thus a system for establishing new behaviors in organisms was developed.

Another major contribution of Skinner was his discovery of *extinction* with respect to operant behavior. He made the discovery one Sunday in his lab and then reported how he was concerned that something would happen to him before he was able to share his results with others (Skinner, 1979). The feeding mechanism for pigeons (that were part of a different experiment) accidently jammed, but their pecking continued to be recorded by a device. Upon inspection of the data that the device recorded, Skinner noticed a sharp increase in the pecking behavior and then a gradual decrease in its occurrence. Thus, a previously reinforced response (pecking) eventually stopped as a result of the termination of the delivery of reinforcers, now referred to as extinction. This same principle has been demonstrated in humans. Consider a child whose whining and crying for a toy in the grocery store results in procurement of those toys. If the caregiver begins to refrain from purchasing toys as a result of the child whining and crying, the child will eventually stop emitting that behavior. It may, however, get worse before it gets better, referred to as an *extinction burst*. But, withholding reinforcement for the previously reinforced response will eventually result in the child no longer emitting the behavior (i.e., whining and crying) to access toys within the grocery store.

As Skinner noted, this should not be confused with other procedures that may result in the same outcome, specifically the use of *aversive stimuli*, which are stimuli that an organism escapes or avoids. When aversive stimuli are presented following a behavior, it is referred to as *punishment*, the technical term for a consequence that results in a decrease in the preceding behavior. Skinner (1953) spoke explicitly of the disadvantages of punishment, noting that it was at that time (and likely continues to be today), one of the most common techniques of control in modern life. At the same time noting, "In the long run, punishment, unlike reinforcement works to the disadvantage for both the punished organism and the punishing agency" (Skinner, 1953, p. 183). In comparing extinction versus punishment, Skinner noted, although punishment reduced the occurrence of behaviors, when discontinued, the frequency of the behavior rose again. Thus punishment was a temporary suppression of the behavior and did not result in a reduction of the total number of responses. If an organism is engaging in an undesirable behavior, that behavior can be reduced or completely eliminated by simply withholding reinforcement. Thus, punishment, a consequence that results in a decrease in the behavior, does not need to be implemented.

Notably, Skinner concentrated on examining and measuring actions (i.e., behaviors) as well as what is referred to as *experimental control*. He carefully controlled the variables and then sought to determine a direct relationship between the dependent variable (the behavior) and the independent variable (that which was systematically manipulated). The study of animal behavior allowed for precise measurement of behavior through mechanical devices, which could be recorded over long periods of time. True, it is far easier to control conditions in animal laboratories than it is with humans. However, the principles remain the same, as Skinner himself clearly stated: "The barest possible statement of the process is this: we make a given consequence contingent upon certain physical properties of behavior ... and the behavior is then observed to increase in frequency" (Skinner, 1953, p. 64). He referred to these learned behaviors as *operants*, as "[t]he term emphasizes the fact that the behavior operates upon the environment to generate consequences" (p. 65). Operants are emitted as a function of the stimulus that follows (i.e., reinforcing stimuli). Skinner's work was thus based on observation, measurement, and induction (Morris, Smith, & Altus, 2005).

Skinner and his classmate from Harvard, Fred Keller, were expanding behavior analysis, Skinner at Indiana University and Keller at Columbia University. In 1946, they came together and organized a conference on the experimental analysis of behavior. What set this group apart from early behaviorists was both their acknowledgment that genetics influenced behavior and their focus on operant conditioning (i.e., the establishment of behaviors using reinforcement principles). In 1958 they started their own journal, the *Journal of the Experimental Analysis of Behavior* (*JEAB*). Over time, this group's work transitioned from basic research, that which is conducted for scientific knowledge alone, to applied research, that which is conducted to solve problems. What followed were more and more applications to human problems, particularly with respect to mental illness, intellectual disability, and education. Thus, in 1968, the *Journal of Applied Behavior Analysis* (*JABA*) began, and was dedicated to the application of behavioral principles to socially important problems (Baer, Wolf, & Risley, 1968).

Applications to Human Behavior

Skinner applied his principles to human behavior while considering ways to enhance the development of his own two daughters. He realized that his baby daughter could move about more freely if there was not a need for clothing and blankets. Thus, he created the *air crib* that regulated the air temperature, allowing the child to move about comfortably in only a diaper. This would also allow for less clothing and blankets needing to be washed, which in turn gave caregivers more time to interact with their toddler. Skinner described the crib in an article for a popular magazine (the *Ladies Home Journal*), referring to it as "the baby tender," but the title of his article was changed and it ultimately featured the "Baby in a Box" (Rutherford, 2009). Unfortunately, shortly after, it was confused with the "Skinner box" which was used to mechanically reinforce animals in laboratories. More misinformation soon followed. Contrary to what was being reported, the only conditions manipulated within the air crib were temperature and humidity. But manufacturers who did not want to be associated with the negative publicity promptly stopped producing the air crib.

As Skinner's daughters matured and entered school, he became interes educational applications and directed his work toward the development of strat that could be used within educational settings (Skinner, 1954; 1963). Specifically, developed a system where students were exposed to small segments of the conten within frames shown in a box-like structure. Students were required to generate answers (i.e., responses) to questions, which could immediately be compared to the correct answer. Although this programmed instruction met with much interest early on, it was not long before it was criticized as being inhuman, cold, and robot-like. However, Skinner did go on to published the acclaimed book, *The Technology of Teaching* (1968), which described how the learning environment can be arranged to enhance instruction and how skills can be taught by breaking them down into small components and delivering individualized reinforcement for correct responding. These are the very basic foundations for evidence-based strategies that exist today.

Throughout his career Skinner made assertions that went against the grain of other noted psychologists. One was that he considered internal events to be behaviors, and similar to other behaviors that can be directly observed, these behaviors were learned through interactions with others and with environmental events (Skinner, 1954). Thus, he viewed thinking, feeling, thoughts, and remembering as behaviors in and of themselves. This was quite a different view to that of many psychologists who, in contrast, viewed these very things as the *cause* of behavior; a human acts in a certain way because the mind directs him or her to do so. Clearly, these were very different perspectives. Another assertion that Skinner made was that language was yet another operant behavior, one which was learned. Throughout his career Skinner analyzed various forms of language, with several studies focusing on examining the language of humans (e.g., Skinner, 1937; 1939). His theory was that language is learned based on how others in the environment deliver consequences to the young child. He wrote about how, throughout a lifetime, language serves a series of functions (i.e., purposes) for the human. Skinner (1957) extensively articulated his theory of language development in the book titled *Verbal Behavior*. In it, he conceptualized language as a series of behaviors that were emitted based on antecedent stimuli and a history of reinforcement associated with those stimuli. In this work he identified each of the functions with elaborate explanations of the stimuli and the consequences that resulted in the human engaging in those behaviors. He proposed that verbal behavior was not just spoken language, but also took the form of written language and sign language.

At the time there were language theorists who also had their own views regarding the development of language, including Noam Chomsky. Upon Skinner's publication of his book on verbal behavior, Chomsky (1959) published an expansive review of the book and articulated several rebuttals. Although there were also reviews in support of Skinner, Chomsky's received the most attention, leading many to dismiss what Skinner himself perceived as one of his greatest contributions to the field. Interestingly, however, as the field of applied behavior analysis has expanded, so too have the supporters of Skinner's work on verbal behavior. So much so, that it is the focus of a journal, *The Analysis of Verbal Behavior*, and the very foundation of numerous interventions that address the communicative needs of children and adults with developmental disabilities, including alternative forms of communication for individuals with developmental disabilities (Frost & Bondy, 2002; Sigafoos, Reichle, & Doss, 1990).

Skinner was quite prolific, even after his retirement from Harvard University in the early 1970s. He continued to conduct research and published extensively on the role of behavior analysis in lives of humans, addressing issues such as world peace, freedom, and dignity (Morris, Smith, & Altus, 2005). He even shared advice for dealing with the day-to-day demands of aging (Skinner & Vaughan, 1983). Skinner continued applying principles of behavior to solve important problems right up until his passing on August 18, 1990.

Applications within Early Childhood Settings

At the very foundation of Skinner's work was the demonstration of a relationship between behavior (the dependent variable) and the external conditions that influence it (the independent variable). This is referred to as *functional analysis*, which demonstrates a functional relationship between an intervention being implemented (i.e., the antecedents and consequences) and the desired behavior. With this approach in place, every child has the potential to learn, and the onus is on the educators and interventionists to adjust and improve upon instruction so that learning does take place. This certainly is an optimistic point of view. Instead of associating poor outcomes with internal characteristics, a behaviorist assumes that poor outcomes are a result of how the environment and experience shaped the behavior of individual children. When environmental factors and experiences are identified, as interventionists, one can design programs that prevent and intervene to improve outcomes. As Strain and McConnell (1992) so eloquently stated, "Thus, the emphasis on external control in the behavioral approach is not dehumanizing; rather it offers a conceptual model that celebrates the possibilities for each individual" (p. 126).

This approach has been applied within early childhood settings for decades. In fact, there was a large longitudinal, government funded study that took place between 1968 and 1976 called *Project Follow Through*. Its purpose was to systematically evaluate different instructional approaches within Head Start programs around the country (see Watkins, 1995). Several instructional approaches were examined, including behavioral approaches, one of which was referred to as *Direct Instruction*. Data were collected from 120 sites across the country. The findings clearly indicated that the Direct Instruction approach yielded the best outcomes across measures associated with basic skills, cognitive-conceptual skills, and self-concept. However, there was reluctance on the part of the government funding agency to support a behavioral approach to early intervention. Thus, conclusions that were in conflict with the actual findings were disseminated (for example, information about models that were not effective was disseminated). As a result, a large-scale adoption of behaviorally based early intervention programs was not and has yet to be realized. However, a lack of broad based adoption does not prevent individual interventionists or individual center-based programs from implementing sound behavior analytic programming.

Data-driven Decision Making

An essential tenet of behaviorally based programming is careful documentation and analysis of child performance, prior to, during, and following the implementation of intervention conditions, also referred to as *data-driven decision making*. This allows interventionists to determine the extent to which the intervention is successful. If the child's behavior is not moving in the desired direction (e.g., desired behavior is increasing and/or undesirable behavior is decreasing), interventionists can examine the intervention and ask the question, "What can we do differently to enhance learning?" Importantly, close and frequent monitoring of the effectiveness of an intervention prevents lengthy implementation of ineffective interventions. The fundamental process in applied behavior analysis is in fact the *analysis*. Thus, if a child is exposed to instruction that is *not* resulting in the child learning, a systematic analysis of the intervention conditions would be implemented. Then, decisions are based on the child's actual performance not subjective opinions on the part of interventionists and caregivers. When a group of individuals is trained systematically to document the occurrence of or lack of occurrences of behavior, it is that information that indicates the success of an intervention. There would be no reliance on the memories or opinions of a group of caregivers. This level of accountability is one of applied behavior analysis' strongest virtues, and one that may prove quite threatening to those who make decisions in other ways.

Effective Teaching Opportunities

Another application of Skinner's work is attention to the *three term contingency* consisting of the stimulus, response, and consequence. Ensuring that interventionists within early childhood settings have a firm understanding that given a stimulus (e.g., a shape, a color, an object, a social opportunity), if a desired behavior follows (e.g., identification of the shape, the color, the object label, a social nicety, such as "thank you"), and it is followed by a reinforcing consequence, there will be an increase in the desired behavior (i.e., the acquisition of skills). Thus, the identification of shapes, colors, object labels, and social niceties (and many more skills) will increase. It is equally important for interventionists to have an understanding of what they can do to increase the likelihood that a desired response will occur. What is done to provide assistance to increase the likelihood that the child emits the desired response is referred to as a *prompt*. Prompts can be delivered at the same time or right after the discriminative stimulus (the stimulus that should occasion the behavior). Prompting procedures include verbal prompts (telling the child what to do), a model (demonstrating for the child what she or he should do either physically or verbally), physical prompts (physically assisting the child), or gestural prompts (using a facial expression or a hand motion to indicate to the child what response should be emitted). These are referred to as *response prompts* as they are directed at the child. Other types of prompts include *stimulus prompts*, which entail the interventionist manipulating a stimulus to ensure the child emits the desired response. Stimulus prompts include moving the correct choice closer to the child, highlighting the correct choice in some way (e.g., colored paper, making it larger) so that the correct choice catches the child's attention, or they can be graphic in nature (e.g., symbols, photos, written words) to indicate to the child what the response is and when it should be emitted.

The implementation of prompts ensures the child engages in the response that can in turn be reinforced. Thus, they are systematically delivered to ensure the child responds correctly, which in turn results in reinforcement, which increases future correct responding. The prompts are then faded. Thus, they are gradually removed so that the controlling stimulus is no longer the prompt, but the natural stimuli in the environment serve this role (the natural discriminative stimulus). There are several prompt fading procedures. The most common consists of *a most to least* fading strategy, where the most *intrusive* prompt is used that establishes the response and then, it is gradually faded, so the child begins to respond to the discriminative stimulus alone. Another very effective prompt fading strategy is called a *time delay* (Halle, Marshall, & Spradlin, 1979). During the initial stages of using a time delay, the prompt is delivered immediately following the discriminative stimulus. Then, across teaching opportunities, the interventionist inserts a delay between the discriminative stimulus and the prompts. If the child responds within the time delay period, reinforcement is delivered; if she or he does not, the prompt is delivered.

Let us consider an example of how these procedures would be incorporated within an early childhood setting. A child is walking down the hall of his or her preschool where there are colored stripes painted on the wall. The adult who escorts the child to the classroom can use this as a teaching opportunity. She or he may point to a stripe and say, "What color is this?" This would be the discriminative stimulus. If the child does not yet know colors, the interventionist would immediately identify the corresponding color (e.g., "It's yellow."). That would be the prompt that would be preselected; if the child imitates verbalizations, that would likely result in the child performing the desired behavior, such that, saying "yellow" in response to being asked, "What color is this?" Once the child has engaged in the desired response, reinforcement would be delivered. Now a misconception associated with Skinner's work is that the reinforcing consequences always take the form of candy (most notably M&Ms) or food items. However, a mere smile, nod of the head, or a comment, "That's right, that is yellow," may function as a reinforcer for many young children. That is not to say that food reinforcers, which are actually primary reinforcers, would never be considered. Some children, particularly those with disabilities, may not find social interaction reinforcing. Thus, food could certainly be used to establish the skill, and then, just as prompts are systematically faded, so too would the use of primary reinforcers.

Speech and Language Instruction

These same procedures (specifically, operant conditioning) can also be applied to teach speech and language skills (a priority within early childhood settings), as can Skinner's procedures for behavior shaping. Thus, the speech and language of each individual child can be shaped into more sophisticated forms. One would first consider the stimuli in the environment. If preferred and/or novel stimuli are placed within the environment, the child's motivation to obtain access to those stimuli will increase. An important factor will be delivering those stimuli (e.g., toys, objects, access to activities) contingent (i.e., "if–then") on specific behaviors (language forms). Thus, "if" the child emits a communicative utterance, "then," she or he can have access to those desired stimuli. At first the utterance could be any sound or an approximation of the corresponding word; but, over time, access to those items would be contingent on more sophisticated utterances. To increase the likelihood that a more sophisticated response is emitted, a series of prompts would be delivered that would result in the child performing a closer form of what would be considered the "terminal response." All the children in a particular setting may not be advancing at the same rate. Thus, one child may be working toward expressing him- or herself with two word utterances, while another child may be working on putting three words together, and yet another child may be working on multi-word sentences with multiple adjectives, for example, "May I have a delicious, crunchy double chocolate chip cookie?" Non-contingent access to those materials may result in a child learning some skills; but if caregivers place contingencies on the children, the expressive language will certainly be enhanced.

Addressing Challenging Behavior

For decades, researchers have demonstrated the application of Skinner's findings to develop a technology to address challenging behavior in individuals of all ages, with and without disabilities. Unfortunately, there is a tremendous lack of implementation of these procedures within early childhood settings. This is evidenced by the high rate at which preschoolers are expelled from preschool settings (US Department of Health and Human Services/US Department of Education, 2015). This is particularly disappointing, as we currently have an extensive technology referred to as *positive behavior intervention and supports* (PBIS) (Carr et al., 1999). It is based on applied behavior analysis, as well as self-determination (one's ability to make one's own decisions), and the principle of normalization (Wolfensberger, 1972), which means making available to people with disabilities the same opportunities that are available to those without disabilities. PBIS takes a three-tier approach to intervention, with evidence based strategies being used system wide (Tier 1), small targeted group interventions (Tier 2), and then highly individualized support systems that meet the needs of a small number of children in a highly individualized and intense manner (Tier 3). This three-tier approach, when applied in early intervention settings, is referred to as the Pyramid Model for Supporting Social Emotional Competence in Infants and Young Children. Within the Pyramid Model, the first tier involves two levels of practice: *nurturing and responsive caregiving relationships* and *high quality supportive environments* (Fox, Dunlap, Hemmeter, Joseph, & Strain, 2003).

When challenging behavior persists in young children, and they have not responded to the first two tiers of intervention, a plan is put in place for highly individualized assessment and intervention. The assessment and intervention strategies that would be implemented at the individualized level have as their very foundation the principles that Skinner demonstrated in his laboratory: specifically, the relationship between behaviors, their antecedents, and the consequences that maintain them. The assessment process consists of a functional behavior assessment (O'Neill, Horner, Albin, Storey, & Sprague, 1990) conducted to determine the function of the behavior, preceding consequences, and the maintaining consequences. Then, an intervention plan, referred to as a *positive behavior support plan*, can be put in place.

One component of a positive behavior support plan is based on Skinner's work demonstrating that communication serves a purpose. Carr and Durand (1985), in their seminal research, demonstrated that challenging behavior served a function for individuals with severe disabilities who lacked the communication skills to indicate their desires to caregivers. Specifically, they demonstrated that challenging behavior occurs based on a history of being *positively reinforced*, thus to either obtain access to an item or an event (e.g., a preferred toy, food item, attention, or access to an activity) or based on a history of being *negatively reinforced*, such as to avoid or escape something or someone (e.g., a non-preferred object, activity, or person). These behaviors can be social in nature, and so happen in the presence of another person in order to have that person serve as a mediator (e.g., the parent who provides access to the toy following a challenging behavior or the teacher who terminates a non-preferred task following a tantrum), or they can serve a non-social function (i.e., be non-socially motivated). When a behavior is non-socially motivated, this means it occurs in the presence of or absence of another person, as there does not need to be anyone there to consequent the behavior. The non-socially motivated behaviors are referred to as being *automatically reinforced*. This means the behavior occurs, and the child immediately receives reinforcement. She or he does not need to wait for the "mediator" to provide the reinforcement.

With an understanding that behaviors actually serve a function (purpose) for a child, professionals and caregivers can then approach the behavior in a systematic way, one that does not increase the future likelihood of the behavior. For example, oftentimes, following a child's challenging behavior, a caregiver will go to the child, establish eye contact, and then explain to the child what she or he did wrong and what she or he should have done correctly. This may occur simultaneously with physical contact (e.g., holding the child's arms or hand). Now, consider the function of the child's behavior. If the child engaged in the challenging behavior to receive attention, the caregiver stopping what she or he was doing, going to the child, bending down to establish eye contact, and coming into physical contact while speaking directly to the child may serve as a reinforcer for engaging in the challenging behavior; and thus the child's behavior is likely to increase. With an understanding that behaviors actually serve a function, caregivers can respond in a way that would decrease the future likelihood of the challenging behavior by refraining from reinforcing it (i.e., implementing extinction) and then systematically reinforcing more appropriate behaviors, which is referred to as *differential reinforcement*.

The interventions to address challenging behavior discussed thus far have concentrated on what are referred to as *consequence based strategies*, as they are implemented after the challenging behavior has or has not occurred. Other types of interventions focus on addressing the antecedents that precede a child's challenging behavior, such as offering a choice among activities (Kern, Vorndran, Hilt, Ringdahl, Adelman, & Dunlap, 1998), engaging the child with stimuli that will distract him or her from the non-preferred task, or delivering a series of easy tasks to which the child is likely to comply just before asking the child to perform a task that would ordinarily result in escape-motivated behavior (referred to as *high probability request sequences*) (Davis, Reichle, & Southard, 2000). These interventions described can be implemented in isolation or in combination, forming the positive behavior support plan. The links to comprehensive resources for positive behavior supports can be found at the end of this chapter. Information is certainly available for caregivers who are interested in systematically addressing challenging behavior in the children they serve.

Intervention (Treatment) Intensity

In general, when an early childhood program utilizes behavior analytic procedures, there would be a carefully designed curriculum in place that specifies a set of skills which are identified for instruction over a specific time frame (a series of days or possibly weeks). Personnel would be aware of the skills that are being addressed at any given time and then would carefully construct teaching opportunities, using the three-term contingency. In any early childhood setting, there will be range of strengths and weaknesses across children. If the program at any given time has one or more children with disabilities in the setting, there is potential for that range to be even wider. Thus, it is very likely that some children will need to receive more intensive instruction in order to acquire skills within a particular setting. For example, some children may learn the identified skills given very few teaching opportunities spread across several days; while other children may warrant many more teaching opportunities within a shorter period of time.

In response to the need for more intensive instruction, intervention can be planned accordingly to meet the needs of each child. This is not to say that the intervention setting must change, nor is it a rationale for removal from settings with typical peers. Rather, a *portion* of the child's programming can be dedicated to intensive instruction. This may consist of an increased number of teaching opportunities, which is only one way to vary intervention intensity. The intensity of behaviorally based interventions can also vary with respect to the type of material (contrived or natural), the type of reinforcement (naturally occurring or not related to the task), and the density of teaching opportunities (many within a short period of time or few spread out across the day) (Yoder & Woynaroski, 2015).

One way to conceptualize intervention intensity is to look at the context in which instructional opportunities are presented. In many early childhood settings, one generally finds these three contexts for instruction: *naturalistic instruction* (which capitalizes on ongoing and naturally occurring opportunities), *instruction embedded within an activity* (which entails embedding teaching opportunities while a small group of children are engaged with a game or a toy), and *discrete trial instruction* (which entails delivering many teaching opportunities within a short period of time, within a one-to-one format). All three of these contexts are applications of behavior analytic technologies to address skill acquisition, and all three are evidence based strategies. Also, it is important to note that individual children may require more intensive instruction in some skill areas versus other skill areas. For example a young child may be physically agile and have met all of his or her gross motor milestones; thus any instruction in physical skills may only require a small number of naturally occurring teaching opportunities. In contrast, that same child may experience difficulty in acquiring expressive communication skills, with that skill area warranting additional and contrived teaching opportunities.

It is this very intense application of behavior analytic principles that has come to be *the* recommended procedure for the treatment of autism spectrum disorders. Having long been demonstrated as an effective technology to address a large variety of needs of the population of learners with disabilities including self-care, communication, academics, and challenging behavior, its specific application to young children with autism spectrum disorders has had profound effects on both the children who receive the intervention as well as their families who deal with the day-to-day demands of this disability (see Chapter 9 on O. I. Lovaas in this volume for further discussion). In the seminal work of Lovaas (1987), the systematic and intense implementation of behavioral intervention resulted in the amelioration of autistic characteristics in a subset of the participants and significant changes in skill levels for all of the participants. This work, referred to as *early intensive behavioral intervention*, has been consistently demonstrated to be an effective treatment for autism spectrum disorders as it specifically addresses the core deficits associated with the disorder during the early years, which changes the trajectory for many children.

Informing Early Childhood Professionals of the Value of Skinner's Work

Knowledge of the principles discovered by Skinner, which have been empirically demonstrated to have profound and lasting effects on humans, will provide professionals in the field of early childhood with the tools they need to enhance learning in the children who cross their paths. Clearly, there is a lack of understanding regarding the effectiveness of behaviorally based interventions within early childhood settings. Thus, an important question is to ask is, "What can be done to dispel the myths associated with behavioral approaches and to lead early childhood interventionists to implement these evidence based approaches?"

One can begin by providing, within personnel preparation programs, accurate information about *all* theorists. The dissemination of misinformation with respect to behavior analysis in early childhood education became apparent through an informal review of textbooks whose purpose was to prepare early childhood professionals (Feeley, 2015). This review revealed blatantly incorrect information about the findings of behavioral theorists as well as about their corresponding applications. In addition, in place of information regarding the empirical support for behavioral applications, there was extensive discussion of why the theory could not and should not be used within early childhood settings. This was in contrast to the structure of chapters on other theorists, who were clearly held in higher regard by the texts' authors. The use of these publications in personnel preparation programs allows for exposure to these misconceptions before the professionals in training enter the field.

Ensuring that preservice programs provide a breadth of accurate information is imperative, as are opportunities to conduct fieldwork in programs that are implementing behavior analytic interventions. Programs should be identified that have close oversight by one or more behavior analysts who are experienced in designing and supervising sound behaviorally based interventions.

Importantly, preservice professionals should be taught the basic tenets of evaluating research so they can become informed consumers. In addition, those responsible for preparing professionals for careers in early childhood should demonstrate a strong commitment to evidence based strategies, which will undoubtedly lead to behaviorally based interventions. Finally, for those individuals who are implementing Skinner's principles with improved outcomes, there should be a commitment to share their findings with others and encourage them to "try it." The improved performance of the child will likely function as a reinforcer for the interventionist; thus, their use of those principles will increase. Yet another application of B. F. Skinner's work.

Conclusion

B. F. Skinner founded a science, that of applied behavior analysis. Starting in his animal laboratories, he systematically demonstrated its utility in solving important problems experienced by humans. He did so over the course of his 86 years and hundreds of publications. Inherent in the application of these behavior analytic principles is the systematic demonstration of their effectiveness in enhancing behaviors. With an increased focus on accountability in our education programs, empowering individuals at both the pre-service and in-service levels with an understanding of these principles, including proficiency in measuring behavior change, will enable them to routinely monitor the impact their interventions are having on the children they serve. This, in turn, allows for timely adjustments providing optimal experiences during the earliest years of children's lives.

References

Baer, D.M., Wolf, M., & Risley, R. (1968). Some current dimensions of applied behavior analysis. *Journal of Applied Behavior Analysis, 1*, 91–97.

Carr, E.G., & Durand, V.M. (1985). Reducing behavior problems through functional communication training. *Journal of Applied Behavior Analysis, 18*, 111–126.

Carr, E.G., Horner, R.H., Turnbull, A.P., McLaughlin, D.M., McAtee, M.L., Smith, C.E., ... Doolabh, A. (1999). *Positive behavior support for people with developmental disabilities: A research synthesis*. Washington, DC: American Association on Mental Retardation.

Chomsky, N. (1959). *Verbal Behavior* by B.F. Skinner. *Language, 35*, 26–58.

Davis, C.A., Reichle, J.E., & Southard, K.L. (2000). High-probability requests and a preferred item as a distractor: Increasing successful transitions in children with behavior problems. Education and Treatment of Children, *23*, 423–440.

Feeley, K. (2015). *A review of early childhood education textbooks for accuracy regarding behavior analytic theorists and interventions*. Unpublished manuscript. Department of Special Education and Literacy, Long Island University, Brookville, New York.

Fox, L., Dunlap, G., Hemmeter, M.L., Joseph, G., & Strain, P. (2003). The teaching pyramid: A model for supporting social competence and preventing challenging behavior in young children. *Young Children, 58*, 48–53.

Frost, L.A., & Bondy, A.S. (2002). *Picture exchange communication system*. Newark, NJ: Pyramid.

Halle, J.W., Marshall, A.M., & Spradlin, J.E. (1979). Time delay: A technique to increase langue use and facilitate generalization in regarded children. *Journal of Applied Behavior Analysis, 12*, 431–439.

Kern, L., Vorndran, C.M., Hilt, A., Ringdahl, J.E., Adelman, B.E., & Dunlap, G. (1998). Choice as an intervention to improve behavior: A review of the literature. *Journal of Behavioral Education, 8*, 151–169.

Lovaas , O.I. (1987). Behavioral treatment and normal educational and intellectual functioning in young autistic children. *Journal of Consulting and Clinical Psychology, 55*, 3–9.

Morris, E.K., Smith, N.G., & Altus, D.W. (2005). B.F. Skinner's contribution to applied behavior analysis. *The Behavior Analyst, 28*, 99–131.

O'Donohue, W.T., & Ferguson, K.E. (2001). *The psychology of B.F. Skinner*. Thousand Oaks, CA: Sage.

O'Neill, R.E., Horner, R.H., Albin, R.W., Storey, K., & Sprague, J.R. (1990). *Functional analysis of problem behavior: A practical assessment guide*. Sycamore, IL: Sycamore Publishing.

Pierce, W.D., & Cheney, C.D. (2013). *Behavior analysis and learning: 5th Edition*. New York: Psychology Press.

Rutherford, A. (2009). *Beyond the box: B.F. Skinner's technology of behavior from laboratory to life, 1950s–1970s*. Toronto: University of Toronto Press.

Sigafoos, J., Reichle, J., & Doss, S. (1990). Spontaneous transfer of stimulus control from Tact to Mand contingencies. *Research in Developmental Disabilities, 11*, 165–176.

Skinner, B.F. (1937). The distribution of associated words. *The Psychological Record, 1*, 71–76.

Skinner, B.F. (1938). *The behavior of organisms: An experimental analysis.* New York: Appleton-Century.
Skinner, B.F. (1939). The alliteration in Shakespeare's sonnets. *The Psychological Record, 3*, 186–192.
Skinner, B.F. (1953). *Skinner science and human behavior*. New York: Macmillan.
Skinner, B.F. (1954). The science of learning and the art of teaching. *Harvard Educational Review, 24*, 86–97.
Skinner, B.F. (1957). *Verbal behavior*. Cambridge, MA: Prentice-Hall.
Skinner, B.F. (1963). Reflections on a decade of teaching machines. *Teachers College Record, 65*, 168–177.
Skinner, B.F. (1968). *The technology of teaching*. New York: Appleton-Century-Crofts.
Skinner, B.F. (1979). *The shaping of a behaviorist: Part two of an autobiography*. New York: New York University Press.
Skinner, B.F., & Vaughan, M.E. (1983). *Enjoy old age: A program of self-management*. New York: W.W. Norton.
Strain, P.S., & McConnell, S.R. (1992). Behaviorism in early intervention. *Topics in Early Childhood Special Education, 12*, 121–142.
Thorndike, E.L. (1898). Animal intelligence. *Psychological Review Monograph Supplements* (Serial no. 8).
US Department of Health and Human Services/US Department of Education (2015). Policy Statement on Expulsion and Suspension Policies in Early Childhood Settings.
Watkins, C.L. (1995). Follow through: Why didn't we? *Effective School Practices, 15*. Retrieved from http://darkwing.uoregon.edu/~adiep/ft/watkins.htm
Watson, J.B., & Raynor, R. (1920). Conditioned emotional reactions. *Journal of Experimental Child Psychology, 3*, 1–14.
Wolfensberger, W. (1972). *The principle of normalization in human services*. Toronto: National Institute on Mental Retardation.
Yoder, P.J., & Woynaroski, T. (2015). How to study the influence of intensity of treatment on generalized skill and knowledge acquisition in students with disabilities. *Journal of Behavioral Education, 24*, 152–166.

Suggested Websites

B.F. Skinner Foundation: www.bfskinner.org
Cambridge Center for Behavioral Studies: www.behavior.org
National Institute for Direct Instruction: www.nifdi.org/?catid=0&id=79
Positive Behavioral Interventions and Supports: www.pbis.org/
Princeton Child Development Institute (PCDI): www.pcdi.org/
The Technical Assistance Center on Social Emotional Intervention for Young Children: http://challengingbehavior.fmhi.usf.edu/

9

OLE IVAR LOVAAS

A Legacy of Learning for Children with Disabilities

Emily A. Jones, Sally M. Izquierdo, and Caraline Kobel

The groundbreaking pioneer of autism treatment, Dr. Ole Ivar Lovaas, was born May 8, 1927, in Lier, Norway. After coming to the United States in 1950, he graduated from Luther College in 1951 and went on to receive his Ph.D. in clinical psychology from the University of Washington in 1958. During his time at the University of Washington he spent three years as a research assistant professor and had the great opportunity to work with leaders in the field of applied behavior analysis (ABA) such as Don Baer, Mont Wolf, Todd Risley, and Sid Bijou.

Lovaas became an assistant professor of psychology at the University of California–Los Angeles (UCLA), in 1961, retiring as an emeritus professor in 2003. After becoming ill with Alzheimer's disease and complications during surgery, Lovaas passed away in Lancaster, California, on August 2, 2010, at the age of 83, leaving behind a legacy of extraordinary, life changing work for children with autism and their families (Smith & Eikeseth, 2011).

In an attempt to broaden the scope of his research on the influence of language, Lovaas began to work with individuals with autism. The first research questions were about the effects of language instruction on other behaviors for children with autism. And so began the focus of his research for the next half-century.

Lovaas' approach to autism challenged the prevailing notions of the time. In the twentieth century, autism treatment took a psychoanalytic approach. Bruno Bettelheim blamed autism on cold, uncaring mothers whom he termed "refrigerator mothers" (Bettelheim, 1967). Treatment involved children's removal from their family home to an institution where they received play therapy while mothers received psychoanalysis. It was revealed much later that most of Bettelheim's claims about the effectiveness of his treatment for children with autism were not supported by empirical evidence (Severson, Aune, & Jodlowski, 2008). In 1964, Bernard Rimland offered a comprehensive discussion of the evidence for a biological explanation of autism (Rimland, 1964). This began the focus on exploring the biological etiology of autism. Unfortunately, this perspective led many to conclude that nothing could be done to change the bizarre and dangerous behaviors, language deficits, or social difficulties often associated with autism.

Lovaas thought differently about autism. Using principles from operant learning theory or the experimental analysis of behavior, he put into practice the premise that behavior is modifiable, and did so with this significantly impaired population of children. Applied behavior analysis (ABA), the term with which many are familiar in education for children with autism, puts that science into practical applications to discover environmental variables to change socially significant behavior.

Whether a child has a diagnosis of autism, another disorder, or is typically developing, the obstacles children present to learning do not mean they cannot learn. In fact, what Lovaas emphasized was breaking down a disorder into behaviors that needed instruction. One of the most exciting things about Lovaas' work and ABA is the focus on what can be changed rather than blaming the child and disorder for difficulties in learning.

Lovaas focused not only on ways to decrease challenging behaviors (e.g., Lovaas, Freitag, Gold, & Kassorla, 1965; Lovaas & Simmons, 1969), but also on how to teach more appropriate behaviors (e.g., Lovaas, Berberich, Perloff, & Schaeffer, 1966) to children, some with autism (also referred to as childhood schizophrenia at the time), others with intellectual disability (referred to as mental retardation), and other labels. In 1973, Lovaas and colleagues summarized work with 20 children with autism (Lovaas, Koegel, Simmons, & Long, 1973). Intervention was effective, though generalization and maintenance varied; children who returned to state hospitals did not generalize gains, but those whose education was conducted primarily by their parents, overseen by Lovaas and his team, fared better. Issues of generalization and maintenance led to changes and improvements in Lovaas' approach.

In 1981, Lovaas published the first comprehensive curriculum for educating children with autism, commonly referred to as *The ME Book*. The curriculum described behavioral strategies to reduce self-stimulatory and self-injurious behaviors and teach compliance, imitation, toy play with peers, expressive language, emotions, and academic skills. His early work on language comes through in the emphasis on language and communication instruction. Years of research in this field have demonstrated that challenging behavior is communicative and learning more appropriate ways of getting one's wants and needs met results in decreases in problem behavior (e.g., Mancil, 2006; Matson, Dixon, & Matson, 2005).

This comprehensive curriculum covered all the skills, across domains of development, and included the stipulation that children needed to participate in their homes, schools, and communities. The teaching approach, discrete trial teaching (DTT), is one way of teaching using the principles of ABA and is the term many people probably associate with autism treatment. DTT involves breaking each skill down into small steps and presenting repeated opportunities to practice skills while systematically helping the child to engage in the correct behaviors and providing consequences to increase newly learned skills.

In 1987, Lovaas published his widely known longitudinal study, "Behavioral Treatment and Normal Education and Intellectual Functioning in Young Autistic Children," demonstrating the effectiveness of the approach to treating children with autism described in *The ME Book*. He compared 40 hours a week of DTT to 10 hours of treatment. Results indicated that the group who received 40 hours of DTT per week showed significant improvements in intellectual and educational placement compared to the group who received only 10 hours of treatment per week.

Intervention in the 1987 study reflected what Lovaas had learned in his previous work and emphasized the importance of instruction all day every day. He also emphasized starting at a young age because he thought it would increase the likelihood of a better outcome, and it would be easier to transition young children into a regular class than older children. Unlike the 1973 follow up study, a 1993 follow up study showed considerable maintenance of improvements (McEachin, Smith, & Lovaas, 1993).

The Lovaas method, referred to more broadly now as early intensive behavioral intervention, represented a turning point in autism treatment. Since 1995, The Lovaas Institute in Los Angeles, California, has provided training for teachers in the "Lovaas method" and services for children with autism. His son, Erik, opened the Lovaas Center in Las Vegas, Nevada, where professionals continue to practice this method. As of 2016, there are 12 Lovaas Centers throughout the United States providing ABA services to children with autism (Lovaas Institute, n.d.). Treatment programs for children with autism go by many different names. Implementation may look somewhat different and the emphasis may focus more on certain behaviors (e.g., language), but those with empirical evidence are based in part in applied behavior analysis (Schreibman et al., 2015).

Since Lovaas' 1987 study, a number of studies have demonstrated the effectiveness of early intensive behavioral intervention, with recent meta-analyses confirming medium-to-large effect sizes across domains of development (e.g., Eldevik et al., 2009; Reichow & Wolery, 2009; Strauss, Mancini, Fava, & SPC Group, 2013). Organizations as well as the surgeon general (U.S. Department of Health and Human Services, 1999) and even states (e.g., New York State Department of Health and Early Intervention Program, 1999) endorse applied behavior analysis in the treatment of autism.

So, what does Lovaas' legacy for the education of children with autism look like in early childhood classrooms?

A Technology of Teaching

DTT involves the structured and systematic application of behavior analytic principles to teach new behaviors. Once a target behavior is identified, it can be plugged into the A-B-C model (Figure 9.1) in which A refers to the *antecedent* or what happens before B, the target *behavior* or skill, followed by C, the *consequence* that happens after the behavior.

Both antecedents (A) and consequences (C) should be tailored to ensure that the child will emit the new skill (B) when he or she should. Figure 9.2 shows the components of DTT plugged into the A-B-C model. In DTT, the programmed antecedents are discriminative stimuli (S^Ds) and prompts. The S^D is an instruction that signals the availability of reinforcement for some response (B). For example, when teaching number identification, the S^D might be, "Point to 5."

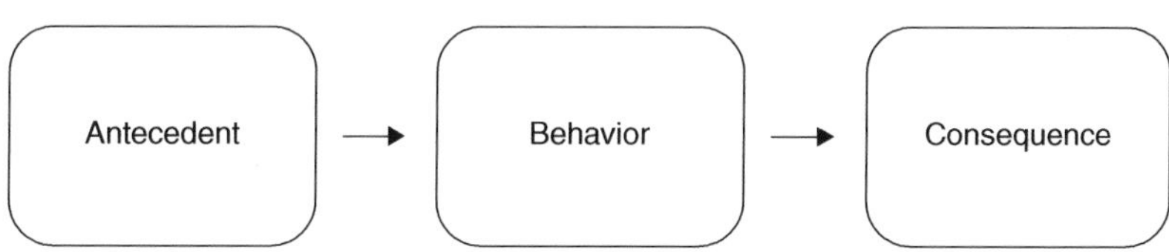

Figure 9.1 The A-B-C Model: A refers to the antecedent, B the behavior, and C the consequence.

Figure 9.2 The Components of DTT Plugged Into the A-B-C Model. The antecedents include SD and prompt, the behavior of interest is the target skill, and the consequence is positive reinforcement.

Prompts are any additional stimuli added to ensure that the child engages in the desired response (B). If a teacher wants a student to identify the number 5, she or he might include prompts such as modeling how to point to 5, moving the number 5 closer to the child than the other numbers on the table, or taking the child's hand and moving it to touch the number 5. Once the child has engaged in the correct response (B), consequences (C) ensure that the correct behavior is repeated in the future under similar conditions. A reinforcer is a consequence delivered contingent upon the target behavior that makes it more likely the behavior will be repeated in the future. So, when the instruction "Touch 5" is given and the child touches the number 5, the teacher might say something like, "Yes! That's 5! You got it! Wonderful!" She or he might also give the child a small piece of a favorite snack, a few moments to play with a preferred toy, or a token to place on his/her token board (Figure 9.3).

One learning opportunity, or trial, consists of one presentation of an S^D, prompt, behavior, and consequence (A-B-C). Prompts are faded out across opportunities until the child performs when asked the S^D (without any prompt). In DTT, many opportunities are presented one after the other, separated by a very short inter-trial interval of 1–5 seconds. Generally, the shorter, the better (Koegel, Dunlap, & Dyer, 1980). Skills may be presented in mass trials, e.g., 10 of one skill, then 10 of another, and so on, or by mixing and varying different skills. The latter tends to be more natural, but also more difficult to implement.

Lovaas originally designed intervention to be conducted at home, where young children spend most of their time. Today, increasingly, even very young children are in school, especially with the availability of disability services in school. The good news is that DTT can be conducted almost anywhere the child spends a good deal of time, including school! In fact, many autism preschools in the United States and around the world use DTT (Harris & Handleman, 2008) with some public preschools following suit and sometimes even extending the technology to children with other disabilities (e.g., Downs, Downs, Johansen, & Fossum, 2007).

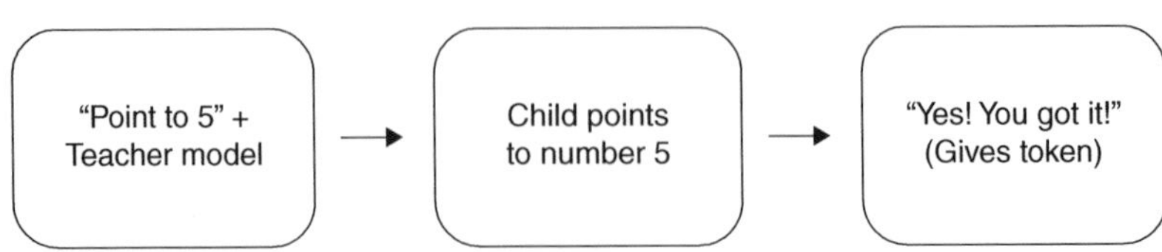

Figure 9.3 An Example of DTT Instruction within the Context of the A-B-C Model.

What Does DTT Look Like in an Early Childhood Classroom?

Similar to home programs, DTT will look a little bit different in each classroom, with programs to meet the needs of specific children.

Step 1: Choose a Target Behavior

The first step is to select behaviors or skills to teach, because each of the remaining components will be designed around those targets. In general, skills should be selected that are developmentally and age appropriate. Lovaas began with basic attending and reduction of problem behaviors by replacing those with communication and imitation skills. These are not only skills that very young children typically acquire early on, but are also relevant, functional, and pivotal. Pivotal skills are those that, once mastered, open the door to other skills with little to no teaching. For example, a child who learns to imitate motor movements may now learn play behaviors by imitating his or her siblings at the park.

Parents can help identify problem behaviors and skill deficits and the contexts in which they are most relevant. An ABA curriculum, along with the child's Individual Education Plan, can also be used to select and sequence skills. The Assessment of Basic Language and Learning Skills-Revised (ABLLS-R) (Partington, 2006), Verbal Behavior Milestones and Placement Program (VB-MAPP) (Sundberg, 2008), Essentials for Living (McGreevy, Fry, & Cornwall, 2012), and Strategies for Teaching based on Autism Research (STAR) (Arick, Loos, Falco, & Krug, 2004) are just a few of many curricula that have been developed since Lovaas and *The ME Book*. Each ABA curriculum may have a slightly different emphasis, but provides guidelines for assessing and teaching skills as well as the writing of IEP goals. Many even have electronic versions.

Step 2: Choose a Location

Schools that have successfully implemented DTT creatively utilize available space, while adhering to the guidelines for least restrictive environment (US Department of Education, 2004). All that is needed to implement DTT is a small table or desk, two chairs, and some materials; therefore, instruction can take place almost anywhere. One might consider a table in the classroom, pull out to a resource or therapy room, or time in a smaller or self-contained classroom. It might also be advantageous to combine the needs of multiple children with similar goals by running some DTT programs in dyads or triads.

Step 3: Choose a Team

Ideally at least two individuals will work with the child on a consistent schedule. More than one person providing instruction increases the likelihood of generalization across people. Instructors might include a classroom teacher, classroom assistant, aide or one-to-one aide, related service provider, counselor, or other available professional willing to learn and implement DTT. Sometimes home therapists conduct some of their sessions at school and may be part of the team. Parents should also be trained to teach skills that are relevant at home. The team, including the parents, should meet often (weekly or bi-weekly) to review the child's performance, make changes to instructional programs, and choose new targets.

Step 4: Choose Reinforcers

It can be challenging to motivate children with disabilities, requiring careful selection and delivery of reinforcing consequences. Children with disabilities may not respond well to instruction, ignore requests for their attention, and, in general, not find teachers all that interesting relative to toys, objects, or engaging in repetitive behaviors. Early and frequent preference assessments can help to identify a number of powerful reinforcers to get started. It is important to realize that what will function as a reinforcer for one skill or for one child may not function as a reinforcer for another skill or another child. The teacher should first pair himself or herself with those reinforcers; engage the child with his or her preferred activities, and provide other reinforcers "for free" every few minutes. The next step is to gradually fade in instructions so that reinforcers are provided following correct responses.

Step 5: Gather and Organize Materials

The materials needed to conduct DTT will vary depending on the skills. Many items are readily available in classrooms or can be made. It will also be important to develop a system for storing and organizing those materials for easy access by instructors. Materials can be shared between children, but this will require more time and organization to make sure that materials are where they need to be when it is time to work with the child. Each child will also need a program book, usually a three-ring binder with sections for each skill containing a description of intervention procedures and forms to track performance.

Step 6: Create an Individualized System of Recording the Child's Performance

All teaching programs require some form of progress tracking to make decisions about mastery, remediation, and the introduction of new skills. Traditionally, data are recorded for each and every opportunity during DTT until mastery criteria are met (set as some percentage of opportunities correct across several sessions or days, usually 80%). The process of recording performance should not, however, interfere with the pace or integrity of instruction. Sometimes it is better to record only the first opportunity in a session for each skill so that instruction then takes place without interference. Data sheets and mastery criteria can be customized to match the target skills and data recording system. With any system, better programming decisions tend to be made when data are graphed and reviewed daily. As a result, children perform better (Hojnoski, Gischlar, & Missall, 2009).

Intervention Intensity: A Continuum from DTT to Naturalistic Instruction

Arguably, DTT and Lovaas' approach are rather intense interventions. Lovaas wanted children to receive intervention during most of their waking hours with intervention involving repeated opportunities to practice skills. He thought that level of intensity was critical to outcomes; in the 1987 study he compared 40 hours of treatment per week to just 10 hours per week, showing much greater gains and better outcomes with 40 hours (Lovaas, 1987). This aspect of intensity is referred to as *dose frequency* (Warren, Fey, & Yoder, 2007). Today, a high level of intensity is seen as a critical component of intervention for children with autism. Between 10 and 40 hours of intervention per week are recommended, although children under 3 years old may receive fewer hours, and school-aged children more (Lovaas Institute, n.d.; National Research Council [N.R.C.], 2001; New York State Department of Health [N.Y.S.D.O.H.], 1999).

There are other dimensions of intensity that may also impact outcomes for children with autism. The number of opportunities per session (*dose*), the overall length of treatment (*duration*), and the quality of intervention, including where intervention occurs and with whom (*dose form*) are also part of intervention intensity (Warren et al., 2007). In fact, Lovaas' DTT is also relatively high intensity in terms of dose and duration, providing many opportunities per session with many sessions occurring over several years. In addition, DTT is traditionally implemented in a one-to-one format, often incorporating powerful reinforcement unrelated to the skill being taught and delivered on a more frequent schedule than would happen naturally, reflecting a high intensity of dose form.

The same ABA principles underlying Lovaas' approach to intervention can be implemented with variations in dose and dose form. For example, a teacher might use prompting and reinforcement to teach a child to identify colors during an art lesson, providing a few opportunities during each art lesson that occurs a few times per week. In this case, intensity varies significantly from Lovaas' approach: only a few opportunities, spaced out during an art lesson, with only a few sessions each week, in a large group art lesson. This more naturalistic approach to instruction (sometimes also referred to as incidental or natural environment teaching) relies on the same strategies that Lovaas used in instruction: careful definition of the target behavior, systematic prompting and prompt fading procedures, and reinforcement. So it is every bit as planned and precise as DTT. That is, within the context of everyday activities and in the presence of naturally occurring S^Ds, adults can seek out and even set up opportunities for children to learn, prompt desired behaviors, and provide reinforcement.

One of the advantages of incorporating opportunities in the natural environment is that the skills are more likely to be generalized across materials, settings, and people, and be maintained over time. It was important to Lovaas that children learn skills that enable them to be successful at home and remain with their families. Generalization and maintenance were obstacles he faced in his initial work in clinics and institutions, leading to his emphasis on teaching children at home.

Some combination of DTT and naturalistic teaching seems desirable. This provides the needed structure, repeated opportunities, use of contrived reinforcers (if natural consequences do not function as reinforcers), while creating opportunities to generalize and maintain skills in settings where they are functional and lead to greater access to natural and social reinforcers. Often the combination can involve naturalistic opportunities within inclusive settings with typically developing peers (e.g., Stahmer, Akshoomoff, & Cunningham, 2011).

What Does Intervention Intensity Look Like in an Early Childhood Classroom?

When designing educational programs for children with disabilities, teachers can arrange the aspects of intensity to match individual child needs. In the steps outlined previously for developing DTT intervention, after identifying skills to teach (step 1), the level of intensity that will be most effective and efficient *for each skill* should be identified. This requires careful consideration of a number of factors. If the skill is related to an area of interest or is a strength, the child may readily engage with naturalistic learning opportunities. If, however, the child has a history of lack of engagement with relevant instructional materials for the task (not interested) or the child has struggled to acquire this type of skill in the past, the repeated practice and teacher-directed structure of DTT may be advantageous. Similarly, DTT may be advantageous to quickly teach more appropriate communicative replacements if the child is engaging in challenging behavior. Once skills are mastered in DTT, they can be transferred to more naturalistic settings to work on generalization.

So, for *each target skill* for a given child, the intensity of instruction including the context of instruction (dose form), how often sessions will occur (dose frequency), and how many opportunities will be provided per session (dose), should be decided. These considerations will vary for different children and different skills along the continuum of intensity (DTT to more naturalistic).

Inclusion

The previous discussion of intensity should have revealed how the principles on which Lovaas' intervention approach rests can be implemented in many different environments. In fact, many think that DTT and education for children with autism must occur outside or away from the community activities and schools that children would have accessed if they did not have a diagnosis of autism. With the first demonstration of comprehensive treatment for children with autism, Lovaas made a big shift from what had been done up to that time: he kept children with autism at home with their families and in their communities where parents also enrolled their children in a regular preschool. The children did not need to go somewhere else to get "better."

The hypothesis of Lovaas' 1987 study was that, with intensive intervention in the early years, children could catch up to their peers by first grade. He measured first grade placement as one of the outcomes; 47% succeeded in a regular first grade class in a public school.

Lovaas succeeded, and subsequent research suggests benefits for children accessing inclusive opportunities in their toddler and preschool years (e.g., Boulware, Schwartz, Sandall, & McBride, 2006; Strain & Bovey, 2008). Often this is a combination of instruction, some with typical peers and some with one-to-one discrete trial teaching (e.g., Stahmer et al., 2011). Studies of inclusive programs show improvements across communication, social, and adaptive development along with decreasing autism symptomatology (e.g., Harris, Handleman, Gordon, Kristoff, & Fuentes, 1991; Stahmer & Ingersoll, 2004; Stahmer et al., 2011). Inclusion of children with disabilities also shows positive outcomes for typically developing peers across the school years (e.g., McDonald, Birnbrauer, & Swerissen, 1987) and no negative effects on academic achievement (e.g., Farrell, Dyson, Polat, Hutcheson, & Gallannaugh, 2007). Much is known about translating the strategies Lovaas used into practice within general education classrooms to support children with autism (e.g., Crosland & Dunlap, 2012; Ferraioli & Harris, 2011; Wagner, 1999).

What Does Inclusion Look Like in an Early Childhood Classroom?

Intervention should, and can be provided within children's natural environments, and the goal should be that children succeed in the environments in which they would have been if they did not have a diagnosis. This means home and community preschools as well as parks, playgrounds, libraries, and gymnastics classes—the places where typically developing children learn and grow in early childhood.

The question then is about *how* to support children's opportunities in their natural environments (home, school, community, with typically developing peers). The task of helping a child with autism participate in inclusive classrooms or community activities will mean drawing on the principles and strategies of applied behavior analysis to find ways to support the child's learning and participation. This will likely include the following:

- teaching social skills to the child with autism and training peers to support social opportunities;
- modifying educational activities and curriculum, providing some individualized instruction, preparing the child with autism ahead of time for new curriculum content and activities, and involving peers as peer tutors;
- utilizing positive behavior supports (Bambara & Kern, 2005) that involves assessing the function of challenging behavior (functional behavior assessment), teaching more appropriate communicative alternatives, strategies to prevent challenging behavior, and consequences that increase the likelihood of appropriate behavior;
- structuring the classroom through seating arrangements that encourage attention to instruction and engagement with sophisticated and trained peers, and even a class-wide visual schedule (and usually a schedule individualized for the child with autism).

Some children with autism will also have paraprofessional support within the classroom and/or a consultant who specializes in autism and behavior analysis whose role is to help the classroom teacher develop the best ways to teach the child with autism.

Parent Involvement

Inclusion does not just refer to schools and classrooms, but all aspects of communities and neighborhoods, and starts with keeping kids at home with their families. When Lovaas did this, it was a radical deviation from the psychoanalytic approach that had pervaded treatment for autism. Not only did Lovaas keep children at home, but he actively involved parents as team members in their children's education. Parents actually learned to implement intervention, acting as co-instructors. As a result, parents could increase the number of hours of instruction their child received to nearly all waking hours. Parent involvement also helped with generalization of skills children were learning during instruction so children demonstrated skills across different environments and with different people. Lovaas taught parents how to implement intervention using the same manual and curriculum he used to instruct teachers and other professionals how to teach (*The ME Book*). Research suggests that early intensive behavioral intervention with parents involved in implementing intervention yields better outcomes than without parent involvement (e.g., Strauss et al., 2013).

What Does Parent Involvement Look Like in an Early Childhood Classroom?

For classroom teachers, involving parents means many things. The process of teaching parents to carry over instruction at home relies on the same principles Lovaas used to design interventions for children with autism. Teachers should break down instruction into steps, show parents what to do (model), help parents practice with their child, and provide feedback about what they did well and what they need to improve on. This process should be repeated until parents are proficient, implementing instruction as modeled. This is referred to as behavioral skills training (e.g., Nigro-Bruzzi & Sturmey, 2010). The child needs to be present during behavioral skills training so the parent can practice instruction with him or her while receiving feedback from a skilled professional. The genuine involvement of parents as team members means that they are taught how to conduct instruction at home and in the community on a regular basis, not as something that happens just a couple of times a year. The outcomes for children are better when parents are taught to implement intervention than when they are just given information about autism and education (e.g., Bearss et al., 2015).

Parents must also be involved in choices about their child's instructional program, ranging from helping to identify reinforcers to deciding what skills to teach their children. Parents can help ensure that the skills are socially significant for their child, meaningful in his or her everyday life, with a positive impact on his or her relationships. In inclusive environments parents can be one of the best resources for talking to typically developing children about autism and what it means for their child. Educating the typically developing children is an important component of supporting a child with autism in an inclusive setting.

Lovaas' Legacy

Lovaas' work is most often associated with autism. His approach to treatment, from the theoretical underpinnings to the choices he made about parents, location, and intensity of treatment remain key components of intervention for children with autism today. But the interventions he developed were developed with individuals with a range of diagnoses, perhaps most often intellectual disability. His curriculum, commonly referred to as *The ME Book*, is fully titled *Teaching Developmentally Disabled Children: The ME Book*. Lovaas himself always made it clear that ABA was applicable to individuals with many needs, not just those with autism. The approach he took shifted thinking several decades ago from institutional care to family and community care, with an emphasis on teaching skills and aiming for inclusion with typically developing peers for *all* children with developmental disabilities.

References

Arick, J.R., Loos, L., Falco, R., & Krug, D.A. (2004). *The STAR Program: Strategies for teaching based on autism research* (2nd ed.). Austin, TX: Pro-Ed.

Bambara, L., & Kern, L. (2005). *Individualized supports for children with problem behaviors: Designing positive behavior plans*. New York: Guilford Press.

Bearss, K., Johnson, C., Smith, T., Levalier, L. Swiezy, N., Aman, M., ... Scahill, L. (2015). Effect of parent training vs. parent education on behavioral problems in children with autism spectrum disorder: A randomized clinical trial. *Journal of the American Medical Association, 313*(15), 1524–1533. http://dx.doi.org/10.1001/jama.2015.3150

Bettelheim, B. (1967). *The empty fortress: Infantile autism and the birth of the self*. New York: The Free Press.

Boulware, G., Schwartz, I.S., Sandall, S.R., & McBride, B.J. (2006). Project DATA for toddlers: An inclusive approach to very young children with autism spectrum disorder. *Topics in Early Childhood Special Education, 26*(2), 94–105.

Crosland, K., & Dunlap, G. (2012). Effective strategies for the inclusion of children with autism in general education classrooms. *Behavior Modification, 36*(3), 251–269. http://dx.doi.org/10.1177/0145445512442682

Downs, A., Downs, R.C., Johansen, M., & Fossum, M. (2007). Using discrete trial teaching within a public preschool program to facilitate skill development in children with developmental disabilities. *Education and Treatment of Children, 30*(3), 1–27.

Eldevik, S., Hastings, R.P., Hughes, J.C., Jahr, E., Eikeseth, S., & Cross, S. (2009). Meta-analysis of early intensive behavioral intervention for children with autism. *Journal of Clinical Child and Adolescent Psychology, 38*(3), 439–450. http://dx.doi.org/10.1080/15374410902851739

Farrell, P., Dyson, A., Polat, F., Hutcheson, G., & Gallannaugh, F. (2007). SEN inclusion and pupil achievement in English schools. *Journal of Research in Special Educational Needs, 7*(3), 172–178. http://dx.doi.org/10.1111/j.1471-3802.2007.00094.x

Ferraioli, S.J., & Harris, S.L. (2011). Effective educational inclusion of students on the autism spectrum. *Journal of Contemporary Psychotherapy, 41*, 19–28. http://dx.doi.org/10.1007/s10879-010-9156-y

Harris, S.L. & Handleman, J.S. (2008). *Preschool education programs for children with autism* (3rd ed.). Austin, TX: Pro-Ed.

Harris, S.L., Handleman, J.S., Gordon, R., Kristoff, B., & Fuentes, F. (1991). Changes in cognitive and language functioning of preschool children with autism. *Journal of Autism and Developmental Disorders, 21*, 281–290.

Hojnoski, R.L., Gischlar, K.L., & Missall, K.N. (2009). Improving child outcomes with data based decision making: Collecting data. *Young Exceptional Children, 12*(3), 32–44. http://dx.doi.org/10.1177/1096250609333025

Koegel, R.L., Dunlap, G., & Dyer, K. (1980). Intertrial interval duration and learning in autistic children. *Journal of Applied Behavior Analysis, 13*(1), 91–99.

Lovaas Institute. Retrieved from www.lovaas.com/lovaasnote.php

Lovaas, O.I. (1981). *Teaching developmentally disabled children: The ME book*. Austin, TX: Pro-Ed.

Lovaas, O.I. (1987). Behavioral treatment and normal educational and intellectual functioning in young autistic children. *Journal of Consulting and Clinical Psychology, 55*(1), 3–9.

Lovaas, O.I., Berberich, J.P. Perloff, B.F., & Schaeffer, B. (1966). Acquisition of imitative speech in schizophrenic children. *Science, 151*, 705–707.

Lovaas, O.I., Freitag, G., Gold, V.J., & Kassorla, I.C. (1965). Experimental studies in childhood schizophrenia: Analysis of self-destructive behavior. *Journal of Experimental Child Psychology, 2*(1), 67–84.

Lovaas, O.I, Koegel, R., Simmons, J.Q., & Long, J.S. (1973). Some generalization and follow-up measures on autistic children in behavior therapy. *Journal of Applied Behavior Analysis*, 6(1), 131–166.

Lovaas, O.I., & Simmons, J. Q. (1969). Manipulation of self-destruction in three retarded children. *Journal of Applied Behavior Analysis*, 2, 143–157.

Mancil, G.R. (2006). Functional communication training: A review of the literature related to children with autism. *Education and Training in Developmental Disabilities*, 41(3), 213–224.

Matson, J.L., Dixon, D.R., & Matson, M.L. (2005). Assessing and treating aggression in children and adolescents with developmental disabilities: A 20-year overview. *Educational Psychology*, 25(2–3), 151–181. http://dx.doi.org/10.1080/0144341042000301148

McDonald, S., Birnbrauer, J.S., & Swerissen, H. (1987). The effect of an integration program on teacher and child attitudes to mentally-handicapped children. *Australian Psychologist*, 22(3), 313–322.

McEachin, J.J., Smith, T., & Lovaas, O.I. (1993). Long-term outcome for children with autism who received early intensive behavioral treatment. *American Journal on Mental Retardation*, 97(4), 359–372.

McGreevy, P., Fry, T., & Cornwall, C. (2012). *Essential for living: A communication, behavior, and functional skills curriculum, assessment, and professional practitioner's handbook*. Winterpark, FL: Patrick McGreevy.

National Research Council. (2001). *Educating children with autism*. Washington, DC: N.R.C.

New York State Department of Health Early Intervention Program (1999). *Clinical practice guideline: Report of the recommendations: Autism/pervasive developmental disorders: assessment and intervention for young children (age 0–3 years)*. Albany, NY: N.Y.S.D.H.E.I.P.

Nigro-Bruzzi, D., & Sturmey, P. (2010). The effects of behavioral skills training on Mand training by staff and unprompted vocal Mands by children. *Journal of Applied Behavior Analysis*, 43(4), 757–761. http://dx.doi.org/10.1901/jaba.2010.43-757

Partington, J.W. (2006). *The assessment of basic language and learning skills—revised*. Pleasant Hills, CA: Behavior Analysts.

Reichow, B., & Wolery, M. (2009). Comprehensive synthesis of early intensive behavioral interventions for young children with autism based on the UCLA Young Autism Project model. *Journal of Autism and Developmental Disorders*, 39, 23–41. http://dx.doi.org/10.1007/s10803-008-0596-0

Rimland, B. (1964). *Infantile autism: The syndrome and its implications for a neural theory of behavior*. New York: Meredith Publishing Company.

Schreibman, L., Dawson, G., Stahmer, A.C., Landa, R., Rogers, S.J., McGee, G.G., … Halladay, A. (2015). Naturalistic developmental behavioral interventions: Empirically validated treatments for autism spectrum disorder. *Journal of Autism and Developmental Disorders*, 45, 2411–2428. http://dx.doi.org/10.1007/s10803-015-2407-8

Severson, K.D., Aune, J.A., & Jodlowski, D. (2008). Bruno Bettelheim, autism, and the rhetoric of scientific authority. In M. Osteen (Ed.) *Autism and representation* (pp. 65–77). New York: Routledge.

Smith, T., & Eikeseth, S. (2011). O. Ivar Lovaas: Pioneer of applied behavior analysis and intervention for children with autism. *Journal of Autism and Developmental Disorders*, 41(3), 375–378. http://dx.doi.org/10.1007/s10803-010-1162-0

Stahmer, A.C., Akshoomoff, N., & Cunningham, A.B. (2011). Inclusion for toddlers with autism spectrum disorders: The first ten years of a community program. *Autism*, 15(5), 625–641. http://dx.doi.org/10.1177/1362361310392253

Stahmer, A.C., & Ingersoll, B. (2004). Inclusive programming for toddlers with autism spectrum disorders: Outcomes from the Children's Toddler School. *Journal of Positive Behavior Interventions*, 6, 67–82. http://dx.doi.org/10.1177/10983007040060020201

Strain, P.S., & Bovey, E.H. (2008). LEAP: Learning experiences, an alternative program for preschoolers and parents. In J.S. Handleman and S.L. Harris (Eds.), *Preschool education programs for children with autism* (3rd ed.). Austin, TX: Pro-Ed.

Strauss, K., Mancini, F., Fava, L., & SPC Group (2013). Parent inclusion in early intensive behavior interventions for young children with ASD: A synthesis of meta-analyses from 2009–2011. *Research in Developmental Disabilities*, *34*(9), 2967–2985. http://dx.doi.org/10.1016/j.ridd.2013.06.007

Sundberg, M.L. (2008). *Verbal behavior milestones assessment and placement program: The VBMAPP*. Concord, CA: AVB Press.

US Department of Education (2004). *Individuals with Disabilities Education Act (IDEA) 2004*. Washington, DC: General Printing Office. Retrieved from http://idea.ed.gov/

US Department of Health and Human Services (1999). *Mental health: A report of the Surgeon General*. Rockville, MD: US Department of Health and Human Services, Substance Abuse and Mental Health Services Administration, Center for Mental Health Services, National Institute of Health, National Institute of Mental Health.

Wagner, S. (1999). *Inclusive programming for elementary children with autism*. Arlington, TX: Future Horizons.

Warren, S.F., Fey, M.E., & Yoder, P.J. (2007). Differential treatment intensity research: A missing link to creating optimally effective communication interventions. *Mental Retardation and Developmental Disabilities Research Rreviews*, *13*(1), 70–77. http://dx.doi.org/10.1002/mrdd.20139

Suggested Websites

The Lovaas approach: www.lovaas.com/about.php

Curriculum guide: www.marksundberg.com/vb-mapp.htm

Curriculum guide: http://starautismsupport.com/curriculum/star-program

http://specialed.about.com/od/ABA/a/Reinforcer-Assessment.htm

Data sheet: https://docs.google.com/viewer?a=v& pid=sites& srcid=cHJhY3RpY2FsYXV0aXNtcmVzb3VyY2VzLmNvbXx3d3d8Z3g6NzMwMWE2MjFmODQyMWFi

Evidence based practice: https://www.pbis.org/Common/Cms/files/Forum14_Presentations/D15_NAC_Ed_Manual_FINAL.pdf

Creating a Safe Environment: https://www.autismspeaks.org/family-services/autism-safety-project/first-responders/teachers-administrators

Tools for Professionals: https://www.autismspeaks.org/family-services/resource-library/tools-professionals

Part IV

CRITICAL THEORIES

10

MIKHAIL BAKHTIN

Dialogic Language and the Early Years

E. Jayne White

> Dialogic relationships are reducible neither to logical relationships nor to relationships oriented semantically toward their referential object, relationships in and of themselves devoid of any dialogic element. They must clothe themselves in discourse, become utterances, become the positions of various subjects expressed in discourse, in order that dialogic relations might arise among them.
>
> (Bakhtin, 1984, p. 67)

Dialogism can be broadly and somewhat ironically described as a unifying means of exploring "voice" and its authorship—its lived construction, enactment, and interpretation by another. As an overarching theory dialogism resists the centrality of certain forms of language and their privileged meaning over others while paying close attention to their delivery. Language is therefore interpreted as social exchange comprised of a collaboration of multiple dialogues which are utilized by the individual in order to communicate to another (even when there is no apparent "other"). Emphasis is placed on the extent to which the strategic employment of voices alter, or transform, meaning in social encounter. As such, language becomes a living event of dialogue in relationship with others.

Brought to bear in the early years, dialogic theory invites a view of language that pays attention to the subtle verbal and non-verbal events that take place on a moment-by-moment basis as a central source of learning. An application of these ideas draws attention to key related concepts of *utterance* as the primary link in a chain of communication, and *heteroglossia* as the complex space in which language gives rise to certain meanings in social discourse. Together they posit an agenda for language that orients attention towards a boiling cauldron of possibilities for meaning-making in the early years context and grants primacy to dialogues with children as a source of agency and growth for all. In this chapter, these possibilities will be introduced to the reader as a means of understanding and enacting a revised pedagogical orientation to the study of language for young children and those who work with them.

Mikhail Bakhtin's Elusive Biography

The life and times of Mikhail Bakhtin (1895–1975) create a somewhat elusive background to a full understanding and appreciation of his vast contributions to the field. Born to liberal parents in the town of Orel, Russia, Bakhtin was second in a family of five children. His childhood was spent in what was described as "the pale of settlement," a boundary that was defined within the Russian empire with separate laws that did not apply to others. As a young boy Bakhtin endured a serious bone infection that caused him a great deal of pain and ultimately resulted in the amputation of one leg as an adult. Elsewhere (White, 2016) it has been speculated that this enduring pain may have led to Bakhtin's emphasis on the body as central to language and communication.

Following the Russian revolution, Bakhtin spent his entire life in various parts of Russia during a tumultuous historical era that included a significant totalitarian period of state control under Stalin. During this time Bakhtin was exiled to Kazakhstan and several of his friends executed in an era of control that was characterized by the censorship of ideas. These events influenced Bakhtin tremendously, shaping the orientation of his work towards an emphasis on creativity and diversity, both of which were unwelcome in this political regime. Given this background, it may not be surprising to discover that Bakhtin's emphasis on the social, lived experience of language—as discourse—became central to his thinking, and formed the basis of his later writing. For Bakhtin discourse was associated with sets of ideologically oriented values that give primacy to certain ways of thinking, speaking, and acting in the world. Since certain values would have been silenced during Bakhtin's lifetime, he had tremendous insight into the negative consequences for society when one discourse is promoted over others.

While Bakhtin can be described as a philologist (that is, someone who studies the relationship between languages) and a "thinker," his scholarship was not always granted legitimacy in formal university settings. What sets Bakhtin apart from many of his peers is his long and varied engagement with society at a practical level also. Indeed, Bakhtin spent a considerable period of his life as a teacher across a variety of educational settings. In Bakhtin's (2004) essay (only recently accessible to English readers), Bakhtin provides significant pedagogical insights into the practical ways grammar could be taught based on his experiences as a teacher of literature. Here, Bakhtin emphasizes the central importance of ensuring that the text is brought into "lively conversation" in order to generate meaning. This, he suggests, is a central dialogic imperative for the teacher. It is also a fundamental principle for all language in his view.

Of special significance in understanding Bakhtin's approach to language are the collaborations he shared during the early phases of his career with his friend and colleague Valentin Voloshinov (1895–1936). In Voloshinov's (1973) book *Marxism and the Philosophy of Language*, he clearly establishes the basis for a dialogic view of language that was to play a key role in Bakhtin's thinking.

Voloshinov's example highlights the ideologic, volitional nature of language as an event that takes place between people in unique social contexts that are laden with meanings. In Voloshinov's analysis it becomes clear that the verbal declaration "well," when considered as *utterance* holds different meanings as a result of the social context in which it is given and received. This thinking gave rise to a broader

Voloshinov argued that popular approaches to language failed to take into account the creative use of language in discourse. His most famous example of the living nature of language begins with two people silently looking out the window and discovering a snowflake.

Eventually one of them declares: "Well? ..."

As Voloshinov explains, those of us looking in on this event as spectators cannot appreciate its meaning unless we have access to its background. He then proceeds to give a lengthy background to the significance of this event, explaining that both people looking out the window had previously expressed disappointment about the arrival of snow in late spring. Their observation of a snowflake on the window, coupled with their disappointment, which we cannot see, orients the meaning of the "Well? ..." Yet it is inaccessible to those outside the event.

Contemplating the nature of language, Volshinov then asks:

> To whom is this reproach addressed? Clearly not to the listener but to somebody else. This tack of the intonational movement patently makes an opening in the situation for a third participant. Who is this third participant? Who is the recipient of the reproach? The snow? Nature? Fate, perhaps?
>
> (1973, p. 103)

definition of language that can be best captured in the overarching theory of dialogism that Bakhtin was to develop. *Utterance* and its relationship to *heteroglossia* represent two key concepts that offer a means of exploring dialogic language as a lived reality in discourse and, in doing so, open up the possibilities for an expanded view of meaning-making. Both are explained in the sections below, followed by some applications for the early years.

Utterance

> Any understanding of live speech, a live utterance, is inherently responsive ... Any utterance is a link in the chain of communication.
>
> (Bakhtin, 1986, p. 84)

By now it is clear that, for Bakhtin (as for Voloshinov), utterance is much more than a spoken word or phrase. Rather it is an *event of dialogue* that seeks and often (but not always) receives a response. It is therefore oriented towards others and takes place only in the between-ness of social discourse. For this reason utterance is a central concept in understanding dialogic approaches to language. Interaction is therefore best portrayed in terms of its capacity for form-shaping dialogues that take place between participants. It is an event of in-between-ness that is never isolated from others. As such, words and actions are jointly constructed in dialogue.

It should also be evident that a dialogic view of language pays attention to meaning-making in social interaction. Language and its meanings both reflect and refract external reality through the interplay of various signs that are utilized to convey meaning. The intention here is not merely to explain the use of sign-use per se, but to understand its utility in society, *as utterance*. What is valued (and, as a consequence is privileged) in a particular social group is likely to promote certain types of language-use over others. As Voloshinov (1973) explains:

> Contexts do not stand side by side in a row, as if unaware of one another, but are in a constant state of tension, or incessant interaction or conflict. The change of a word's evaluative accent in different contexts is totally ignored by linguists and has no reflection in its doctrine on the unity of meaning. This accent is least amenable to reification, yet it is precisely a word's multiaccentuality that makes it a living thing.
>
> (pp. 80–81)

These ideas signal the importance of paying attention to lived meanings rather than "dead foreign language" (Gogotishvili, 2004, p. 29). Such meanings are generated in the "between-ness" of social spaces as discourse and require dialogue partners to take time to understand their significance rather than asserting any single (or what Bakhtin calls "monologic") interpretation.

Speech Genres

The related concept of "speech genres" is an expansion of utterance and, in doing so, offers a route to the broader interpretation of language and its meanings in social discourse. Bakhtin described speech genres as certain socially sanctioned and stable combinations of language form and language content that establish routes to meaning because they betray the ideology of the speaker and their social orientation in language-use:

Model 1: Speech Genres

Language form + Language content + Language context = Meaning

For example, genres might be summoned to the dialogue in order to make a particular claim, or assert a "professional" position. There are certain genres for talking on the telephone (and cellphone for that matter), conversing over drinks with friends, or presenting a lecture. Each establishes particular types (combinations) of language forms coupled with certain meanings—many of which are unstated but learned through social intercourse and ascribed to certain contexts. Misunderstanding a particular genre in a specific context may have serious consequences for an individual. Imagine, for example, shouting loudly from the audience during a traditional church sermon. You might be asked to leave the premises! Yet shouting at a rugby match seems to be entirely acceptable (at least in my culture!). These genres are learned over time and established according to the social group and addressees to which they are oriented (and which sometimes may be in conflict with others in the same heteroglossic space).

Fortunately, Bakhtin does not suggest that certain genres should be privileged over others. Indeed, he argues strongly and convincingly for the creative potential that lies in the disruption of certain genres over others in dialogue. Nonetheless, genres play a vital role in shaping utterance and, by association, what gets "heard" in any dialogue (and what does not). In this conceptualization a much more complex view of language as multi-lingual, muti-layered, and multi-discursive is asserted than Bakhtin's predecessors ever considered. As Bakhtin (1981) explains, "The word lives, as it were, on the boundary between its own context and another, alien, context" (p. 284). It is this boundary that holds much potential for understanding language in the early years.

Heteroglossia

> not all words for just anyone submit easily to the appropriate, to this seizure and transformation into private property: many words stubbornly resist, others remain alien, sound foreign in the mouth of someone who appropriated them and who now speaks them; they cannot be assimilated into his context and fall out of it; ... the speaker's intentions—it is populated—overpopulated—with the intentions of others. Expropriating it, forcing it to submit to one's own intentions and accents, is a difficult and complicated process.
>
> (Bakhtin, 1981, p. 293)

In the quote above an expansion of utterance, genre and its boundaries is now posed. Instead of merely anticipating the class struggles of utterance, Bakhtin (1981) now enters into the specific relational aspects of language and its complex usage by individuals within discourse(s). In doing so a second key concept in understanding a dialogic approach to language is introduced (in loose translation) as "heteroglossia," which Bakhtin describes as "another's speech in another's language, serving to express authorial intentions but in a refracted way" (p. 324).

Given Bakhtin's earlier assertions that language is always half someone else's, and that it exists in social discourse, heteroglossia provides a means of analyzing the different forces that give rise to one type of language-use (or genre) over another *and* the multiplicity of meanings granted to each within an utterance. For Bakhtin it is a constant battle between what he describes as centrifugal and centripetal forces:

Centripetal forces pull towards shared meaning and consensus (which might loosely be described as "intersubjectivity"). They are often characterized by authoritative voices which hold great sway in defining meaning.

Centrifugal forces pull away from shared meaning or consensus (which Bakhtin described as "alterity"). They are characterized by the presence of alternative voices which invite diverse, perhaps even oppositional, interpretations and meanings.

In the heteroglossic spaces where all language takes place, the battle between both forces is very important. Where either force is absent there is either absolute obedience (where only the authoritative voices are heard) or there is absolute anarchy (where there is no consensus whatsoever). The extent to which any language, and its associated meanings, can be heard in a social space (as heteroglot) is influenced by these forces which determine the language, and genres, that are "heard." More importantly, they shape their meanings and determine the extent to which alternative approaches to language might be granted legitimacy.

A heteroglossic approach to language paves the way for consideration of voice as a plural and discursive concept. An individual might, for instance, use one type of language (i.e. genre) in a classroom discussion with adults as opposed to playground chat. They may even use both interchangeably in the same context or event for different purposes, a bit like what is now described as "code-switching" except with an emphasis on the purposes of linguistic shifts. Bakhtin (1984) described this type of language use as "double-languagedness" (or double-voicedness) in representing or borrowing the words of others to speak to a particular addressee or convey a certain meaning. Language use and the selection of genres that are employed offer insight into the heteroglossic spaces of language that surpass any narrow definition of transmission or reception by paying attention to their discursive use. Taken together, they represent what I have come to describe as "a boiling cauldron of living relationships for adults and children alike" (White, 2016, p. 154).

Bringing these concepts to bear in the early years offers much scope for contemplating language well beyond the acquisition of privileged words of certain cultures and individuals. A dialogic view of language opens up possibilities for viewing very young children as competent and complex language users in their own right who are as capable of shaping others through utterance as they are being shaped themselves. It is to them we now turn.

Bakhtin and the Language of the Child

Though Bakhtin never set out to promote language-use in the early years specifically, Bakhtin's earliest works provide important insights concerning the role of language in the life of a child and, by association, the role of the adult. It is one of few references to young children in Bakhtin's writing, but sets the scene for an emphasis on language and the developing consciousness:

> The child receives all initial determinations of himself and his body from his mother's lips and from the lips of those close to him ... they are the words that for the first time determine his personality from outside, the words that come to meet his indistinct inner sensation of himself, giving it a form and a name in which, for the first time, he finds himself and becomes aware of himself as a something ... The child begins to see himself for the first time as if through his mother's eyes, and begins to speak about himself in his mother's emotional-volitional tones.
>
> (Bakhtin, 1990, pp. 49–50)

In this excerpt Bakhtin suggests that language plays the most central role in shaping the way a child begins to view him (or her) self as a personality. Giving both form (that is, words, sounds, body movements) in tandem with content (that is, the imbued meanings of the forms, influenced by aspects such as tonality) marks the earliest origins of language development. As one will recall, for Bakhtin, as for Voloshinov, forms cannot be divorced from their location in discourse, hence he draws attention to the complex and highly nuanced dialogic spaces in which the young child receives meaning. These social spaces are imbued with complexity and take into account language-use beyond the spoken word. They encompass the many features of language that orient their meaning, their subsequent (often creative) use by the child, and their influence on his or her developing personality.

Taking a dialogic view, language in the early years is no longer seen as simply a case of transmitting language for the purposes of learning certain codes as a precursor to effective communication in the world. Instead, Bakhtin suggests that language between people—as dialogue—is a life-long journey of "ideological becoming." What is "learned" is less concerned with linguistic or cognitive acquisition (although this may be a by-product of the experience), but focuses instead on the developing and creative personality as they engage with a complex and multifaceted social world. This is not an agenda for the young child alone, but for all—adults and children alike.

Dialogic Approaches to Language and the Early Years

Bakhtin's dialogic theory is particularly relevant for considering language in the early years for (at least) two key reasons:

1 Despite a very strong developmental legacy suggesting that language is merely transmitted from expert to novice in the early years, Bakhtin's concept of utterance supports the view that language is "dialogised," that is, it is both "caught and taught" in relationships with others. It is therefore always addressed to someone else and anticipates a response.
2 Contrary to traditional views that there is a generic sequence of language acquisition, dialogism upholds the view that language is used strategically in social discourse. Language is discourse or, as Bakhtin describes it, "skaz," which can be interpreted as a kind of narrative that represents voices in discourse. It both reveals and conceals meaning and presents itself in many subtle forms. Therefore meaning is not fixed and exists within and between heteroglossic spaces. It is comprised of much more than words and influenced by the values of those involved. Even the tonation of voice or the flick of a hand plays a vital role in language and all are implicated in its use.

But why (and how) are these dialogic principles of relevance to early years pedagogy? First, because Bakhtin's view of language opens up possibilities to view the young child as much more than merely a receiver or transmitter of language. Given his broad emphasis on language beyond merely words, Bakhtin invites a view of the child that situates him or her as a dialogic partner in language rather than a novice. While there is no doubt that there is much to be learned at an early age concerning the languages of adults, a dialogic approach suggests there are other languages, seen and unseen, that also contribute to the heteroglossic space. In this regard a much richer, more expansive view of dialogue, in contemplation of young children, is offered. Moreover, Bakhtin provokes an interpretation of language that invites consideration of dialogue as a living event that is laden with emotion and in relationship with others. Adults are seriously implicated in this conceptualization.

Second, in keeping with Bakhtin's dialogic imperative, dialogic theory establishes a framework for contemplating the central role of the early years teacher in engaging with the "dialogicality of language" in the life of the child as the central source of understanding. This is an important agenda for contemporary early years pedagogy since the role of the teacher is so heavily caught up in interpreting and engaging with children's language as a primary source for identifying learning in early childhood education curricula. Much emphasis is now placed on teacher dialogues with young children as an exclusive source of intersubjectivity leading to shared understanding with the view of promoting greater learning. This view is conveyed in popular movements, such as Reggio Emilia, who promote a "dialogue pedagogy" which argues for children's active verbal and non-verbal engagement in the construction of their own learning (Pramling-Samuelsson & Carlsson, 2008). Dominant approaches to dialogue as pedagogy in early childhood education internationally now promote the role of the teacher as a dialogue partner whose task it is to extend language through "proven" techniques such as questioning. Siraj-Blatchford's (2007) promotion of sustained shared thinking as "a particularly effective pedagogic strategy" (p. 3) is an example of this pedagogical orientation. A dialogic approach takes a different view by inviting adults to "linger lovingly" with learners in an effort to engage wholeheartedly with language-use to its fullest extent. A dialogic agenda is therefore oriented to the meanings that can be generated in dialogue that is relevant to its participants (García-Carrión & Villardón-Gallego, 2016), rather than a means of advancing an adult agenda of language transmission or delivering prescribed educational outcomes, referred to in contemporary early childhood education (ECE) practice as "pedagogic progression" (Siraj-Blatchford, 2007, p. 3).

Applying Dialogic Concepts in the Early Years

Dialogic concepts have now been applied to the study of early years experience by several early years researchers internationally. In one way or another these studies orient us away from an exclusive emphasis on received forms of language in order to contemplate the rich nature of children's voices in play. Paying attention to these subtle language events has presented a greatly revised view of children's language worlds and, by association, the potential to appreciate the heteroglossic experience of language-use in early years settings as complex social spaces. Throughout the remainder of this chapter examples are presented to illuminate dialogic concepts of utterance and heteroglossia in particular, as a route to reconceptualizing language and its multiple uses in interactions within and beyond early years settings.

Applying Utterance to the Early Years

Understanding children's language as part of a complex chain of utterances emphasizes the unique meanings that each child may bring to language and the shifting meanings that might arise from an appreciation of these. In the context of an early years setting it also highlights the important role of families in the life of a child, and implicates the teacher to engage fully with their interpretations of language as a tremendous source of insight too.

The following dialogue between a researcher, mother, father, and teacher in New Zealand highlights this challenge for adults in the early years. Together they are earnestly trying to interpret the language forms of an 18-month-old child based on video footage shot from the point of view of an 18-month-old child (Zoe), teacher, and myself:

> RESEARCHER: ... she lifts her top and, I felt sure, she said "button" but when she does that same action with [her mother], her mother made the suggestion that she was saying "whoop whoo."
> MOTHER: Whoop whoo. Yeah.
> RESEARCHER: And I'm going "what ...?"
> TEACHER: I thought she said "puku" [Maaori word for stomach] ...
> MOTHER: (laughs) Well it could be that too, yeah.
> RESEARCHER: And [the teacher] said "we don't use that [word] here, I wonder if they do at home?"
> FATHER: (smiles and puts his forefinger in the air)
> Everyone laughs.
>
> (White, 2009a, p. 116)

This dialogue further reinforces Bakhtin's claim that language is always half someone else's—a point we will return to repeatedly throughout this chapter. Whether or not the father is correct in his silent assertion is less important than the *effort* these adults are making to try to understand that draws on events well beyond this moment. For Bakhtin it is in this effort of trying that meaning can be generated—not to establish the "truth" but to engage in fuller expressions of language and its centrality to understanding "other." In the early years it establishes an important agenda for engaging with language forms beyond the exclusive domain of adult interpretation or dominant cultural understandings. Moreover it reinforces the view that dialogue with families with and about young children are of central importance to a fuller appreciation of the child. These call for close attention, often beyond our own ideologic stance in contemplation of multiple layers of meaning.

Taking Bakhtin's view that language is never isolated in any social event, it becomes impossible to contemplate children as language-users who draw from multiple discourses (Dore, 1995). This is especially important for children entering into early learning contexts away from home. A child, no matter what his or her age, does not arrive at the early years setting without a wealth of genres that have already been successfully deployed in chains of utterance beyond this context. In Bakhtin's conceptualization, these utterances can then be strategically employed to generate new meanings (or, as I have found in my studies, to thwart certain meanings). They may even become personally and professionally confronting for the teacher who realizes that they are not always in control of what is learned, or the interpretations that might be given to language.

Several early years researchers have explored genres in ECE settings (see, for example, Sawyer, 1997; Marjanovic-Shane & White, 2014). Some have identified specific early years contexts, such as block play (Cohen & Uhry, 2007; Cohen, 2015), that can be characterized in terms of genre-use. In my studies with Zoe (White, 2009a), her teacher and family, we identified at least five different genres that were strategically employed by Zoe in a New Zealand center catering for children aged birth to five years of age:

1 Outside-in genres: Typically expressed in words with reference to resources that are child-initiated.
These genres are drawn from experiences outside of the ECE setting. For instance Zoe watches a peer ride past on his bike and calls out. The teacher does not notice but when I asked Zoe's mother she instantly recognized the vocalization in terms of a game that is played at home chasing the family dog: "Go Taylor Go!"

2 Inside-out genres: Typically expressed in referential pointing, sounds, words with reference to resources that are teacher-initiated.
Examples of this genre are found, and privileged, in assessment documentation that is closely aligned with the center plan which predetermines certain activities, such as art or stories. Mat time is a particularly rich example of this genre, where children are expected to sit obediently in response to teacher initiations. In Zoe's case, such obedience was not always evident as many ways of disrupting the genre were tried out!

3 Symbolic play genres: Again, resources were used in tandem with sounds or words. This genre was often initiated by Zoe but fully supported by the teacher.
Symbolic play was discoverable on occasions when Zoe utilized resources (such as bark chip or an egg carton) to represent something else. Often this was based on cues from her peer group or the teacher.

4 Free-form genres: Here whole body movements, onomatopoeic sounds, use of a fist or biting are utilized by the child, seemingly for no particular purpose.
On several occasions Zoe would run across the outdoor area, making long sounds. She would often be joined by her peers who would imitate the sounds. It appeared as if the peer group were fully acquainted with these language forms and their potential for meaning.

5 Intimacy genres: Facial gesture, watching, upturned arms, touch, and sound are utilized here, initiated always by the child.
One example is found in Zoe's careful observation of her teacher comforting an older child. She imitates the facial gestures and sounds in order that she might receive a cuddle too. On other occasions she would stroke her teacher's body or raise her arms in attempts to be picked up.

The significance of this identification was found in discussions with the teachers who paid little, or no, attention to some genres (in this case # 1 & 4) or, in other cases (# 5) downplayed them because they were personally confronting for the teachers; while others were privileged in the center heteroglot. Those that were privileged (# 2 & 3) responded to the authoritative educational discourse that set an agenda for knowledge transmission through "activities" and sanctioned forms of play drawn from a developmental paradigm, both of which prioritized adult forms of language (and associated meanings). While those that were ignored or trivialized represented genres drawn from either the child's home life or their embodied language encounters with peers. When recognized, sounds became words and words became a source of subsequent dialogue between teachers and parents, and, with this understanding, the child.

The awareness that followed such identification altered the nature of dialogue for these teachers in their pedagogical work. They now recognized how much they were missing in their understanding by privileging their own developmental, pedagogical and linguistic agenda rather than taking the time to engage with the genres at the disposal of the young child:

> it's deeper and there's a lot more meaning. You can see progression in their relationship and as a result we are all viewing her a lot more directly and intently ... We are getting to know the Zoe that's deeper.
>
> (Researcher's journal: May staff meeting comment by supervisor, in White, 2009a, p. 190)

Applying Heteroglossia to the Early Years

Since, for Bakhtin (1981), "the word in language is half someone else's" (p. 293) it stands to reason that a dialogic approach to meaning would also take the time to understand the seen and unseen addressees within any language exchange in order to contemplate its relevance. Not only does this emphasis highlight the multiple interpretations that might be given to meaning, but also entertains the idea that even the same language will be received differently by others. Language thus becomes a very creative event indeed.

In a New Zealand study, 18-month-old Jayden shares a fist action with his teacher during several play events. In this action he looks at his teacher and appears to shake his fist at her, with a very stern expression on his face. The teacher responds to this language act by lifting her arm into a fist and making a grunting sound. When I asked her what this meant and why she had responded in this way, she explained that she thought Jayden was trying to be a "he-man" and her response was to mimic his actions. I asked Jayden's mother about this movement and she immediately laughed, explaining that this was the fist action used by actor Jim Carrey in a favorite family movie "Liar Liar." In this movie the actor uses his fist as a mark of achievement when he has tricked his wife so that he can spend more time with his son on a telephone call. The mother told me that this was a favorite joke in the family and one that was frequently shared at home. With this additional information the language act took on a completely new meaning and, upon further consideration by the teacher, explained why Jayden employed this particular language after completing a task, such as building a tower or completing a puzzle. These insights oriented the teacher towards a very different response and, as a consequence, a much more appreciative relationship with Jayden.

(White, 2009b)

Several ECE researchers have revealed some of the deeply confronting language events that take place in early years settings by adopting a heteroglossic approach to their understanding. Their discoveries disrupt traditional views of both language *and* conceptions of the child. They range from preschoolers' deployment of double-voiced strategies to imitate the teacher taking a formal group time (De-Vochdt, 2015) to Po-Chi Tam's (2013) realization that preschool children were altering their language when they perceived the teacher was close. In each case their investigations reveal the sophisticated ways young children engage in discourse through language.

During an interview session with Zoe's mother when we were discussing our understandings of her language use, Zoe appeared to be playing independently in the background. However, access to video after the event highlighted a very different story! During my dialogue with Zoe's mother, I shared my interpretations concerning Zoe's interests in shoes based on previous observations, suggesting that Zoe appeared to like only certain (pink) shoes that she would try on regularly. In the background (and outside of our visual perspective at the time) Zoe listened carefully to the discussion. The video highlighted her very deliberate movement to the dress-up box where she strategically pulled out a pair of sparkly golden shoes, looked at me quite sternly, and put them on. I have since speculated that Zoe was exercising her "dialogic loophole" in this instance by altering the narrative that was being told about her as a personality. In so doing, she was able to assert agency over her life without uttering a single "word."

(White, 2011)

These examples highlight the point that all language is imbued with thoughts and feelings that are conveyed through tone (and its interpreted meanings) as much as word or even the body for that matter. Language is not merely *received* in this conception, but *it is experienced* in the between-ness of the event itself: the dialogic space. It is axiologic, emotionally imbued and responded to by a thinking, feeling "other." As Bakhtin explains, the use of language is thus much more than simply learning to speak the words of others, but a way of speaking of the self and others in the world as shifting subjectivities in a complex heteroglot. It is much more complex than adults typically give children credit for.

Language as Dialogue between Teachers, Children, and Their Peers

In contemplating dialogic language for the early years it is important to emphasize that Bakhtin includes the broadest possible view of dialogue—far beyond the spoken word. For Bakhtin whispered or even unspoken languages play a vital role in utterance, as we saw for Zoe and her deployment of "free-form" genres. This is an important consideration for any dialogue, but especially helpful in contemplating language in interactions between infants and teachers who do not necessarily share the same semiotic clues to meaning through selected language forms and associated genres, let alone the same social world of their genesis.

A study with eight-month old Lola in a New Zealand Education and Care service highlights the importance of both the nuanced details of language and the importance of prior dialogues in relationships between teachers and infants:

> Teacher responses called for a combination of forms that drew from the familiar, embodied language of the infant rather than their own (verbal) language preferences ... At times, infant gestures were very subtle, such as a gaze or wave of the hand, but were nonetheless seen as highly significant pedagogical cues by the teachers who oriented their responses accordingly ... Teachers' responses varied in accordance with their understanding of infant priorities, ranging from expansions of non-verbal initiations with verbal and non-verbal combination responses or, conversely, teachers' non-responses which they described as pedagogically oriented acts of "standing back" or "being present."
> (White, Peter, & Redder, 2015, p. 170)

Such a view places serious implications on adult communication with young children and its centrality to pedagogy. Bakhtin explains the way a young child comes to a positive view of themselves through the playful language of an adult who speaks endearingly of their "footsie-tootsies," and in turn comes to speak of themselves in similar, embodied, tones that form a positive view of themselves and others:

> He determines himself and his states in this case through his mother, in his mother's love for him, as the object of his mother's cherishing affection, her kisses; it is his mother's loving embraces that "give form" to him axiologically.
> (Bakhtin, 1990, p. 50).

There is now much evidence for this claim in psychological research (see for example the work of Malloch & Trevarthen, 2009, among others) but seldom have teachers been implicated in this understanding.

Thus we can see that, in dialogic approaches to language, the body as much as the voice betrays such tones; for instance, it might be possible that positive words are spoken but they are not underpinned by positive tones or body language. Conversely, seemingly negative words can be given positive meaning when they are conveyed in loving tones (or vice-versa, as the following example portrays). Paying attention to tonality therefore provides a broadened view of language-in-discourse, and its meaning for young children.

The event below highlights the importance of the tonality of the body as much as the voice in orienting children's responses. It takes place in the block play area, after 18-month-old Zoe has carefully observed her teacher harshly reprimanding a four-year-old by wagging her finger, frowning, and raising her voice. The teacher (Teacher A) leaves the area. Here's what happens next:

> Zoe approaches Wayne and takes one of the blocks from his pile. Wayne turns to Zoe and says "NO." Zoe looks across the room to Teacher A, who is now occupied elsewhere, picks up a block, and hits Wayne on the head. Her arm is used in full force and she repeats "NO" in the same tone as Teacher A has used. Wayne cries and hits her back. Teacher B enters the scene and removes the block from Wayne, explaining, "We don't hit. We don't hit smaller children," and asks Wayne to say sorry, which he does. Teacher B leaves. Zoe turns to a second boy, then repeats the action, using the same tones, saying "NO" and hitting him with the block. Teacher B returns and repeats the phrase "We don't hit."
>
> The following week Zoe enters the block area where four-year-old Elsa is building a tower. Zoe picks up a block to add to the tower but Elsa puts her arm in front of the tower and says "no." Zoe promptly picks up a block and hits Elsa on the head in the same action as the previous week. Elsa cries very loudly and for an extended period of time. During this time Zoe peers closely at Elsa's face. Eventually Teacher B arrives and softly explains to Zoe that she should say "sorry" to Elsa, and models rubbing her head. Zoe dutifully rubs Elsa on the head and says "sorry." The teacher leaves. Zoe repeats the act of hitting Elsa on the head, immediately followed by the word "solly" and a rub on her head. Elsa stops crying and they build the tower together.
>
> (White, 2013, p. 70)

Learning language is presented here as much more subtle than words or body language in the absence of relationships. It is nuanced and imbued with meaning that others give it in its delivery, based on what has gone before as well as how it might be anticipated into the future. It is therefore wholeheartedly interpretive, in many ways making a mockery of traditional claims adults make concerning their knowledge of children's language development. And most certainly implicating adults for *their* language-use also.

Ana Marjanovic-Shane presents an "up-close" dialogue between herself, her three-year-old nephew Jay, and other adults in the family. It begins when a great-uncle asks Jay who he loves the best:

> Not stopping to run around the table for even a moment, Jay looks at his mother and father, and then at me and loudly declares: "Nobody!" Then, he runs straight to me, his aunt, pulls my head to his mouth and whispers in my ear so that no one else can hear: "YOU're nobody!"
> (Marjanovic-Shane, 2011, p. 201)

Taking a dialogic stance Ana speculates that Jay is expertly avoiding the question while taking into account the feelings of others, feelings that we as spectators cannot see. At the same time he provides a means of sharing his own position with his aunt (or, conversely, he sees that his aunt would like to have this recognition and responds accordingly, we can never really know for sure). Whatever Jay's meanings, we can see a very sophisticated dialogue representing a chain of utterances taking place. It is saturated with meaning and a repertoire of language forms that are utilized for strategic relational purposes (content) and addressed to seen and unseen others.

As with Voloshinov and the snowflake, we can now begin to see a view of language as utterance in a dialogic sense. Meaning is determined by its interpreted and enacted delivery in the social world, intended and unintended. This is not only concerned with the people who are physically present, but will also be influenced by prior dialogues—seen and unseen—and addressed to others beyond the immediate exchange whom we may not know of or appreciate. In this sense the challenge for early childhood teachers is especially great, since they do not necessarily share in the social world of young children outside of the early years context.

Elin Odegaard (2007), in her study of Norwegian preschoolers' dialogues, tells of what she calls a "co-narrative" that took place one afternoon in the early years setting in response to teacher (Maritt's) curriculum goals of counting:

Maritt: Yes, what happened to the Billy Goat? Andreas [aged 2.7] looked at Maritt and sat down again. "Yes." Maritt tries again: "What happened?" Andreas was occupied with chewing his bread and did not respond. Maritt tried one more time: What had he learned? Vidar [1.6] rose up to reach for the billy goats. Then Maritt changed the direction of the co-narrative: "Yes! That other billy goat. The one that bit your finger!"

Elin explains how the dialogue now shifts to a much more engaged and lively narrative in which both Andreas and Vidar are able to contribute to their fullest extent. They are able to draw from their own understandings and use their own language forms (for example, Vidar points and makes sounds which are interpreted as orienting features of the dialogue) to participate. Elin describes the teacher's role here as "seizing an opportunity" to empower children to become actively involved in the narrative. That the teacher is willing to notice, recognize, and respond to these language cues is central to her pedagogy.

Dialogue in this sense is also reciprocal learning in that the adult is also obligated to try to "learn" the language of the child just as the child is negotiating his or her way through the heteroglot. As such, early childhood teachers are called upon to not only listen but to look carefully at every language event as a potential source of insight.

We took this notion very seriously in a study of infants (White, Redder, & Peter, 2015), summoning Bakhtin to an analysis of "the work of the eye" in teacher pedagogy. Analysing the significance of a "look," a "watch," and a "gaze" as part of utterance, it became possible to interpret the significance of the eye in establishing and maintaining dialogues between infants and their teachers. We found that each "look" played an important role in reciprocal dialogues with infants. ECE contexts that call upon the infant and teacher to negotiate their way in and out of multiple relationships require both parties to engage with language forms that do not necessarily share the same meanings.

> From a Bakhtinian standpoint, this is a positive thing because the language event is creative and ungraspable by another, yet represents opportunities for creativity and transgradience. As such, like other language forms (and indeed in tandem with other language forms), the eye is an important source of communication for the infant who is seen (and heard) as a dialogic partner.
>
> (p. 297)

Taking a dialogic approach to language in this way allows us to contemplate language as a complex, interactive, and living event that takes place in the "between" social spaces of the early years setting. These include peers as well as adults which are beyond the scope of this chapter. Suffice to say that teachers are also fully implicated in peer interactions (White & Redder, in press) and dialogue *is* learning. Clearly, across all dialogue contexts, the adult is called to account for his or her own language use as much as for that of the child in a dialogic approach. In this approach it is clear that relationships are central to how language might be enacted and interpreted; and that all encounters—direct and indirect—are important in the ideological becoming of life-long learners. As Bakhtin (1993) reminds us, "my non-alibi in Being" (p. 40).

Conclusion

Bakhtin's dialogic theory of language invites teachers to contemplate the complexity of dialogue that takes place every day in early years settings. Utilizing key concepts of utterance and heteroglossia, it becomes possible to adopt a deeper appreciation of the subtleties of language with young children and, in doing so, recognize the significance of their initiations and responses in everyday learning events. In taking this approach attention is oriented to the genres that are employed and their location within the social arena rather than the acquisition or transmission of privileged forms of language. Paying heed to the fullest expression of language use and its orientations, beyond the exclusive domain of words, it becomes possible to see even the youngest child as a competent dialogic partner. Taking a dialogic view of these dialogues it also becomes possible to see the discursive layers that might (and indeed are) employed by children using complex combinations of language drawn from multiple places as they negotiate their way through the early years heteroglot. These discoveries set the scene for a lively and deeply confronting re-visioning of language *as dialogue* in the early years—where all are implicated.

References

Bakhtin, M.M. (1981). *The dialogic imagination.* Austin: University of Texas Press.

Bakhtin, M.M. (1984). *Problems of Dostoevsky's poetics* (C. Emerson, Trans., vol. 8). Minneapolis, MN: University of Minneapolis Press.

Bakhtin, M.M. (1986). *Speech genres and other late essays.* Austin: University of Texas Press.

Bakhtin, M.M. (1990). *Art and answerability: Early philosophical essays* (M. Holquist & V. Liapunov, Eds.; V. Liapunov & K. Brostrom, Trans.). Austin: University of Texas Press.

Bakhtin, M.M. (1993). *Toward a philosophy of the act* (V. Liapunov & M. Holquist, Eds., V. Liapunov, Trans.). Austin: University of Texas Press.

Bakhtin, M.M. (2004). Dialogic origin and dialogic pedagogy of grammar: Stylistics in teaching Russian language in secondary school. *Journal of Russian and East European Psychology, 42*(6), 12–24.

Cohen, L. (2015). Layers of discourse in preschool block play: An examination of children's social interactions. *International Journal of Early Childhood Education, 47*(2), 267–282. doi: 10.1007/s13158-015-0138-9

Cohen, L.E., & Uhry, J. (2007). Young children's discourse strategies during block play: A Bakhtinian approach. *Journal of Research in Childhood Education, 21*, 302–315.

De-Vochdt, L. (2015). Reconceptualising teacher–child dialogue in early years education: A Bakhtinian approach. Doctoral dissertation, Canterbury University, New Zealand.

Dore, J. (1995). The emergence of language from dialogue. In A. Mandelker (Ed.), Bakhtin in contexts: Across the disciplines (pp. 151–176). Evanston, IL: Northwestern University Press.

García-Carrión, R., & Villardón-Gallego, L. (2016). Dialogue and interaction in early childhood education: A systematic review. *REMIE Multidisciplinary Journal of Educational Research*, 6(1), 51–76.

Gogotishvili, L.A. (2004). Introduction to the notes (with the assistance of S.O. Savchuk). *Journal of Russian and East European Psychology*, 42(6), 25–49.

Malloch, S., & Trevarthen, C. (2009). *Communicative musicality: Exploring the basis of human companionship.* Oxford: Oxford University Press.

Marjanovic-Shane, A. (2011). You are "Nobody!" The three chronotypes of play. In E.J. White & M.A. Peters (Eds.), *Bakhtinian pedagogy: Opportunities and challenges for research, policy and practice in education across the globe* (pp. 201–226). New York: Peter Lang.

Marjanovic-Shane, A., & White, E.J. (2014). When the footlights are off: A Bakhtinian analysis of play as postopok. *International Journal of Play*, 3(2), 119–135. doi: 10.1080/21594937.2014.931686

Odegaard, E. (2007). "What's up on the teachers' agenda?": A study of didactic projects and cultural values in mealtime conversations with very young children. *International Journal of Early Childhood*, *39*(2), 39–45.

Pramling-Samuelsson, I., & Carlsson, M.A. (2008). The playing learning child: Towards a pedagogy of early childhood. *Scandinavian Journal of Educational Research*, *52*(6), 623–641. doi: 10.1080/00313830802497265

Sawyer, R.K. (1997). *Pretend play as improvisation: Conversation in the preschool classroom*. Mahwah, NJ: Lawrence Erlbaum.

Siraj-Blatchford, I. (2007). Creativity, communication and collaboration: The identification of pedagogic progression in sustained shared thinking. *Asia-Pacific Journal of Research in Early Childhood Education*, *1*(2), 3–23.

Tam, P.C. (2013). Children's bricolage under the gaze of teachers during dramatic play. *Childhood*, *20*(2), 244–259. doi: 10.1177/0907568212461036

Volshinov, V.N. (1973). *Marxism and the philosophy of language* (I.R. Titunik & L. Matejka, Trans.). New York: Seminar Press.

White, E.J. (2009a). Assessment in New Zealand early childhood education: A Bakhtinian analysis of toddler metaphoricity. Doctoral dissertation, Monash University. http://arrow.monash.edu.au/hdl/1959.1/198069

White, E.J. (2009b). A Bakhtinian homecoming: Operationalizing dialogism in the context of an early childhood centre in Wellington, New Zealand. *Journal of Early Childhood Research*, *7*(3), 299–323. doi: 10.1177/1476718X09336972

White, E.J. (2011). "Now you see me, now you do not": Dialogic loopholes in authorship activity with the very young. *Psychology Research*, *1*(6), 2–9. ISSN 2159-5542

White, E.J. (2013). Cry, baby, cry: A dialogic response to emotion. *Mind, Culture, and Activity*, *20*(1), 62–78. doi: 10.1080/10749039.2012.692107

White, E.J. (2016). *Introducing dialogic pedagogy: Provocations for the early years*. With video companion website. London: Routledge. www.routledgetextbooks.com/textbooks/9780415819855

White, E.J., Peter, M., & Redder, B. (2015). Infant and teacher dialogue in education and care: A pedagogical imperative. *Early Childhood Research Quarterly*, *30*. doi: 101177/0907568212461036

White, E.J., & Redder, B. (In press). A dialogic approach to understanding infant interactions. In C. Hruska & A. Gunn (Eds.), *Interactions and learning: Interaction research and early education*. The Netherlands: Springer.

White, E.J., Redder, B., & Peter, M. (2015). The work of the eye in infant pedagogy: A dialogic encounter of "seeing" in an education and care setting. *International Journal of Early Childhood*, *47*(2), 283–299. doi: 10.1007/s13158-015-0139-8

Suggested Websites

White, E.J. (2016). *Introducing dialogic pedagogy: Provocations for the early years* (with video companion website). www.routledgetextbooks.com/textbooks/9780415819855

Journal of Dialogic Pedagogy: http://dpj.pitt.edu/ojs/index.php/dpj1/index

The Bakhtin Centre, University of Sheffield: https://www.sheffield.ac.uk/bakhtin

"The Bakhtin Circle." *Internet Encyclopedia of Philosophy*: www.iep.utm.edu/bakhtin

11

EDUCATIVE EXPERIENCES IN EARLY CHILDHOOD

Lessons from Dewey

Denise D. Cunningham and Donna Adair Breault

Biography

John Dewey is one of the most noted American philosophers of all time. While he is known for his wide range of work spanning philosophy, psychology, and educational theory, he is most known for his work in education. Dewey is not only one of the most popular philosophers of education today, but he was also somewhat of a celebrity in his own time. In the June 4, 1928 issue of *Time Magazine*, Dewey is featured on the cover as one of the most influential forces of the period. They refer to him as "the Second Confucious" and note how his influence was spreading internationally, particularly in China. In other magazines of the era, advertisers used him as a sponsor, including his quotes about society, democracy, and progress. In his June 2, 1952 *New York Times* obituary, the author notes that Dewey had written more than 300 books, essays, and articles by the time he retired from Columbia University in 1930, but they also add, "By the time he was 90, his published works must have totaled 1,000."

Dewey was influenced greatly by the era in which he was born and educated. Darwin's *Origin of Species* was published the year Dewey was born, 1859, and this work profoundly influenced his education and his perspective regarding social evolution. He even wrote the book, *The Influence of Darwin on Philosophy and Other Essays* (1910) where he connects his views regarding the evolutionary nature of the scientific method to knowing and the nature of reality. As Dewey began to pursue his degree at the University of Vermont at age 15, he became interested in philosophy. At the time, much of the instruction in American universities involving philosophy was still closely tethered to religion. He chose to pursue his doctoral degree at Johns Hopkins University because it was a secular program. Even with this in mind, philosophy was not a common pursuit in the early 1880s. The president of Johns Hopkins encouraged him to pursue another field. Nevertheless, Dewey completed his degree with a focus in philosophy and psychology in 1884, and shortly thereafter followed his mentor, George Sylvester Morris, to the University of Michigan where he began his academic career as an instructor (Westbrook, 1991).

During the early years in the academy, two key individuals influenced Dewey: his wife Alice Dewey, and T. H. Green, a philosopher who died in 1882, but whose work became very important to Dewey. Alice challenged Dewey to pay attention to the social issues surrounding them. She also influenced his views regarding religion and shifted his focus from institutional religion to a more organic and lived experience based on concern for others. At the same time, Dewey was challenged by Green's writings that promoted an active philosophy, a "philosophy of citizenship" (Westbrook, 1991, p. 36). The multiple influences of Dewey's formal training, Darwin's work, and new ideas regarding social responsibility became a solid foundation for his theories regarding inquiry, democracy, and the relationship between school and society. These ideas, in particular, impacted Dewey's work when he left Michigan to teach at the University of Chicago in 1894. This was his first experience of living in an urban area. Not only could he see first-hand the impact of industrialization, but he was also able to get involved with a number of social activists in the city, including Jane Addams.

It is not surprising that Dewey's interests led him to study and write about education. Prior to entering graduate school, Dewey taught high school for three years. During that time he struggled with classroom management, and this could have influenced his decision to change professional courses and pursue his doctorate. Further, both Dewey and his wife grew frustrated with the education their children were receiving in public schools in Chicago. They were not alone. A number of notable individuals in the Chicago area were interested in school reform, and among them was Colonel Frances Parker, who was able to start a school that promoted progressive ideas. Not only did Dewey support Parker, but he also sent his own children to Parker's school. Shortly thereafter Dewey began to advocate for a school that would be associated with the University of Chicago where he could apply his ideas about education. The university agreed, and what was to be known as the "Dewey School" opened in 1896, with Alice Dewey serving as principal (Westbrook, 1991).

Dewey's laboratory school opened with 16 children and 2 teachers. By 1903 the school served 140 students with 23 teachers and 10 graduate students (Westbrook, 1991). The school, as noted throughout this chapter, was very progressive for its time. It is important to emphasize, however, that the school's curriculum was *society-centered*, not *child-centered*. The latter is a common misinterpretation of Dewey's work in educational foundation textbooks. While there was an educational movement during the industrial period that romanticized the child and indulged his or her individual interests, Dewey's school organized its curriculum around socially significant and relevant experiences that children as members of a larger community would share. While growth was a critical factor for Dewey, the growth he sought in schools was simultaneously personal and social. The purpose of schooling was to prepare children as valuable citizens who would work together to make their collective lives better.

The curriculum of the Dewey School was organized around occupations. Occupations involved a series of activities that reflected a period in social and/or cultural life. Some of the periods were past periods. For example, children worked in gardens and in a textile lab. They sheered sheep, carded and spun wool, and dyed the wool to create blankets and other items as if they lived in a pre-industrial, agrarian society. At other times children engaged in occupations that were more contemporary. For example, each age group learned different aspects related to transportation that were connected to what they experienced in and around Chicago (Mayhew & Edwards, 1936).

This work was influenced by one of his strongest students in Chicago, Ella Flagg Young. Young was the first female superintendent of Chicago Public Schools. She was 50 when she took a seminar course from Dewey, and, according to one student, the course was largely a two-way conversation between Dewey and Young in which other students were merely spectators (Condliffe Lagemann, 1996). The period in which Dewey became directly involved with schooling and started working with Young was a period of tremendous change in America. More and more children were staying in school beyond the elementary years, and as numbers grew administration became more and more important. Young recognized the challenges and was able to use her experience as a teacher to help Dewey respond to challenges emerging within the laboratory school. She worked with both Deweys to make administrative changes that included adding a departmental structure; and the new structure promoted a better environment for collaboration and reflection (Mayhew & Edwards, 1936).

Dewey left the University of Chicago in 1904 because of conflicts between him and the university's president, William Rainey Harper, most of which related to the school and Alice's role as principal. Dewey joined the faculty at Columbia University, where he remained for 25 years. While his time in Chicago was the only period in his academic career where he was directly involved in the work in schools, it nevertheless influenced his work for the remainder of his career. Dewey's influence continued to expand to address labor issues and international unrest, particularly in the period leading up to, during, and following World War II; but he also continued to write about education, and he was consulted internationally regarding educational systems. Now, more than a century after his work in Chicago, educators recognize his influence regarding the purpose of schooling and how curriculum and pedagogy should reflect that social purpose. At the heart of his work are the key ideas of experience and growth. For Dewey, a school's curriculum should be based upon shared experiences, and the purpose of schooling should be continuous growth.

Dewey (1938a) argued that the idea of learning together was integral to the curricular experience. He often posed questions about the role of learners (both students and teachers) regarding growth and development and the relationship of that growth and development to freedom itself. Frequently he questioned whether textbooks challenged or stifled children's development. Textbooks could be seen as boring by both learner and teacher if not connected to meaningful experiences. Misuse or overuse of textbooks, in lieu of experiences, may be counterproductive to critical thinking and overall learning. Instead, cognitive connections and learning made through interaction were intricately linked to the experiential education Dewey valued. Dewey challenged the traditional education process with a progressive and humanistic ideal that he considered to be in harmony with democracy.

Learning experiences should enhance curiosity and inspire a sense of momentum that moves one toward enhanced thinking and initiative (Dewey, 1938b). At the heart of progressive, humanistic education, nurturing students to explore the depth and passion of learning in caring environments is still vitally important or "educative." Effective education is found in environments where teachers maintain a focus on how young children develop, and reflect on how children think and can physically represent their cognitive and affective experiences about life, and these include choices to pursue their interests yet push their boundaries of thinking and develop language skills. Ideally, environments are enriched by the interaction of learners among a pluralistic population of co-learners, including the teacher.

Instruction is transacted through processes of in-depth investigations and a democratically managed curriculum.

What Constitutes an Educative Experience?

Researchers find that specific curricula, particularly curricula focused on children's development, have impacted the degree to which children improve in terms of social-emotional skills, self-regulation, math, language, and literacy (Bierman et al., 2008; Clements & Sarama, 2008; Fantuzzo, Gadsden, & McDermott, 2011; Preschool Curriculum Evaluation Research Consortium, 2008). To this end, curriculum will be addressed as the lived experience of children, and the basis of the framework on the degree to which that experience is *educative* in a Deweyan sense. Like Dewey's ideas regarding curriculum and schooling, the following framework and the rubric used to assess key elements for educative experiences focus on students' experiences and how those experiences can lead to even more growth.

Before presenting the framework and rubric, it is essential to focus on the conditions teachers create in order to facilitate educative lived experiences for children. As Dewey (1916) notes, "We never educate directly, but indirectly by means of the environment" (p. 19). This is particularly critical in an early childhood context where the setting itself provides much of the impetus for what and how children learn. Children make connections based upon the objects within their environment and the degree to which they are supported in the exploration of those objects. However, merely having objects accessible does not guarantee learning. Blocks, texture books, and sand tables, while certainly concrete in appearance, do not, by virtue of their existence, ensure growth and development. Dewey (1933) makes this critical distinction:

> If physical things used in teaching number or geography or anything else do not leave the mind illuminated with recognition of means beyond themselves, the instruction that uses them is as abstract as that which doles out ready-made definitions and rules for it distracts attention from ideas to mere physical excitation.
>
> (p. 140)

There is a phenomenological connection between the lived experiences of children and the space within which those experiences are facilitated (Seamon, 2000). Therefore, it is important for the early childhood educator to keep the "natural resources" of the children in mind when creating conditions for learning within their classrooms. Dewey (1976a) identifies four key impulses or resources of the child which educators must consider in planning and in instruction.

First, *children are social*. Dewey contends that language is the simplest form of social expression, and, as such, it is a very important educational resource. He notes, "the child always has something in mind to talk about, he has something to say; he has a thought to express, and a thought is not a thought unless it is one's own" (1976a, p. 56). Dewey chastises traditional educational settings where children are kept silent other than at rare points in the day when they are expected to recall a predetermined answer to a question. In Dewey's (1916) mind, the classroom is a miniature community, and community is impossible without communication. Therefore, teachers should recognize and play into the communicative nature of children. Children need to have a reason to communicate, and the nature of the communication should be guided, not merely indulged, to lead to growth in social relationships as well as a growth in understanding of the child's world and his or her role in that world. For example, when children in Dewey's laboratory school in Chicago learned a foreign language, they would use it in actual social situations. They would use French words related to food as they sat together at lunch (DePencier, 1967).

Second, *children like to construct*. Dewey believes that children construct using play, movement, and make-believe. Their construction also takes on concrete forms in order to communicate something. Much of this is seen in children's play. According to Dewey (1910/1991), children use physical objects in play to enlarge their understanding of and relationship with the world. He notes, "they are subordinating the physically present to the ideally signified" (p. 161). He argues that playfulness, an attitude to objects and experiences, is more important than play. Curiosity and playfulness are intellectual qualities. They provide the starting point from which children can explore possibilities. He also contends that the subject matter of play needs to be closely connected to children's experiences. With this in mind, young children in Dewey's laboratory school had games and activities related to the home, including making furniture, tending a garden, and making a playhouse equipped with a kitchen, its utensils, and so forth. Later, the children extended their activities to learn about their community and the different forms of transportation within their communities. To achieve this, they built a model of a city complete with different forms of transportation. As they progressed from kindergarten into early elementary grades, they would extend these experiences. For example, they later built a model of a city that included a deeper understanding of zoning and patterns of growth (DePencier, 1967).

Third, *children like to investigate*. Dewey (1976a) notes that children are active and curious, and, he contends, that it is the responsibility of teachers to direct these impulses toward educative ends. Teachers must create spaces in their classrooms where possibilities are guided, but not predetermined. Further, they must resist the urge to focus on what they already have settled in their own minds, whether that concerns a specific disciplinary category (e.g., this is a math lesson only) or specific answers. Starting with where the adult mind is, according to Dewey, will surely stifle a child's ability to investigate, and it will shortchange the possible outcomes of an investigation.

In Dewey's laboratory school, young children would explore the nature of primitive weapons (e.g., arrowheads). From these initial explorations, the children would test different materials to determine their hardness and pliability. After discussing the Iron Age, they began to explore different metals and other materials. From these experiences, the children studied principles of combustion in order to determine the best way to construct a smelter. Their initial designs did not work, so they had to go back and study the effects of drafts as well as different fuels in order to improve their design. Regarding this line of investigation, Dewey (1976a) noted the following: "Yet the instruction was not given ready-made; it was first needed, and then arrived at experimentally" (p. 53). The children then used materials like copper and experimented with forging various tools. They forged the same tools with different metals (e.g., iron) and then imagined the implications for different geographic regions where access to some materials was limited. They further explored what geological conditions would be needed for farming communities, for military advantage, and so on. After these discussions, they mapped out different communities in sand molds. Thus, very young children were guided through significantly educative experiences in order to understand and make connections between geology, physics, geography, anthropology, and history. How could this kind of work happen in an early childhood classroom? Dewey noted that the children worked on this for five hours per week for an entire year.

Finally, *children love to express themselves through art.* Dewey (1976a) contends the rhythms of life become manifest through artistic expression, and it is important for educators to be aware of the dynamic between art and life in order to create the spaces through which children can find their places within those rhythms. Dewey (2005) states:

> There is a rhythm in nature before poetry, painting architecture and music exist. Were it not so, rhythm as an essential property form would be merely superimposed upon material, not an operation through which material effects its own culmination in experience.
>
> (p. 153)

He further contends that children are not mere spectators of this rhythm; they are a part of it; it is part of what connects them to people through time and region. As such, early childhood educators need to provide opportunities for children to express themselves within the context of that rhythm.

In Dewey's laboratory school they used a textile lab as one means to achieve this while integrating multiple disciplines in the process. Children were given flax, cotton, and wool to examine and compare. They then processed the materials while learning how this had been done in earlier times. They compared the fibers of each material and how the fibers worked together to produce different textures and functions in fabric. They participated in the entire process of taking the raw products and producing fabric (carding, spinning, and weaving). Dewey (1976a) noted, "Then the children are introduced to the invention next in historical order, working it out experimentally, thus seeing its necessity, but upon modes of social life ..." (p. 21). The children also studied chemical properties as they dyed wool. In addition, they studied patterns of Native American blankets in order to design their own patterns and weave their own blankets. Because of their connection to the rhythm of production and creating something of beauty, a process that had been exercised for centuries, the children were able to express something of beauty that was also historically and socially significant.

The conditions created in order to promote growth and development of children matter. To this end, teachers are responsible for changing conditions within their classrooms to ensure that the children's experiences are even more educative. In other words, their development as teachers needs to grow simultaneously with the growth of the children. For this to happen, they need to develop the habit of asking "How can I make these experiences even more educative?" and then systematically reflect on the elements of their lessons and of the conditions within the classroom that may achieve this. However, it may be challenging to engage in this level of inquiry without some sort of tool or support: a platform or framework which helps scaffold the degree of thinking needed to address various elements of an early childhood classroom, so that the teacher may achieve sound judgments regarding that context. To help achieve this, a rubric for focusing on educative experiences in early childhood classrooms has been developed and will be presented in the next section.

Rubric for Educative Experiences in Early Childhood

Development of a rubric based upon Dewey's work offers a practical tool through which early childhood educators can judge the degree of quality education within their specific contexts (see Table 11.1). The rubric has a specific focus on the following three Deweyan dimensions that make up educative early childhood experiences: active learning, democratic learning, and inquiry-based learning. Each dimension will be explained in detail below.

Active Learning

By referencing active learning, one explores the degree to which experiences within early childhood education settings engage children in meaningful work whereby they experience satisfaction of that work. It was Dewey's (1938a) belief that intellect develops through these lived experiences. Young children's thoughts are still closely associated with action; therefore, active learning is critically important in early childhood classrooms. Children are more mentally active when they are more physically active in the discovery and exploratory process. Research indicates improved self-regulation and increased on-task behaviors in classrooms using active learning that engages many aspects of a child's intellect (Cunningham, 2009). Active learning is valued not only for stimulating the child's cognitive development, but also for promoting the dispositions associated with the child's role as an active learner.

How do teachers know they are providing active learning experiences in their classrooms?

Four characteristics of active learning have been identified that describe the nature of the child's involvement with the learning experience. First, to what degree are activities both immediately useful and connect to future work and potential usefulness in other contexts? Second, learning subject matter and active learning are not mutually exclusive. Instead, the activities connect students to the world around them and to an enlarged and deeper understanding of that world. Dewey (1976a) points out that children do not think in terms of academic categories (e.g., math, science, and reading); instead, young children think of learning in more personal and active terms. Children will describe what they *do* in school rather than what they *learn*. Also considered is the degree to which active learning connects children socially. As Dewey notes (1976a), active learning is more effective when it honors the embryonic community that exists within educative contexts. Opportunities for children to share their experiences and compare ideas with peers augment a student's learning. Third, while it is acknowledged that Dewey believed the curriculum should consider the child and his or her experiences, the early childhood curriculum should not indulge idiosyncratic whims and interests of children, but, instead should direct their natural interests to shared experiences (Dewey, 1976b). Fourth, it is imperative that active learning lead to growth and this must include consideration for continued growth. Children's active learning is important because it is the catalyst for cognitive

Table 11.1 Rubric for Educative Experiences in Early Childhood Classrooms

To what degree does my classroom promote:	*Key elements for educative experiences*				*Then, to what degree do I see the following:*
	Time	*Space*	*Relationships/interaction*	*Teacher's role*	
Active learning?	Provide adequate time each day to explore concepts and materials; ensure time for reflection on activities; ensure students see how experiences connect to real life; opportunities for in-depth investigations lasting for weeks or months.	Make space as authentic as possible; ensure that resources are accessible and appropriate; provide adequate space for movement and monitoring children's activities; establish spaces for specific learning (e.g., art, construction, library).	Develop and sustain mutual trust and respect; establish clear expectations; promote confidence; evidence that teaching and learning are occurring for teacher and children.	Manage resources effectively; provide meaningful experiences; stay out of the way; provide opportunities for both individual and small group activities; recognize and stimulate children's interests; create a nurturing and respectful environment where children feel safe to explore.	Growth in motor development; growth in symbolic representations; growth in confidence to engage in learning; growth in language skills.
Democratic learning?	Provide time to relate to one another; provide time to develop more complex language to connect concepts; provide time to build shared understandings and to see one another's perspectives; provide time for children to express ideas and choices.	Make space optimal for communication (where children can talk and work simultaneously); create expectations for children to be responsible citizens; make the space welcoming to families and members of the community; provide space where children can work through conflict.	Promote mutual trust and respect; provide opportunities for children to negotiate with one another; help children understand others' perspectives; promote a cosmopolitan perspective.	Encourage questions; allow children to have control; provide choices on a regular basis; redirect intolerance; scaffold negotiations among children; allow children to make mistakes.	More productive and positive relationships; increased pro-social behavior; increased cultural sensitivity; more effective conflict resolution.

Inquiry-based learning?	Provide time to know, to hypothesize, to be curious; provide sufficient time to test hypotheses and to consider bigger contexts; provide time to see how things connect across the curriculum and across the world; provide time to see how current experiences connect to past experiences; allow time for thinking and time for making mistakes.	Secure a safe space for children to ask questions; provide space for children to be alone and think; provide large spaces where children can playfully consider ideas; provide spaces where children can explore without a predetermined objective; provide appropriate tools/materials for children to safely explore and experiment.	Promote mutual trust and respect; scaffold how to ask questions; support the children's interests and connect those interests to bigger ideas; have meaningful conversations; ensure proper balance between asking questions and giving facts/answers.	Introduce problems and support the need to solve problems; allow for inquiry to emerge; model inquiry by acknowledging when you do not know/understand something and then work to better understand it; avoid dogmatic statements; protect your classroom from too much coverage.	Growth in curiosity; more hypothesis testing; more and more thoughtful questions; more "aha" moments where children see connections; more interesting conversations with and among children.

restructuring, and hence development. Not only should the early childhood experience acknowledge the current experiences of the child, but it should also prepare the child to encounter future experiences in meaningful ways (Dewey, 1938/1988).

Democratic Learning

This section of the rubric explores the degree to which early childhood classrooms help children see themselves as a vital part of their communities. Children imagine the kind of communities in which they wish to live, and they see themselves as active agents creating these desired communities. Democratic spaces have faith in the capacities of human nature and the realization that everyone, individually and collectively, is a work in progress. It is through their efforts as works in progress that members of a community make the world better. As Dewey (1916) notes, "Democracy is a way of life controlled by a working faith in the possibilities of human nature" (p. 226). Ayers (2014) described this as a dialectical push and pull where we change the world and are thus changed in the process. He notes that this process of humanization requires social connection. Children learning in democratic spaces see how their growth contributes to the growth of their communities, and these communities are not limited to the confines of the center walls. They see themselves as active agents in their families and larger communities within which their families live and work (Noddings, 2013).

How do teachers know they are promoting a democratic classroom? They need to consider how they use their time and space. Do they provide adequate time for children to interact? Do they offer enough time for children to move beyond the descriptive conversations and begin to talk about what they are experiencing in more complex ways? Do they provide enough time for children to help each other see things differently? When children are working at tables or centers, do they have time and opportunity to talk with one another about what they are learning? Teachers should also consider the kinds of relationships between themselves and the children, as well as relationships between children and the community. Teachers need to consider too the degree to which children see ways in which they are responsible for one another. How often do parents and community members engage with children within the classroom? Do teachers provide support to help children work through conflicts? In what ways do children work to understand each other's perspectives? If teachers see evidence of intolerance of others, how do they redirect it? Are children allowed to make mistakes, and are they encouraged to think about those mistakes and learn from them?

Inquiry-based Learning

By referencing inquiry-based learning, teachers explore the degree to which the learning environment supports conditions through which children can explore ideas playfully, engage their imaginations, and remain awed by endless possibilities. Within inquiry-based early childhood education, teachers and children share an "unseen power of the ideal" (Dewey, 1934/1991, p. 36) by rejecting the "cut and dried logic of an adult" (Dewey, 1933, p. 60) and embracing a reverence for life and for one another (Rud & Garrison, 2012). When children engage their imaginations, they are not necessarily and exclusively addressing imaginary things. For example, using their imaginations should not be relegated to fantasy images and make believe. They should also engage their imaginations in relation to the world around them. Further, a critical element within an inquiry-based learning environment is a shared felt need. When children share a need, they are able to suspend judgment and work together to solve the problem. Finally, it is essential within early childhood classrooms to honor and support the potential of a child's curiosity. As Scheffler (1985) warns,

> [T]he child's curiosity, sufficiently blocked, may be dulled beyond awakening. The impulse to question, thwarted repeatedly, may eventually die. The flexibility of mind, adventuresomeness, and confidence required for exploring the novel are precious and fragile learning instruments that lose their edge with disuse or abuse.
>
> (pp. 12–13)

How do teachers know if they are promoting inquiry-based learning? To what degree do they provide time and opportunity for children to be curious and experiment? How often do children in the classroom see connections between what they are doing and other different and bigger ideas? How often do children ask questions related to their experiences? Do teachers provide time and space for children to think? Do they help children ask better, more thoughtful questions about their experiences? To what degree do teachers direct children's curiosity toward more and deeper understanding? If teachers feel or if they have ever felt as if their curriculum is too crowded with surface learning, have they been able to revise that curriculum to focus on spending more time learning about less content at a deeper level? Have teachers modeled the inquiry process for their children? Do they acknowledge when they do not know something and then show the children how they systematically work to learn?

How to Use the Instrument

At one level, a teacher or group of teachers could use this instrument to reflect generally on their classrooms, and this might serve as a helpful introduction to the instrument, but this kind of reflection has limitations. Relying on recalled anecdotes based on one's perception may or may not reflect what is actually happening in the classroom. Even if it is somewhat accurate, it lacks specificity and cannot address frequency of choices and behaviors. This is why it is important to collect data about the lived experience in each teacher's classroom in order for this instrument to achieve its potential to promote professional growth. Therefore, pedagogical documentation (Dahlberg, Moss, & Pence, 1999) is required for systematically capturing what teachers do and the conditions they create within their classrooms.

Observing one's practices is one of the most effective and efficient ways to collect data regarding the experiences children have in the classroom (Kawulich, 2005). Teachers are encouraged to have a director or fellow teacher visit their classrooms three times in which three different common experiences occur. For example, the observer could come during circle time, center time, and a structured lesson. The observer could take detailed notes about what he or she sees including quotes from the teacher and students, movement around the room, materials used, and so on. The teacher could then review the notes with the observer to ensure that he or she understands what the observer saw. Then, the teacher could add his or her own notes to the observation documents to fill in gaps or to provide context for what was observed. The teacher could then consider the notes in relation to the rubric.

Another effective way to collect data includes gathering artifacts to review. The artifacts should represent the nature of experiences children have in the classroom, and the teacher should be able to write a descriptive account of what preceded the creation of the artifacts. Artifacts could include student work, center manipulatives, inventories of materials used throughout the room, sign-in sheets for parent and community volunteers, and other items. For each artifact, the teacher could write a description that helps connect the item(s) to the lived experiences within the classroom. The teacher could then consider those descriptions in relation to the rubric.

Another method teachers can use is photo elicitation. Similar to Reggio Emilia's "documenting children's learning" (Edwards, Gandini, & Forman, 1998), visual documentation in the form of photo elicitation can document the experiences being provided to children by teachers. Harper (2002) notes that photo elicitation helps the person engaging in a study to evoke feelings, memories, and information that might otherwise go unnoticed. Teachers can take pictures in the classroom throughout a period of time (e.g., a week) or have someone else take pictures. Each teacher could then pick out ten to twenty images that seem to capture something regarding the experiences within his or her classroom and write a reflection/response for each. The teacher could then tape the written reflections to the pictures and analyze them according to the rubric.

While there are other ways to collect data within a classroom, these three methods are an effective way to gather data without interrupting the instructional process. Individually or together, these methods could provide rich information from which a teacher could study the degree to which he or she is promoting educative experiences for children. It should be noted that the rubric does not promote yes or no responses to each element. Instead, it asks "to what degree" in order for teachers to determine ways to grow in relation to the elements. To this end, teachers are encouraged to consider the degree to which they support the factors related to time, space, relationships, and their roles ultimately to judge the degree to which the experiences they provide in their classroom are highly educative, moderately educative, minimally educative, or mis-educative. By examining the elements according to degrees as well as their overall assessment of their classrooms, they can better explore the complex nature of teaching and determine areas where they can consciously work to make their classrooms even more educative.

Conclusion

In the past several years, policymakers and the general public have focused more attention on public preschool education. Following President Obama's 2013 State of the Union Address where he called on Congress to expand access to high-quality preschool education for every child in America (Office of the Press Secretary, 2013) a bipartisan group in Congress introduced legislation, "Strong Start for America's Children," and several governors put forward proposals to expand access to prekindergarten within their states.

The research regarding the potential impact of high quality prekindergarten education is clear. Studies indicate that the poverty gap evident within our communities mirrors the achievement gaps in schools, and, in particular, children of poverty score significantly worse on cognitive ability tests in early grades when compared to children from higher income families (Duncan & Magnuson, 2011; Reardon, 2011). In addition, children of poverty who lack quality preschool experiences demonstrate more difficulty paying attention and exhibit more behavior problems. In contrast, students who participate in high quality preschool programs experience academic gains of six months to one year in both math and reading (Camilli, Vargas, Ryan, & Barnett, 2010; Wong, Cook, Barnett, & Jung, 2008).

While access to public preschool is expected to expand given the efforts of Congress and state initiatives, issues of quality remain. Research indicates that very few public preschool programs provide the level of excellence called for by the president, and far too many programs demonstrate poor quality of care and education (Cunningham, 2009). More than half a million children, or 40% of the nationwide enrollment, were served in preschool classrooms that were identified as low-quality (Barnett et al., 2015). Head Start programs are also implicated in the call for reform where research indicates that their programs, on average, do not meet expected standards for quality (Mashburn et al., 2008; Moiduddin, Aikens, Tarullo, West, & Xue, 2012).

Defining and subsequently assessing quality is challenging. The National Institute for Early Education Research (N.I.E.E.R.; Barnett et al., 2015) identified 10 quality benchmarks that include criteria such as teachers' credentials, in-service training, student-to-teacher ratios, etc. While these measures provide a means through which the quality of early childhood education can be judged state-by-state, they fall short of providing meaningful means by which centers and even classrooms within centers can judge the degree to which they are providing high quality experiences for the children in their care (Kearney & Harris, 2014). Kearney and Harris (2014) note, "While on average these characteristics may be positively associated with higher-quality programs, they are not necessarily the causal pathway to a high-quality classroom experience" (p. 25). In other words, the benchmarks provided by the N.I.E.E.R. and others offer broad strokes regarding program quality, but they do not address the experiences themselves, in other words, the early childhood curriculum.

As policymakers and community leaders work to increase access to public preschool education, it is essential that leaders in the field work to maintain a high level of quality in the midst of the growth. The challenges are similar to the growth of elementary and secondary education faced during the time when Dewey and Young worked together in Chicago. There are a number of commissions and agencies speaking to the nature of center quality. We contend that we need an equally strong voice that addresses the nature of curriculum quality. Yes, centers need to be safe and inviting spaces. Yes, teachers need to have appropriate credentials. Yes, classroom size matters. In addition, the kinds of experiences children have in these safe and inviting spaces with these highly qualified teachers need to be highly educative. For this to happen, teachers and directors need a way to measure the degree to which the experiences their children have are active, inquiry-based, and rooted in democratic principles. More importantly, directors, center staff, and other stakeholders need ways to talk about their work using clear and concrete measures in order to make important decisions about resources and professional development needs.

It can be argued that the two most important foci of early childhood curriculum are the same foci Dewey emphasized within his laboratory school in Chicago: experience and growth. As Dewey noted throughout his writings about education, educators need to plan highly educative experiences for children that will promote both individual and social growth. As he demonstrated in the Chicago laboratory school, teachers can achieve this when they have some degree of structure within which to base their planning and discuss their results. The proposed rubric can serve these functions in very practical and meaningful ways. As noted in Dewey's biography above, his work is expansive and dense. We recognize that it is unlikely that most early childhood educators will have the opportunity (or the desire) to engage in an in-depth study of the numerous volumes of his work regarding learning, inquiry, and democracy. It is also recognized that many sources that attempt to summarize his work often fall short, or worse, misrepresent his ideas. With the context provided here as well as the online resources included, it is hoped that early childhood educators will use the rubric as a means through which they can evaluate the experiences they are providing for their students, and explore ways through which they can make those experiences even more educative.

References

Ayers, W. (2014). Education for a changing world. In D. A. Breault and R. Breault (Eds.), *Experiencing Dewey: Insights for today's classrooms*. New York: Routledge.

Barnett, W.S., Carolan, M.E., Squires, J.H., Clarke Brown, K., & Horowitz, M. (2015). *The state of 2014: State preschool yearbook*. New Brunswick, NJ: National Institute for Early Education Research.

Bierman, K.L., Domitrovich, C.E., Nix, R.L., Gest, S.D., Welsh, J.A., Greenberg, M.T., & Gill, S. (2008). Promoting academic and social-emotional school readiness: The Head Start REDI program. *Child Development, 179*, 1802–1817.

Camilli, G., Vargas, S., Ryan, S., & Barnett, W.S. (2010). Meta-analysis of the effects of early education interventions on cognitive and social development. *Teachers College Record, 112*, 579–620.

Clements, D.H. & Sarama, J. (2008). Experimental evaluation of the effects of a research-based preschool mathematics curriculum. *American Educational Research Journal, 45*(2), 443–494.

Condliffe Lagemann, E. (1996). Experimenting with education: John Dewey and Ella Flagg Young at the University of Chicago. *American Journal of Education, 104*(3), 171–185.

Cunningham, D.D. (2009). Second grade students investigate instructional approaches and behavior through action research. *The Constructivist, 19*(1). Available at: https://sites.google.com/site/assocforconstructteaching/journal/the-constructivist-archive

Cunningham, D.D. (2010). Relating preschool quality to children's literacy development. *Early Childhood Education Journal, 37*, 501–507.

Dahlberg, G., Moss, P. & Pence, A. (1999). *Beyond quality in early childhood education and care: Postmodern perspectives*. London: Falmer.

DePencier, I.B. (1967). *The history of the laboratory schools: The University of Chicago 1896–1965*. Chicago: Quadrangle Books.

Dewey, J. (1910). *The influence of Darwin on philosophy: And other essays*. New York: H. Holt.

Dewey, J. (1916). *Democracy and education*. New York: Macmillan.

Dewey, J. (1933). *How we think*. Boston: D.C. Heath. (Original work published in 1910).

Dewey, J. (1938a). *Experience and education*. New York: Macmillan.

Dewey, J. (1938b). *Logic: The theory of inquiry*. New York: Henry Holt and Company.

Dewey, J. (1976a). The school and society. In J.A. Boydston (Ed.), *John Dewey: The middle works, 1899–1924: Vol. 1. 1899–1901* (pp. 5–112). Carbondale: Southern Illinois University Press. (Original work published in 1899).

Dewey, J. (1976b). The child and the curriculum. In J.A. Boydston (Ed.), *John Dewey: The middle works, 1899–1924: Vol. 2. 1902–1903.* (pp. 271–292). Carbondale: Southern Illinois University Press.

Dewey, J. (1988). Experience and education. In J.A. Boydston (Ed.), *John Dewey: The later works, 1925–1953: Vol. 13. 1938–1939* (pp 1–62). Carbondale: Southern Illinois University Press. (Original work published in 1938).

Dewey, J. (1991). *A common faith.* New Haven, CT: Yale University Press. (Originally published in 1934).

Dewey, J. (2005). *Art as experience.* New York: Penguin. (Original work published in 1934).

Duncan, G., & Magnuson, K. (2011). The nature and impact of early achievement skills, attention skills, and behavior problems. In G.J. Duncan & R.J. Murnane (Eds.), *Whither opportunity? Rising inequality, schools, and children's life chances* (pp. 47–69). New York: Russell Sage Foundation and Spencer Foundation.

Edwards, C., Gandini, L., & Forman, G. (1998). *Hundred languages of children: The Reggio Emilia approach to early childhood education.* Westport, CT: Ablex.

Fantuzzo, J.W., Gadsden, V.L., & McDermott, P.A. (2011). An integrated curriculum to improve mathematics, language, and literacy for Head Start children. *American Educational Research Journal*, 48, 763–793.

Harper, D. (2002). Talking about a picture: A case for photo elicitation. *Visual Studies*, *17*(1), 13–26.

Kawulich, B. (2005). Participant observation as a data collection method. *Forum Qualitative Sozialforschung / Forum: Qualitative Social Research*, 6(2). Retrieved from www.qualitative-research.net/index.php/fqs/article/view/466/996

Kearney, M.S., & Harris, B.H. (2014). *The Hamilton Project: Policies to address poverty in America.* Washington, DC: Brookings Institution.

Mashburn, A.J., Pinata, R.C., Hamre, B.K., Downer, J.T., Barbarin, O.A., Bryant, D., & Howes, C. (2008). Measures of classroom quality in prekindergarten and children's development of academic, language, and social skills. *Child Development*, *79*, 732–749.

Mayhew, K.C., & Edwards, A.C. (1936). *The laboratory school.* New York: Appleton-Century.

Moiduddin, E., Aikens, N., Tarullo, L., West, J., & Xue, Y. (2012). *Child outcomes and classroom quality in FACES 2009 OPRE Report 2012-37a.* Washington, DC: Office of Planning, Research, and Evaluation, Administration for Children and Families.

New York Times (June 2, 1952). Dr. John Dewey dead at 92: Philosopher a noted liberal. www.nytimes.com/learning/general/onthisday/bday/1020.html

N.I.E.E.R.: National Institute for Early Education Research. www.nieer.org

Noddings, N. (2013). *Education and democracy in the 21st century.* New York: Teachers College Press.

Office of the Press Secretary (2013). State of the Union Address. The White House. www.whitehouse.gov/state-of-the-union-2013

Preschool Curriculum Evaluation Research Consortium (2008). *Effects of preschool curriculum programs on school readiness* (N.C.E.R. 2008–2009). U.S. Department of Education, National Center for Education Research. Washington, DC: U.S. Government Printing Office.

Reardon, S. (2011). The widening academic-achievement gap between the rich and the poor: new evidence and possible explanations. In G.J. Duncan & R.J. Murnane (Eds.), *Whither opportunity? Rising inequality, schools, and children's life chances* (pp. 91–116). New York: Russell Sage Foundation and Spencer Foundation.

Rud, A.G., & Garrison, J. (2012). *Teaching with reverence: Reviving an ancient virtue for today's schools.* New York: Palgrave Macmillan.

Scheffler, I. (1985). *On human potential: An essay in the philosophy of education.* Boston: Routledge & Kegan Paul.

Seamon, D. (2000). Phenomenology, place, environment, and architecture: A review of literature. *Phenomenology Online*, *36*.

Westbrook, R.B. (1991). *John Dewey and American democracy*. Ithaca, NY: Cornell University Press.

Wong, V.C., Cook, T.D., Barnett, W.S., & Jung, K. (2008). An effectiveness-based evaluation of five state prekindergarten programs. *Journal of Policy Analysis and Management*, *27*, 122–154.

Suggested Websites

The Center for Dewey Studies: http://deweycenter.siu.edu/

Deron Boyle's Lecture on Experiential Education for Chrysalis School: https://www.youtube.com/watch?v=V_fzsNnA57I

The John Dewey Society website: www.johndeweysociety.org/

12

THE WHOLE WORLD IS A CHORUS

Paulo Freire's Influence

Elizabeth P. Quintero

Where I'm really from is a place full of spirit
And culture is everything
And Todo el mundo es un coro ...
[the whole world is a chorus]
(Martinez, personal communication, 2009)

A teacher education student wrote the above stanza in her "Where I'm from" poem assignment as a way to describe Freire's principles about the importance of family history and culture.

Paulo Freire (1921–1997)

Who was Paulo Freire and what does his work have to do with teaching young children? What does his work have to do with "The whole world is a chorus"? Many early childhood educators work in preschools and early elementary schools in multilingual communities, a chorus of multiple languages and histories, often with people living with challenges of poverty and other issues. Paulo Freire's work relates dramatically to their work. The best known of Freire's writings is *Pedagogy of the Oppressed* (1970), and with the publication of *The Politics of Education* (1985), his intellectual, philosophical, and pedagogical ideas became more accessible to more readers. Originally in the United States, Freire's ideas were most often used in programs of adult literacy and adult language education. Gradually community activists started to use Freire's ideas and methodology for their work in a variety of contexts. And, in the early 1990s in the United States, there were even a few in early childhood studies who resonated with the philosophy, theory, and application of Freire's work as relating to our work with children, families, and adults who work with children, this author included.

Freire's work in Brazil and around the world has influenced our work in the context of early childhood programs, especially those working with multilingual children and families from a variety of historical backgrounds. While Freire worked mostly with adults, his ideas, theoretical influences, and generative methodologies for practice have illuminated the promise of the varied languages, multiple histories, and diverse life experiences that young children and their families bring to our field of early care and education, both in the United States and worldwide. It is through the prism of a specific, yet varied, group of teacher education students and children with whom they work that this chapter illustrates a few examples of Freire's teachings with concrete examples of teacher education students participating in critical complex education.

I often encounter skepticism about the possibility of Freire's lofty, intellectual, and activist ideas relating to young children when I introduce his work to teacher education students. Yet, with information and support, teacher education students investigate and put into action many of Freire's concepts as they work with children. They collaborate with each other and with the children to make Freire's theory concrete. Early childhood teacher candidates and young children participate in transformative action in their own ways, according to their contextual realities. Freire's theoretical stance suggests the importance of each child's individual experience of creating meaning from experience, relationships, and learning. And through interactions with peers and adult student teachers, the individual experiences become communal, collaborative learning. The collaborative, interactive learning among children, among adults, and between children and their adult student teachers across roles, is an important, generative aspect of meaning-making. For example, a young child labeling a drawing of herself or himself and a friend in her or his home language and in English is an example of Freire's theoretical stance. A student teacher working with a parent and her child who are refugees recently resettled in a new place, demanding that information from the child's school be written in the child's home language exemplifies Freire's interpretation of critical theory. Both are forms of critical transformative action.

Early childhood work stands clearly on the shoulders of many great scholars and activist educators over the past decades, from Vygotsky, Bronfenbrenner, and Lucy Sprague Mitchell to Reggio-inspired teachings of Malaguzzi. In the past few decades, many educators, working in the complicated world of learners with multiple languages, multiple strengths, multiple histories, and multiple needs, have worked to add to the more traditional approaches for working with children and families, a study of critical theory and critical pedagogy (Freire, 1985; Kincheloe, 2000; Kincheloe, McLaren, & Steinberg, 2012).

A look at Paulo Freire's personal history and then a brief definition of the major concepts of his work are introduced here. Later, this rich personal and sociopolitical history, and the brief definitions of the concepts will be connected to work with young children in the dynamic world of early childhood through a few brief stories and vignettes of young children and their student teachers, many of whom are just beginning their work with children.

Early Life

Paulo Freire was born in Recife, Brazil, in 1921. He was the youngest of four children. His father was a military officer and his mother was a seamstress. They were considered an educated, middle-class family. His mother had great faith in Paulo's intellect and his father would sing him to sleep and read children's storybooks to him (Smidt, 2014). "Paulo learned to read with his parents, in the shade of the trees in the yard of the house in which he was born" (Gadotti, 1994, p. 2). When Paulo Freire went to his first school, a small private school, he already knew the alphabet and was able to write well and copy words. He was there only a little over a year, but would never forget something that his teacher called "making sentences" (Gadotti, 1994, p. 2). The teacher asked the children to write two or three words and then asked them to say something with those words. She had a very definite intuition of the importance of children expressing personal meanings through writing (Gadotti, 1994).

Freire's family moved from Recife to Jaboatão when he was 10 years old. Freire maintained always he had a happy childhood, but like most children in northeastern Brazil in the early 1930s, he knew poverty and hunger. Living in Jaboatão, Freire played soccer and other games in the street with children and teenagers from extremely poor rural families and the children of workers who lived in the hills or near the canals. He commented later on his life about this time as a teenager:

> My experience with them helped me to get used to a different way of thinking and expressing myself. This was the grammar of the people, the language of the people, and as educator of the people I devote myself today to the rigorous understanding of this language.
>
> (Gadotti, 1994, p. 3)

Freire was 12 years old when his father died. So he had to interrupt his studies. He finally was able to start high school at 16, whereas most of the other students began high school at 12 or 13 (Gadotti, 1994).

Early Professional Life and Beyond

As Freire continued to study after high school in university, and during his early years as a teacher, several activist intellectuals influenced his work. One was a lawyer and philosopher, R. Barbosa, who was an activist against slavery. Another was a physician, C. Ribeiro, who wrote a book in a sociolinguistic framework that investigated the political, historical, sociological, educational influences on the development of the Portuguese language (Smidt, 2014). During his early career, Freire taught Portuguese in secondary school. In 1944–45, he married Elza Maria Oliveira, with whom he had five children. Elza was consistent in her encouragement of Freire's devotion to his studies. In 1959, Freire finished his doctoral thesis on adult literacy (Smidt, 2014). Freire became a professor of history and philosophy of education at the University of Recife, and held that position until 1964.

During the1960s Freire worked with a multitude of adults who had not had formal schooling and were not literate. In 1963/4 there were courses for coordinators in all Brazilian states and a plan was drawn up for the establishment of 2,000 cultural circles. Freire's "culture circles" were where learners used their own ways of speaking to articulate their shared understanding of how their world came to be and how it could be changed through transformative action in their future. This work reached 2,000,000 people (Freire & Macedo, 1987). However, following the 1964 coup d'état in Brazil, Freire was imprisoned for 70 days for the "subversive" elements of his teaching. He was in exile for years, living in Bolivia, Chile, Geneva (Switzerland), and the United States. He returned to Brazil in 1979 and led the Workers' Party in Sao Paulo's literacy project for six years. In 1988, Freire was appointed as Sao Paulo's Secretary of Education (Smidt, 2014).

Throughout the 40 years of Freire's dramatic evolution of his philosophy and his methods, his constant and creative collaborator was his wife, Elza. Sadly in 1986, "after 40 years of being sweethearts" (Gadotti, 1994, p. 5), Elza died, and Freire was devastated. Paulo's friends and colleagues worried that this tragedy would change him, make him lose his passion for his work and life. And then, after some years, Freire was reacquainted with Ana Maria Araújo. They married, and years later he explained to his friend Donaldo Macedo:

> Nita not only taught me that it is possible to love again, but she gave me a new and renewed intellectual energy. I feel reenergized intellectually. ... she also impressed upon me the importance of revising my earlier ideas so as to reinvent them.
>
> (Macedo, 2001, p. 4)

Paulo Freire continued his critical intellectual and activist work until his death in 1997. One of his last publications was a compilation of critical dialogues with a range of scholars and practitioners who felt the impact of his work. These scholars represented different critical perspectives, racial backgrounds, approaches to teaching and learning, and life experiences, and all of them were mentored by Freire. *Mentoring the Mentor* (Freire, 1997b) ends with Freire explaining the intention of this edited volume:

> My aim here in this response is not to exhaust all the questions that may be raised, ... but to give examples of how I answer some of the questions. The challenge for the readers is to repeat the questions of the book in order to answer the questions I have not answered, and to do so in their own lives and in their own concrete historical context, ... Once again we are in the spirit of our understanding of dialogue and reinvention. ... It is for the reader to reinvent what is here and make it alive in history.
>
> (Freire, 1997b, p. 329)

Major Concepts

Paulo Freire has become known for major contributions to teaching and learning, human rights and social justice, and ideas about transformative action inside and outside the classroom. His ideas are considered central to critical social theory (often labeled critical theory) and the related pedagogy known as critical pedagogy. Several of his concepts are briefly defined here, and then in the next section of this chapter, vignettes of early childhood teacher education students and the children they work with will help to illustrate what these concepts may mean for work with young children.

Praxis: Reflection and Action

Freire (1970) is most known for his theory of praxis, which includes both reflection and action. In *Pedagogy of the Oppressed*, Freire defines praxis as "reflection and action upon the world in order to transform it. ... [Through] praxis, oppressed people can acquire a critical awareness of their own condition, and, with their allies, struggle for liberation" (p. 36). This reflection and action is directed at policies and structures that need to be transformed. Through praxis, people can acquire a critical awareness of their own situation, and with their allies, struggle for transformation of aspects of this situation that they want to change. This theoretical and methodological approach to the struggle is comprised of several related components and is considered, and often labeled as, critical social theory (McLaren & Giroux, 1994).

Conscientization

Learning is a critical process that depends upon uncovering real problems and actual needs. Freire created a method for this work that he called conscientization. This consisted of developing a critical awareness of one's social reality through reflection, questioning, dialogue, and action. Action is fundamental because it is the process of changing reality (Freire, 1985). Conscientization is sometimes explained as recursive praxis that generates more learning.

Codification

This is a way of gathering information in order to build up a picture (codify) around real situations and real people in a particular context. "It is like a photographer bringing a picture into focus" (Freire, 1983, p. 6). Codification makes the action or object explicit in a purely taxonomic form. De-codification is a process whereby the people in a group begin to identify with aspects of the situation they feel themselves to be in and so are able to reflect critically upon its various aspects, thus gathering understanding. De-codification thus transforms what was a way of life in the real context into an objective theoretical context and participants in the dialogue reflect on and discuss "what is really going on here?"

Dialogue

In the Freirean sense, a dialogue situation, talking with people and collaborators, presumes equality among all participants. Participants must trust each other, and there must be mutual respect and care and shared commitment. Each person must question what he or she knows and realize that through dialogue existing thoughts will change and new knowledge will be created (Freire, 1973).

Generative Themes

In the 1950s, in the Movement for Popular Culture in Recife, Freire established "Cultural Circles." Themes were discussed in a group and the group would decide on the theme that should be developed in their work. Freire wanted to encourage the groups to move beyond popular knowledge and popular wisdom to gain a greater solidarity in understanding the themes that make up the knowledge for a specific group of participants. In other words, Freire "had discovered that the *form* of learning, the process of the act of learning, was a determining factor in relation to the *content* of learning" (Gadotti, 1994, p. 18). As data on these issues were brought into the class, Freire became a *problem-poser*. He used the knowledge he and his students had produced about the generative themes to construct questions. The questions he posed through problem-posing were designed to teach the idea that no curriculum, or knowledge in general, was beyond examination. He firmly believed that all knowledge is shaped by the context and the individuals who produce the information (Kincheloe, McLaren, & Steinberg, 2012, p. 16).

The Banking Concept of Knowledge

The concept of education known as the "banking concept" that Freire criticized was, and still is, practiced in many places. This is the practice of knowledge being given by those who consider themselves knowledgeable to those whom they consider to be ignorant. The metaphor is that "Education becomes an act of depositing (as in banks); 'knowledge' is a donation from those who know to those who don't know anything" (Gadotti, 1994, p. 52). Banking education, thus, perpetuates the status quo of inequality, and maintains the division between the oppressors and the oppressed. This practice in education is considered to be the antithesis to problem-posing education and critical social theory, as Freire illuminated it. As described above, Freire advocated for a dialogical relationship between the educator and the pupils where learning is multidirectional. Freire (1970) was adamant that the teacher's primary role is to facilitate educational changes for individual learners and for groups of learners collectively.

Praxis Illustrated

According to Freire's teachings, defined as praxis, it is not enough for people to come together in dialogue to learn about their social reality. They must come together for dialogue to reflect critically upon their reality and then act together to transform the environment and promote their own needs and desires (Freire, 1973).

University students, early childhood teacher education candidates in our program, study teaching with Freire's framework to exemplify praxis both in terms of their own professional learning and their planning for the learning of the children. They explore ways that the theoretical framework of praxis supports an integrated curriculum that leads to young children's meaningful learning (Quintero, 2015). The problem-posing format we use is comprised of *listening*, *dialogue*, and *action*. In the university classes that use this method, teacher education students listen to their own histories through reflective writing and sharing of participants' stories, and gather new information about teaching and learning in the form of mini-lectures, expert presentations, and scholarly research.

During the *listening* section, the adult student teachers use platforms of story, literature, and art to reflect on and build upon their own history of learning as a way to construct a collaborative path to plan their work with children.

Then, they *dialogue* in small groups to share their personal information and make connections to information presented in the university class during the *listening* activities. In these discussions they explore issues of power that have shaped their identities and the current contexts of families, schools, and communities. Then, either in small groups or as a class as a whole, they are asked to make connections from these discussions to the situations of the children with whom they currently work. They then dialogue more about planning future curricular activities that encourage and support action, or transformation, on the part of children, families, and educators.

Then, in the *action* section of the class, the teacher education students practice assignments focused on learning to observe and listen to children in order to prepare and to collect information for informed action-taking and collaboration with children. For example, in the beginning of their work with the children, they participate in writing narrative descriptions of children's participation, strengths, and interests and the context of the early childhood classrooms. They write brief accounts of children participating and playing in ways that show their interests. They notice children using their home language (and English), and address the following questions: "What do the children say?" "What do they do that shows their own interests?" "When do they use their home language?" They also are tasked with noticing details about children's literacy, mathematics, and other content knowledge, answering the following questions: "What do you see as the children's strengths?" "What do they know?" "How do you know they know this?"

A student teacher in a kindergarten class in a bilingual school in an economically challenged urban area in southern California wrote a reflection about what happened after she shared her own family history with the children. She wrote that she wanted to encourage children in the class to use family stories as a way to make connections to the class assignments in their school curriculum. In our university class there had been extensive discussions about the sharing of personal history as a way to build trust with learners. She explained,

> In my small group I wanted to focus on family story and bookmaking. I started out by sharing that my mother had come to California two months before I was born, and that many of my cousins still live in Mexico. I hoped to get to know the students better and thought maybe they would share their stories if I shared mine. When I asked if anyone had family members that lived or currently live in a different location from our city, one student shared with me that her father is in Mexico. I thought this was interesting because this child refuses to speak Spanish at times and seems to be ashamed of her Spanish language.
>
> And there were two other students who are not very outspoken and did not share as much about their family. But to make sure they wouldn't feel left out, I made sure that everyone got a turn to talk about family by asking them each a few specific questions in Spanish. And I did see that they became more engaged when I asked the questions in Spanish. I finally did get a response from one of these students who shared with me that her grandparents lived in Mexico.
>
> (Santos, 2015)

Through observations, documentation, and participation with children, student teachers begin collaborating with the children on engaging in integrated content-learning experiences focusing on children's interests and the history and culture of the children's families (critical pedagogy). It is important that the student teachers "tune in" to the children and their families and build upon their strengths, never minimizing their responsibility to provide opportunities for teaching strong academic foundations for future educational success (critical theory).

Conscientization Illustrated

As previously described, the university students begin thinking about early learning by thinking of their own family histories. They are asked to consider, discuss, and document: What was meaningful in their interactions with loved ones and other people? What did play look like in their families? In what ways did play and stories intersect? What were examples of the beginnings of understanding story and communication? The information from these memories clearly influences the learners' choices for both process learning preferences and content learning passions (critical theory).

The reflections of our own stories, often raw and dramatic, give us perspective about our approaches to designing and implementing curriculum (critical pedagogy). In the sense of critical theory, problem-posing, and critical pedagogy, this listening to memories is *listening*, the sharing with peers is *dialogue*, and *transformative action* comes in to play as the information from memories and dialogue is connected to new learning from educational research and other course information as the students delve into collaborating with young children in curriculum design. A teacher education student wrote about her family history and the dynamics of learning:

> A memory I have of my mother with literacy is singing and dancing while doing chores. I remember her dancing around with a broom and whistling. She taught me how to whistle and hum to music. My mother did not read or write (I now know), but she would always sit down with us to do our homework. She would also buy the newspaper and read it. Little did I know that all she did was look at pictures and cut out the coupons? Now I understand a lot of things that happened when I was younger and appreciate my mother more.
>
> (Quintero, 2015, p. 40)

The mother mentioned above later nurtured a family tradition that involved imagination and pretend story. This is told by the same student teacher; the young boy with the magic book is the grandson of the mother mentioned above.

> In my family we have a "magic book." The magic book got its name because everyone in my family tells a different story every time it's told. Our family members have different types and levels of education and life experiences. My nephew was given this magic book when he was a few weeks old. It is a wordless storybook, and my sister made it a habit to read to him this "magic book" every night. As he got older he would carry his book around and ask different family members to read him this wordless book. We explained to him that anyone could use imagination and make up a new story every time. The reasons we started this tradition was because children tend to memorize a story, and when someone else reads the story a different way, not as they know it, the child corrects the adult. My nephew is 6-years-old now and he has a 1-year-old sister. He continues the tradition with his younger cousins and his sister. The rest of the family also continues the tradition, but now my nephew likes to read them the "magic book" himself. It's amazing to me that he never repeats the story; it's always different. What I find more interesting

> is that he individualizes the story according to whomever he reads the story to, someone different.
>
> (Quintero, 2015, p. 40)

Again, considering critical theory, the family story of the mother (now grandmother), the student teacher, and her nephew, all reflect vivid family participation in learning history and educational experiences, multiple sources of knowledge (homework, newspapers, coupons, wordless story book, the imaginations of all who read the "magic book"), and transformative action through the art, the storytelling, the sharing of meaning and memories. This is a specific example of conscientization on the part of the adult student teacher, as she reflected on and noted how her mother who was not literate supported the literacy development of the children in her family at the time the student was growing up. Then the student connected these literacy support strategies and intentions of her mother to her mother's creating the "magic book" for her grandchildren. Notably, the little boy (the student's nephew, and the student's mother's grandson) developed a critical awareness of both his reality and that of his various family members to whom he read the "magic book." He learned at an early age to change the story depending on social reality of the listener. He was practicing reflection and action. This conscientization through the ongoing retelling of the "magic book" story was a recursive praxis that generated more learning.

Codification Illustrated

Some years ago, while working with master's level early childhood teacher education students, I had begun a class session by introducing Freire's work internationally and in the United States with adult learners. I quickly, through dialogue and problem-posing using learners' actual lived experience, jumped to our immediate task of considering this approach with young children. The students in the class politely listened, and had questions during our dialogue that ranged from skepticism to outright disbelief. At the end of that evening's class, I made the assignment for students to observe children in any aspect of their lives (in schools, in shops, in trains, on playgrounds, or wherever) and to document examples of what might be considered children illustrating critical theory for us to analyze in class the following week.

One student from the class, who had expressed sincere discomfort because she wasn't sure what this might look like, wrote to me just a couple of hours after the class dismissal. She wrote:

> I observed a child and his father riding the subway together. The train was very crowded and there was only enough room for the child to sit down, so the father stood in front of him holding the bar over the seat to steady himself. He put the child in the seat and gave him some paper and a pen to draw with. The child looked around for a while and then finally began drawing. (He was codifying his current situation.) After some time (it was rush hour and the train between Manhattan and New Jersey took almost an hour) the father asked the child what he was drawing. The boy said he was drawing the father riding on the subway. The father looked at the drawing that depicted figures of people in seats on the train. The father replied, "But

> I'm standing, not sitting down," The child then said, "Not on this train; *my* train has seats for everyone to sit down."
>
> (Quintero, 2009, p. 10)

This is a vivid example of a young child practicing critical theory through codification and de-codification. For this 4-year-old, his experience on the subway with his father, and his action through his artwork, transformed a crowded uncomfortable train into one with sufficient seats for everyone. He was de-codifying the uncomfortable train situation to a better, more comfortable, one. Children often have questions and ideas that they do not verbalize that become communicated through art. Often this communication is transformative action for young children.

Dialogue Illustrated

Reading the word and the world is one of Freire's well-known descriptions of what he believes literacy learning must be. This "reading of the world" includes what he calls problem-posing (or questioning of) existing knowledge. Critical educators reconceptualize the notion of literacy. Myles Horton of the Highlander Folk School in Tennessee spoke of the way Paulo Freire read books with students in order "to give testimony to the students about what it means to read a text" (Horton & Freire, 1990, p. 149) and what questions the act of reading together raises in terms of the validity of the information. Going beyond the status quo in terms of accepting knowledge and insisting on questioning and connecting the knowledge to students' current reality is central to Freirean problem-posing. Just as important is the necessity to speak out if there is no connection or relevance to the lived experiences of the group. This position contends that all school curricula should be, in part, shaped by problems that face teachers and students (Kincheloe, McLaren, & Steinberg, 2012).

For example, in university classes teacher education students are encouraged to connect critical theory, early childhood theoretical information, personal histories, family and community information, and educational research to give them background information to prepare for participant observation in early childhood programs. Then, they begin collaboratively planning and implementing a participatory curriculum in their teaching contexts with 3-year-olds to 8-year-olds. Students actually engage in the critical theory through participation, use of multiple sources of knowledge, and transformative action.

A student teacher, Leila (all names in this chapter are pseudonyms), tells us a story of her student teaching experience that illustrates the importance of curriculum in the early years reflecting family history and current lived experience, and dialogue, in Freire's words. Her journal reflections reveal her own learning history first and then her experiences with 3- and 4-year-olds participating in collaborative dialogue. First, in terms of her own learning, she had been studying Spanish, but was not yet bilingual, and she wrote of her worries about her lack of language knowledge:

> Last semester I feared that I wouldn't be able to teach children who shared a different primary language than I did. I shared this concern with one of my professors and she told me that language should not get in the way of my

> teaching. She said that if I planned well *with* the children, the language wouldn't be a problem and that the materials and the children would create the language. I didn't understand this at all. Probably because of teaching practices I've seen before where teachers talk a LOT and children talk a little. What I ended up learning was how true the things my professor had told me were.
>
> The scariest lesson plan I implemented this semester was a long piece of butcher paper rolled out across a wall with the words "Family Wall" and, in Spanish, "la pared de la familia" written across the top and with crayons on the ground below. Amazingly, and much to my surprise, the conversation came. The children spoke to one another about their work. They spoke to me about their work. They spoke to other teachers about their work. I learned more about the few children that I saw working over three days than I had about them over the course of a semester.
>
> (Quintero, 2015, p. 101)

In terms of the children's learning and dialogue, an excerpt of her description of the children working on the Family Wall activity illustrates dialogue and many other positive aspects of the learning. Above, she mentioned the "Family Wall" that was an initial activity which would become a series of activities that she called "Neighborhood Maps." Here is another excerpt from her research journal where she begins to develop the rationale for the activities she was planning and supplies some of the specifics of the children's responses.

> Through the series of activities available, children were given the opportunity to understand differences among people as well as similarities. Children had opportunities to learn about themselves and their peers, they were exposed to print in Spanish and English and concepts through literature. They experienced information about both home communities and global communities, and they had the opportunity to express themselves in the language they felt most comfortable using.
>
> Before bringing a map of North America into the classroom, I sent home a note, written in both languages, to families, asking them to share with their children where they are from, where their parents are from, where the majority of their family members still live. Once all the notes, and oral information was collected, we posted sticky notes on the big map with names of the children and families in the different locations. I talked to the children during morning welcome about the information that was collected and let them know that anyone interested could help work on the map by talking about it and adding additional information to it.
>
> We then taped that map on to a big sheet of butcher paper and renamed it "the Family Wall/la pared de la familia." We brought this in to the classroom so the children could see it and talk about it. After the map had been displayed for a couple of days, I suggested a drawing activity to the children that would be a creation of a "neighborhood map." We added another big piece of butcher paper that was placed on an adjoining wall of the classroom, at children's eye level, and placed a bucket of markers and crayons for them to use to create the neighborhood map.

Dialogue is illustrated as Leila went on to explain:

> Suela approached me while some children were looking at books and she asked me if she could write on the "neighborhood map." The map had just been introduced in to the environment that day. I hadn't intended for it to be written on, but I answered Suela that she could begin writing on the map. I noticed that she began making shapes on the map that looked like a backward "C." I scooted closer, and I heard her whisper, "A." I looked and she had just written a perfect capital "A." Soon Suela moved to the Family Wall and continued to write the same letter shapes and then began drawing. I asked her what she had made. She said, "Un rainbow." I said, "Hmmm, a rainbow on the Family Wall." She said, "Si, un rainbow es una familia."
>
> (Quintero, 2015, p. 103)

Generative Themes Illustrated

Generative themes arise through problem posing in the teacher education students' university class. These generative themes often address research and methodologies regarding bilingual children. These themes often overlap with sociological and political realities for multilingual families in schools and communities that bring up the need, as Freire suggested, to explore which knowledge is correctly relevant to family history. A class session for the early childhood teacher education students began with a student volunteer reading the bilingual storybook *I Love Saturdays y Domingos* by Alma Flor Ada (2004), which tells the story of a girl's life with both her English-speaking grandparents and her Spanish-speaking grandparents. After the story, the university students, talking in small groups, are asked to relate the story to issues discussed during the previous class and the research done over the past week where the focus had been issues in dual language acquisition and current research for effective practice for supporting multilingual young children.

The students read together another storybook, *Friends From the Other Side: Amigos Del Otro Lado* by Gloria Anzaldúa (1997), which is a story about a young girl befriending a boy who had recently moved to an American neighborhood from Mexico with his mother but without documentation. The story includes issues of friendship, coping with bullying, experiences related to how political situations in communities may affect children, and cultural traditions supporting children including sharing food and natural healing. After the story is concluded, the students gather in small groups again for another dialogue section, to debrief about the difficult topics surrounding immigration, discrimination, bullying, and differing family histories. Then the university students reconvene in the whole group to address appropriate ways to negotiate contentious issues and move to transformative action surrounding some of the issues.

In the class, after what often is a heated discussion, the action section of the problem posing assigns students to read and share some teacher research articles addressing controversial issues from the journal *Rethinking Schools Online*. Then, in groups, they are asked to plan collaborative activities (based on their observations of children's strengths and interests) that could be introduced to go with the themes addressed in story. These activities, through using multicultural children's literature and problem-posing in the university class, exemplify Freire's concepts of conscientization, codification, de-codification, generative themes, and praxis.

Banking Concept of Knowledge Illustrated

A brief synthesis of one of the early childhood curriculum classes shows adults learning about the banking concept of knowledge and connecting it to their own family stories and to their work collaborating with children. In the *listening* section opening for class, there is a viewing of a short video clip of an interview with author Sandra Cisneros discussing her revelation about her family when she entered graduate school (https://www.youtube.com/watch?v=nXO8a6HYttw).

She explained that her own Latina history, language, and set of cultural experiences in Chicago were never included in the narratives she studied in school. She noted that in her early schooling right up until her time at graduate school at the University of Iowa, writers and artists never wrote about or depicted *her* house and *her* neighborhood. The "banking education" of all those years and experiences promoted inauthentic visions and possibilities (for her and her community) to describe "home." So, through personal narratives, she began the basis of her writing for *The House on Mango Street* (1991) that won the American Book Award. The book is the story of a girl, Esperanza, growing up in the Latino section of Chicago. The neighborhood is one of stark realities and stunning, complex strengths as seen through families, friends, and *la gente* (the people) in the community.

In the *dialogue* section, students are asked to discuss with a partner their chosen memories of their family literacy and learning history. There is much discussion of the university students' telling personal stories of teachers who had mispronounced, or even insisted on "changing" a student's name that was difficult for the teacher to say and remember. I then invite students to discuss any such experiences among children in the early childhood programs where they are currently working. Then I ask questions about whether the students are familiar with a large group of indigenous learners in our county who speak Mixteco (their indigenous language from Oaxaca, Mexico) as a first language, Spanish as a second language, and learn English as a third language.

Following the discussion, information is distributed related to the history, language, and culture of the Mixtec people (an indigenous community comprising many of the agricultural workers in our country). Research readings disseminated in class explore the fact that children come to early care and education programs from a multitude of family histories and from a multitude of experiences in which global interactions play a part. This is a vivid reality in California. As previously mentioned, many preschool-age children in southern California are of Mixtec heritage.

Following this, in the *action* section of the class, students then work in small groups to consider ways to incorporate some of the information into the curriculum activities that they are collaborating on with children and their friends who may be from this group of families, or neighbors with the families, in our community.

An example is supplied by a two-year collaboration of university students with some Mixtec parents and children that provided an alternative to "banking education" for young Mixtec children in our county through transformative action. Several early childhood student teachers participated in an applied-research project in which student teachers interviewed parents and children from the Mixtec community group about family history, educational goals and preferences for children, and issues of access. The students then created activities that reflected a combination of Mixtec family history, Mixteco language, early childhood activities that children chose, folk tales, and bilingual storybooks. The activities and storybooks were sent home with children who requested them, and then placed in the university library where all the families had been given access for entry and use.

Connecting Freire's Work to History in the Making

According to Freire (1997a), those who adopt critical theory and pedagogy need to be aware that it is not made up of techniques to save the world; rather, he felt that "the progressive educator must always be moving out on his or her own, continually reinventing me and reinventing what it means to be democratic in his or her own specific cultural and historical context" (Freire, 1997a, p. 308). In other words, a critical theory framework supports working with learners from a variety of historical contexts, language groups, and life experiences.

Many of the student teachers participating in the work with children described here are first generation college students, and a large number of them are from families and communities of migrant farmworkers in California. They have truly lived biculturally, with many loved ones located in Mexico and Central America. Many of the children in the early care and education programs in the county also are from families of farmworkers. And, in fact, we now know (Park & McHugh, 2014) that one in four children in the United States lives in a family of immigrants, which gives many of the children we work with expertise from deep, rich historical traditions. For these reasons, we pay attention to the many families with young children who have migrated to California, and also to families with children in crisis transition around the world in 2016.

As we view mass migrations around the world, in particular in response to terrible wars and severe natural disasters such as droughts and earthquakes, we see children experiencing and learning from day-to-day situations of survival. It is not surprising that in our ongoing reinvention of ourselves as critical educators (according to Freire's ideas) and our study as lifelong learners, we are compelled to constantly make connections, in empathy, and in documentation of possible potential, strengths and needs, of the families and children in transit across the world. We strongly agree with the director of the Migration Policy Institute, who emphasizes to policymakers and diplomatic teams that, regarding refugee families, they should think about "*What happens tomorrow?*" (Papademetriou, 2015). Once people have arrived in a resettlement situation, survival depends on food, shelter, and education. We have hope that through our critical analysis of our own work, we can add to the data of possibilities that policy experts and educators may provide for families in the way of critical learning environments and supports for families and children caught in this ongoing and traumatic situation.

Going back to Freire's teenage years when his family moved to Jaboatão, and he played games in the street with children and teenagers from extremely poor rural families and the children of workers who lived in the hills or near the canals, he knew at a very young age that by interacting with others and by building relationships through trust and communication, he could better understand all learners at home and around the world. May we take action to do so ourselves.

References

Ada, A.F. (2004). *I love Saturdays y domingos*. New York: Atheneum Books for Young Readers.

Anzaldúa, G. (1997). *Friends from the other side / Amigos del otrolado*. San Francisco: Children's Book Press.

Cisneros, S. (1991). *The house on Mango Street*. New York: Vintage.

Freire, P. (1970). *Pedagogy of the oppressed* (M. Ramos, Trans.). New York: Herder and Herder.

Freire, P. (1973). *Education for critical consciousness*. New York: Seabury Press.

Freire, P. (1983). The importance of the act of reading. *Journal of Education*, *165*(1), 5–11.

Freire, P. (1985). *The politics of education*. Granby, MA: Bergin & Garvey.

Freire, P. (1997a). *Pedagogy of hope*. Granby, MA: Bergin & Garvey.

Freire, P. (1997b). *Mentoring the mentor*. New York: Peter Lang.

Freire, P., & Macedo, D. (1987). *Literacy: Reading the word and the world*. South Hadley, MA: Bergin & Garvey.

Gadotti, M. (1994). *Reading Paulo Freire: His life and work*. New York: Peter Lang.

Horton, M., & Freire, P. (1990). *We make the road by walking: Conversations on education and social change*. Philadelphia, PA: Temple University Press.

Kincheloe, J. (2000). Certifying the damage: Mainstream educational psychology and the oppression of children. In L.D. Soto (Ed.), *The politics of early childhood education* (pp. 75–84). New York: Peter Lang.

Kincheloe, J., McLaren, P., & Steinberg, S.R. (2012). Critical pedagogy and qualitative research: Moving to the bricolage. In S.R. Steinberg & G.S. Canella (Eds.), *Critical qualitative research reader* (pp. 14–32). New York: Peter Lang.

Macedo, D. (2001). Introduction. In Freire, Ana Maria A., *Chronicles of love: My life with Paulo Freire* (p. 4). New York: Peter Lang.

McLaren, P., & Giroux, H. (1994). Foreword. In M. Gadotti, *Reading Paulo Freire: His life and work* (pp. xii–xvii). New York: Peter Lang.

Papademetriou, D. (2015). *What happens tomorrow? The day after*. Washington, DC: Migration Policy Institute. www.migrationpolicy.org/multimedia/refugee-crisis-europe-qa-demetrios-papademetriou

Park, M., & McHugh, M. (2014, June). Immigrant parents and early childhood programs: Addressing barriers of literacy, culture, and systems knowledge. Migration Policy Institute. www.migrationpolicy.org/research/immigrant-parents-early-childhood-programs-barriers

Quintero, E.P. (2009). *Critical literacy in early childhood education: Artful story and the integrated curriculum*. New York: Peter Lang.

Quintero, E.P. (2015). *Storying learning in early childhood: When children lead participatory curriculum design, implementation, and assessment*. New York: Peter Lang.

Santos, I. (2015). Unpublished research journal. Camarillo, CA.

Smidt, S. (2014). *Introducing Paulo Freire: A guide for students, teachers, and practitioners*. London: Routledge.

Suggested Websites

www.freire.org/
www.genderandeducation.com/issues/relaunch-of-the-paulo-freire-institute-uk/
https://carlosatorres.com/paulo-freire/
www.unesco.org/education/aladin/?menuitem=20&language=spa&member=48
www.vu.nl/ecn/about-vu-amsterdam/faculties-and-institutes/cpf/index.aspx

13

WORKING WITH DELEUZE AND GUATTARI IN EARLY CHILDHOOD RESEARCH AND EDUCATION

Gail Boldt

Introduction

The theories of the French philosophers Félix Guattari and Gilles Deleuze are an increasing presence in early childhood research. Although they were publishing together in French from 1972, and their major works became available in English from 1977, a search for references demonstrates that their theories have been mostly unknown in early childhood research published in English. In the past seven years, however, there has been a small explosion of citations. For example, in the journal *Contemporary Issues in Early Childhood*, from its founding in 2000 through 2008, there were nine citations of Deleuze and Guattari. Since 2009, citations number in the dozens. Programs for the annual Reconceptualizing Early Childhood Education conference show a similar surge in the presentation of papers that reference Deleuze and Guattari. What, one might wonder, is the cause of all of this interest? What are the theories of Deleuze and Guattari providing to early childhood researchers and theorists? And what, if any, implications might these theories have for early childhood classroom practices?

This chapter will provide readers with an introduction to a few of the major theories of Félix Guattari and Gilles Deleuze, with attention to how these theories are being applied to research about early childhood education. I will begin with an example of a child at play drawn from my research with Kevin Leander (Boldt & Leander, in review). I will then move on to a brief biographical sketch of the two philosophers and a discussion of some of their important theoretical concepts related to early childhood, which will be used to analyze the episode of the child playing. I will conclude with a consideration of how three researchers, Liane Mozère, Sheri Leafgren, and Liselott Mariett Olsson, have used Deleuze and Guattari's theories to think about practices in early childhood research.

A Child at Play

The following excerpt is from a much longer play episode in which six-year-old Mike and his father, Kevin, sit on the floor of their home playing LEGO®. Kevin has set up a camera to record their play as part of the work he and I are doing together to rethink children's interactions with material objects and spaces through the use of concepts from the work of Deleuze and Guattari.

The play is just beginning, and Mike has distributed figures and space ships built from various LEGO® Star Wars sets. In an effort, perhaps, to assert his fairness and magnanimity and to deny that the outcome of the battle is already known—that he will win, as he always wins these battles with Dad—Mike begins by explaining that the firepower of the alien figures and ships he has assigned to his father are superior to his own. He describes the only strength of his guys as being "really agile," which he demonstrates by darting his figures over his head and around the space ship his father is holding. The battle commences and Mike throws tiny, pre-fab missile pieces at his father's big ships. The pieces are too small to do any actual damage to Kevin's ships. While his father initially is cooperative with Mike's battle plan, good-naturedly crashing his ships into the carpet in response to a missile hit, he has now begun to assert the superiority of his fleet. He no longer crashes his ships and begins to advance on Mike's fighters. Mike changes tactics. First, he tries to use his proclaimed agility to land a fighter on his father's ship and pry open the hatch to destroy its alien driver. This does not work and his father's ship now menaces his lone alien warrior. Frustrated, Mike tosses his warrior behind his back, proclaiming "Change back!" and grabs a large crane from a pile of LEGO® objects that had not previously been part of the game. As he attaches a large base to his crane, presumably preparing to smash his father's ship, he says, "You can change if you want to." His father expresses confusion so Mike clarifies:

M: You can change to ... You can get another person. Uh, like let's say you have this guy, but you want someone bigger. You can not use that guy. Just use one and put that guy back in your pile.

K: Okay. I guess I understand that. That's a little complicated. So are you changing back?

M: Yeah, I change into this [indicating the crane].

K: Whoa! So now I'm fighting that?

There are many ways we could consider this brief episode of play. For example, a Vygotskian analysis might provide a focus on the function of play, considering how Mike's play supports his growing cognitive skills and acquisition of language. An analysis making use of a cultural studies lens might focus on Mike's taking up of affordances made possible by the corporate strategy of LEGO® that, beginning in the mid-1990s, shifted from an open-ended construction toy to the production of kits that feature both recognizable characters (e.g., Star Wars, Minecraft, Marvel Superheroes) and those of LEGO®'s invention (e.g., Ninjago, Bionicles), with massive marketing tie-ins. My own training in post-structural performance theory suggests yet a third approach to analysis, one that considers the ways that Mike and his father take up and enact or challenge pre-existing subject positions such as gender, race, and social class. This analysis would consider the cultural expectations for what it is supposed to look like to be/act like a white, middle-class boy or man; a professor and researcher or a six-year-old child; a parent or child who is being parented; or many other possible identifications.

A Deleuzo-Guattarian analysis of Mike and his father's play does not necessarily deny or overwrite any of these (or other) perspectives. Rather, what their theories offer is a way to expand our view of what might be happening. While there are many aspects of their work that I could apply to analyzing this instance of play, for this chapter I will focus on two major points. First, the Deleuzo-Guattarian perspective attends to play as wrapped up in desire and the production of affect. The second has to do with attending to play as characterized by movements between that which is known and that which is improvisational, as being, in a word, emergent. These considerations, which I will describe in the next section, allow for the recognition of events in preschool classrooms that are sometimes implicitly understood as important but often not explicitly named or considered. Particularly in an era when playfulness, spontaneity, and improvisation are crowded out of preschool classrooms in favor of increased time for seatwork and a curriculum of narrowly defined skills acquisition, thinking about flows of desire in a classroom may create some space for the unexpected to emerge. A Deleuzo-Guattarian perspective does not preclude skills work nor does it privilege play, but it does call our attention to what space exists for children and teachers to engage in enlivening ways within the confines of existing activities.

Deleuze and Guattari: Some Major Ideas

Félix Guattari (1930–1992) was a French philosopher and psychotherapist, as well as a radical political and social activist. He spent much of his life working at a psychiatric clinic called La Borde, where patients, doctors, nurses, and other staff lived as a collective, sharing the tasks, daily life, and responsibility for governance equally. Gilles Deleuze (1925–1995) was a French philosopher who, in addition to writing about philosophy, also wrote about politics, culture, and art. He spent most of his career teaching at the University of Paris VII at Vincennes/St. Denis, which was established in response to the May 1968 civil unrest in France, to experiment with education reforms. Deleuze and Guattari began their collaboration in 1969. They shared a fervor for enabling revolutionary political and social change. Their best known collaborative writing is a major two-volume work, *Anti-Oedipus: Capitalism and Schizophrenia*, published in 1972 in French and 1977 in English; and *A Thousand Plateaus: Capitalism and Schizophrenia*, published in 1980 in French and 1988 in English.

Deleuze and Guattari's theory is, above all else, a theory of desire. The two major volumes of their work represent their effort to wrest the definition of desire away from the dominant understanding of it organized through capitalism and enunciated through classical and Lacanian psychoanalysis. Desire in their formulation is everywhere and passes through everyone and everything. They characterize desire as impersonal. It is not something that one owns. Rather, desire is the unconscious forces and drives that occur because things come into relation with one another and cause something new to happen (1972/1977). Desire produces and is produced by movement and momentum through time and space. Movement is not just human movement; it is that the world is in constant motion. Because of movement, any number of disparate elements—people, material objects, events, histories, and ideas—are constantly brought into relation with one another. Deleuze and Guattari call this temporary bringing together an assemblage (1980/1988). Assemblages are random; they exist moment-to-moment. A given assemblage constitutes a given time and place. Assemblages lack organization and are open-ended. They create something that didn't exist before, thereby opening up multiple possibilities for what might happen next.

Desire itself lacks organization and is open-ended. There is no inherent object of desire; nothing desire is pursuing. Desire is not owned by anyone. Desire therefore represents both never-ending transformative potential and a problem. Deleuze and Guattari (1972/1977), following Marx, argue that capitalism reproduces itself through the use of two forces: the constant incitement of desire and the harnessing and containment of that desire into forms and expressions that work to its advantage, to constantly reproduce capitalist structures, forms, and, of course, consumption. They name the first force, the generation of the new, deterritorialization. In deterritorialization, there is a breakdown and reorganization of known patterns, expectations, norms, and authorities, and the production of new, and in the case of capitalism, usable desires. The second force, the effort to constrain or channel what emerges, they name "territorialization." The force of territorialization is the effort to constrain the inherent, unlimited nature of desire into specific forms, and in the case of capitalism, into expressions of desire that do not undo capitalism itself.

While desire has no limits, it is constantly being channeled or territorialized into becoming something specific, to connect it into networks that produce specific things, what they called desiring machines (1972/1977). Desiring machines are produced not just by capitalists but also by revolutionaries and by anyone or anything that works to organize and channel desire toward specific outcomes. In other words, territorialization and deterritorialization are not limited to capitalism. It is the nature of social organization. We are all constantly involved in movements of territorialization or the organization of desire in the attempt to produce specific outcomes and deterritorialization, the production or emergence of the new.

Deleuze and Guattari (1972/1977, 1980/1988) look especially to how the psychoanalytic theory of desire, whether Freudian or Lacanian, tells a story about a very constrained version of desire that works on behalf of capitalism. That is, they argued that the psychoanalytic version of desire that reduces it to a constant struggle to overcome Oedipal losses (loss of the desired mommy/daddy) has the effect of individualizing struggles, taking them out of the social context and depoliticizing them. It also tamed desire, tying it to unconscious repetition and lack, or in other words, assuming that desire is always attached to the same old thing. The important point here is that for Guattari and Deleuze, the unconscious, rather than being individual as it is in psychoanalysis, can better be understood as ceaselessly productive, constantly combining flows of desire to produce new energy that impels us forward (1972/1977). This unconscious is not contained within the individual but rather is more like undirected flows of energy that are fueled through the moment-by-moment encounters of all the human and non-human material of daily life with objects, environments, feelings, forces.

The nature of what happens, for Deleuze and Guattari, is characterized by emergence (1972/1977). What will happen next is not known in advance but emerges out of the elements that are brought into the moment-by-moment assemblage. The elements in any given assemblage are shifting and a matter of happenstance, and each has virtual potential to set into motion what Deleuze and Guattari (1980/1988) called "a line of flight," the emergence of something new and unexpected.

With these ideas in mind, we will now return to Mike and Kevin's LEGO® play. We will analyze their play through the concepts of assemblages, territorialization and deterritorialization, emergence, and desire.

Analyzing the LEGO® Play

Considering Mike and Kevin's play through a Deleuzo-Guattarian lens is first of all a consideration of how desire is enunciated and organized. Desire herein is conceptualized as the momentum produced through the ongoing production of affect; in this case, experienced as pleasure, frustration and excitement—through engaging both the familiar and the new, or, in other words, the territorialized and the deterritorialized.

The play engaged in by Mike and Kevin is partly organized through its relationship to pre-existing or already territorialized roles and rituals. There is a father and a son with an existing play relationship that both find gratifying. They occupy additional subject positions: male, middle class, American, child and adult, to name just a few, that have provided norms and limitations in the ways they experience themselves and one another. There are familiar storylines suggested by the materials themselves—LEGO® Star Wars kits—and by their shared knowledge of science fiction/fantasy narratives. These territorializations provide a shared language and set of patterns for relating to one another, the narratives and materials, the time and space, that organize the event of playing together. However, they do not tell the whole story; and they are not in themselves adequate to sustain momentum.

Clearly an important feature of what happened was the deterritorializing or unexpected things that happened and the improvisational moves Mike and Kevin made in response. Mike begins the play with the assertion that he has given his father an advantage by handing over the more formidable looking ships. This is not the first time they have played this game; and the storyline of Mike's previous victories based on claiming the more dominant pieces has been played out. Because the outcome of that scenario is known, it does not generate the excitement it once did; it has lost its ability to produce satisfactory momentum. Mike improvises, handing his father what appears to be the advantage, in order to bring fresh energy to the game. He looks at what he has available to him and names a new skill, agility, and his tiny missiles as the thing that will provide excitement to their David and Goliath contest. Initially, Kevin goes along with providing Mike an easy victory, but that storyline too plays out in terms of what might happen next, so Kevin changes his response, adding new life to the play by acknowledging that the missiles do no damage and advancing menacingly on Mike's fleet. This, too, is improvisation, making use of the affordances of the materials that are present to maintain the excitement and momentum of the play.

What, then, of desire? Liane Mozère (2014), a French sociologist and feminist activist who worked with Guattari and Deleuze, wrote of children's desire as moments when children are able to snatch something that empowers their own "forces of life" (p. 102). She characterizes it as the child's ability to sustain or increase the power and intensity of their actions (Boldt, Lewis, & Leander, 2015). The same is, of course, true of adult desire. Throughout the action of their moves and countermoves, neither Kevin nor Mike knew what would happen next. Each line of flight shifted what was happening, brought new assemblages and therefore new virtualities—or in other words, new openings toward what might happen next—into being. The movement created energy, pleasure, frustration, excitement, and momentum.

While rules of play, the corporate history and material affordances of LEGO®, and the roles provided by identities or subject positions, all forms of territorialization, contributed to the assemblage, they could not guarantee the outcomes. They were participants in the assemblage, but as Kevin and I wrote elsewhere (Leander & Boldt, 2013), such activities are:

> not determined by past design projected toward some future redesign, but as living its life in the ongoing present, forming relations and connections across signs, objects, and bodies in often unexpected ways. Such activity is created and fed by an ongoing flow of affective intensities that are different from the rational control of meanings and forms.
>
> (p. 36)

Brian Massumi (2002), perhaps Deleuze and Guattari's foremost North American interpreter, writes that because the nature of reality is imminent and change is a moment-to-moment reality, the question we need to ask is how we account for the production of sameness. In other words, given that new things can happen at any moment (and indeed do), how do we account for the fact that in so many instances, what gets produced are versions of the same old thing? What this suggests is the kind of analysis of how it comes to be that of all the possible lines of flight, the path taken was the familiar one. The purpose of such a project is not so much to bemoan the powers that maintain the status quo but rather to allow us to see that other things are possible.

Deleuze and Guattari (1972/1977) propose a project of schizoanalysis, which likewise demonstrates the heterogeneous possibilities of any moment. Deleuze and Guattari developed the concept of schizoanalysis to counter analyses that posit humans as primarily driven by the need to pursue and acquire the object, whether that be the conformity of our desires and actions to the norms of the family and society as described through Freud in the Oedipus myth, or its parallel in desire-driven consumption under capitalism. They understand that these narrative practices are powerful, territorializing representations, but they are not the whole story.

Biehl and Locke, in their 2010 reflection on the implications of Deleuze and Guattari's work, state that much of the social analysis emerging from critical perspectives in the past half century has missed what they term "the open-endedness of life" and with it, "the life in things" (p. 323; see also Boldt & Valente, 2014). Rosi Braidotti (2013), a feminist theorist who studied with Deleuze, argues that what is needed is an affirmative politics, a politics that takes notice of what all sorts of bodies, traversed by all sorts of energies, can do.

We now shift to the final section of this chapter, considering a few of the applications of Deleuzo-Guattarian ideas to early childhood research and practice to get a glimpse at how they focus on "the life in things."

Deleuzo-Guattarian Theory in Early Childhood Research and Practice

There is no way to do justice to the many scholars who are using Deleuzo-Guattarian theory to reframe their thinking about early childhood education. For interested readers, I recommend accessing the online journal, *Contemporary Issues in Early Childhood*, and searching "Deleuze" or "Guattari" to get a number of pertinent articles. In what follows, I will highlight just a few applications of this work in order to demonstrate some of the potential of this theory for early childhood research and practice.

One of the most prominent contributions to Deleuzo-Guattarian scholarship in early childhood education has been that of Liane Mozère, mentioned above. Mozère worked with Guattari as a member of his Centre for Studies, Research and Institutional Training and as a worker at the La Borde clinic. As a professor at the University of Metz, Mozère conducted research about childcare and about female childcare laborers. In a 2007 study, Mozère considered how the largely untrained and poorly paid women who staffed French childcare centers contended with the directives of "experts" that represent territorialization in the direction of what Delueze called "a society of control." Mozère states:

> It is obvious that all these injunctions, these orders, have concrete and material consequences on the way to handle children and their bodies, but there are also impacts on the way adults interact with them. In other words, what space is there left for the child's desire; i.e., its singular language that is verbal, non-verbal, corporeal, sensitive, perceptive?
>
> (2007, p. 295)

But such a space is left, she argues, in the lines of flight from the promises of authority:

> [T]hese great unrecognized inventions the staff in the crèches [childcare centers] enabled the children to experience ... practical arrangements, where each time some of what is supposed to be their identity or the normal way of seeing things is revisited, is questioned, and so the normalization system is partly forced to give way to emancipatory forces of desire.
>
> (2007, p. 295)

Describing moments when the staff are able to "find the energy and subjective strength to resist the injunctions of these psychologists" (p. 297) to support the children's playful and spontaneous inventions, Mozère argues that it matters that the staff supported the children's verbal and non-verbal initiatives, recognizing and enabling "the liveliness and the happiness of these magic moments when children's desire emerges and they feel, as they say, that 'something happened'" (p. 297).

In her last publication before her death, Mozère (2014) joined a reflection on her long friendship with Félix Guattari and Gilles Deleuze with thoughts about teaching and learning in classrooms. She argued that real learning always addresses the child's desire, which means that it increases the child's sense of power and her or his intensity for life. She described learning through a description of learning to swim. A swimmer enters the water already territorialized by the knowledge of how to move on land. It is when the swimmer is able to immerse herself or himself in the specificity of movement through in the water that she or he is able to increase the power of her or his actions. In classrooms, this kind of learning happens all of the time, and it may or may not have anything to do with the official curriculum. That is, the curriculum is just one element in the assemblage of the classroom, and the question for the teacher is whether it is part of the the materials that allow the child (and the teacher) to enunciate desire, whether it interferes with desire, or is simply irrelevant (Boldt, Lewis, & Leander, 2015).

Mozère's interest in desire in early classrooms is echoed by the work of Sheri Leafgren (2009), an American teacher turned early childhood professor. Leafgren's book, *Reuben's Fall*, is a study of the co-existence of discourses of "the good student" and "the good teacher" and the many lines of flight from those discourses that compose any given day in a kindergarten classroom. Presented as a study of children's disobedience in kindergarten, Leafgren looks for multiple ways teachers might consider and respond to children's acts. As an example of Deleuzo-Guattarian inspired research, she understands the assemblic or emergent nature of unfolding events to require a non-linear and non-causally determined analysis. She looks at how meanings and power relations become organized and disorganized throughout the happenstance of what comes together in a given moment. Her descriptions of the minutia of a classroom provide an awareness of the vibrancy of that sensory world, the life in things. Recognizing that compliance and non-compliance move in relation to one another, Leafgren paints a portrait of the capacities of children and teachers to occupy simultaneously the homogenizing space of territorialization and the space of heterogeneous emergence. Leafgren offers teachers a way to think about the fact that multiple things are happening in any one act, and she calls us to responses that are steeped in generosity, curiosity, kindness, and a respect for the transformative potential of desire in the classroom.

Liselott Mariett Olsson, a professor at Stockholm University, published *Movement and Experimentation in Young Children's Learning: Deleuze and Guattari in Early Childhood Education* in 2009. Olsson's project, as the title suggests, is to insert an understanding of the implications of movement and experimentation into what she sees as the dramatic over-regulation of young children's lives. Sharing both Mozère and Leafgren's concern with "the control society" and disciplinarity (see Foucault, 1975), Olsson draws on Deleuze and Guattari to critically examine the effects of the ways that early childhood education is organized through "taming, preparing, supervising, and evaluating learning" (Olsson, 2009, p. xiii) that produce normalizing and marginalizing discourses and practices. By calling attention to movement and experimentation, Olsson works to affirm the power of unpredictability and emergence in early childhood classrooms. Desire is present in her work. Her focus is not simply on the learning that happens in the classroom, but on the ways that composing classrooms as spaces where children's desires are acknowledged and intensified sets up reverberations that can transform their lives more broadly.

Conclusion

While there are many other things that could be said about how the work of Deleuze and Guattari can influence our consideration of practices in early childhood research and education, this chapter has been concerned with how a few of their key concepts provide a focus on the unfolding of desire as it operates in and through the people, materials, ideas, histories, and happenstance events in the early childhood classroom. In a way, they help us to center what many have long considered the heart of teaching and living with young children. A bird crashes into the closed window of a preschool classroom. Its loud thump draws everyone's focus from the teacher, who is reading a book to the children at that moment. The teacher tries to return to the book, but she has lost the attention of several of the children, who continue to stare at the window with obvious distress, confusion, or excitement. The teacher must decide at that moment whether to set the book down and go with the children to investigate whether there is any sign of the bird's fate outside the classroom or to try to pull the children back to her planned activity. With either choice, the class is set on a trajectory that did not exist before that moment, as the bird's dramatic entrance into the life of the classroom interrupts not just that activity, but also returns in obvious and subtle ways throughout the day. A child begins crying during lunch, but cannot explain why; two friends suddenly fight over who gets to hold the class hamster; a child begins to sing "Rockin' Robin" in the house corner and three others join in, later asking for the song to be played as they clean up the classroom; and on and on. This is the stuff of the life in things as it emerges from the random and the planned materials that compose time and space in any classroom.

As Mozère, Leafgren, and Olsson additionally demonstrate, the work of Deleuze and Guattari also brings a critical edge to the consideration of how as a profession we have come to be dominated by the same stories of what young children, their families, and their caretakers must be like. While this question is one that is pursued by researchers using other critical and post-structural theories, Deleuze and Guattari add to this an attention to affect and desire, not as individual attributes or experiences, but as flows of energy that bring us together not just with other humans, but with objects, events, and relationships as they unfold in ever changing assemblages. To imagine happenings in a preschool classroom from a Deluezo-Guattarian perspective requires not a linear tracing of cause and events but a map of the numerous connections that flow in and out of any one space or activity, time, person, or object. Their work also suggests an affirmative politics of what else might be possible for children and their teachers and caregivers.

References

Biehl, J., & Locke, P. (2010). Deleuze and the anthropology of becoming. *Current Anthropology*, *51*(3), 317–351. doi.org/10.1086/651466

Boldt, G., Lewis, C., & Leander, K. (2015). Moving, feeling, desiring, teaching. *Research in the Teaching of English*, *49*(4), 430–441.

Boldt, G., & Leander, K. (In review). Becoming through the "break": A post-human account of children's play. *Journal of Early Childhood Literacy*.

Boldt, G., & Valente, J. (2014). Bring back the asylum: Reimagining inclusion in the presence of others. In M. Bloch, B. Swadener, & G. Canella (Eds.), *Reconceptualizing early childhood care and education: Critical questions, new imaginaries and social activism* (pp. 201–213). New York: Peter Lang.

Braidotti, R. (2013). *The posthuman*. New York: Wiley.

Deleuze, G., & Guattari, F. (1972/1977). *Anti-Oedipus: Capitalism and schizophrenia*. New York: Viking Press.

Deleuze, G., & Guattari, F. (1980/1987). *A thousand plateaus: Capitalism and schizophrenia* (B. Massumi, Trans.). Minneapolis: University of Minnesota Press.

Foucault, M. (1975). *Discipline and punish: The birth of the prison* (A. Sheridan, Trans.). New York: Vintage.

Leafgren, S. (2009). *Reuben's fall: A rhizomatic analysis of disobedience in kindergarten*. Walnut Creek, CA: Left Coast Press.

Leander, K.M., & Boldt, G. (2013). Rereading "A pedagogy of multiliteracies": Texts, identities, and futures. *Journal of Literacy Research*, *45*, 22–46. doi: 10.1177/1086296X12468587

Massumi, B. (2002). *Parables for the virtual: Movement, affect, sensation*. Durham, NC: Duke University Press.

Mozère, L. (2007). In early childhood: What's language about? *Educational Philosophy and Theory*, *39*(3), 291–299. doi: 10.1111/j.1469-5812.2007.00327.x

Mozère, L. (2014). What about learning? In M. Bloch, B. Swadener, & G. Canella (Eds.), *Reconceptualizing early childhood care and education: Critical questions, new imaginaries and social activism* (pp. 99–105). New York: Peter Lang.

Olsson, L.M. (2009). *Movement and experimentation in young children's learning: Deleuze and Guattari in early childhood education*. London: Routledge.

Suggested Websites

https://en.wikipedia.org/wiki/Deleuze_and_Guattari
www.critical-theory.com/deleuze-guattari-biography/
http://plato.stanford.edu/entries/deleuze/
www.parrhesiajournal.org/parrhesia02/parrhesia02_smith.pdf
https://en.wikipedia.org/wiki/Assemblage_%28philosophy%29
https://larvalsubjects.wordpress.com/2009/10/08/deleuze-on-assemblages/
https://en.wikipedia.org/wiki/Deterritorialization
https://deterritorialinvestigations.wordpress.com/2013/05/15/how-does-schizoanalysis-work-or-how-do-you-make-a-class-operate-like-a-work-of-art/

INDEX

A-B-C model 117–18
ABA *see* applied behavior analysis (ABA)
activism 165, 167, 182
activity 7–13, 28, 45–55, 62, 67, 75–78, 88–90, 123, 141, 150–55, 168–78, 184–88. *See also* behavior; learning; play
Addams, Jane 150
Adequate Yearly Progress reports 27
adolescents xix, 12–13, 32, 37, 46, 62, 65, 91
adults *see* language; learning; parents; teachers
affect xvii, 180–88. *See also* Deleuze, Gilles; Massumi, Brian
agency 85, 94, 131, 142, 158, 177. *See also* autonomy; learning
alert state 89–91, 93–94. *See also* newborn states
All-Soviet Research Institute for Preschool Education 68
anthropology 19, 21, 31, 154
applied behavior analysis (ABA) 104–5, 107, 116–17, 119, 121, 123
Araújo, Ana Maria 168
arithmetic *see* math
arousal 89–93
art 31, 154, 173–74
assemblages 182–88. *See also* Deleuze, Gilles
assessment xi, xiv, 27, 41, 67, 106–7, 109, 120, 152, 159–60, 171–72, 178
Assessment of Basic Language and Learning Skills-Revised (ABLLS-R) 119
assimilation 7–10
Association for Women's Weal 21
Associazione Femminile di Roma 20
attachment theory 73, 79–80, 85, 91, 93, 96
attention 25, 76, 88. *See also* focused attention
authenticity 74–75, 81–83, 85, 177
autism spectrum disorders 74, 88–89, 111, 115, 117, 120, 122, 124
auto-education *see* self-regulation
automatic reinforcement *see* reinforcement
autonomy 10, 13, 35–36, 40, 50–51, 54, 61, 68, 75, 77–78, 80, 85
aversive stimuli *see* punishment

Baccelli, Guido 18–19, 21
Baer, Don 115
Bakhtin, Mikhail xiv, 131–48
balance (in development) 8, 34, 85, 89–91
banking concept (of knowledge) 170, 177–78
Barbosa, R. 167
behavior 13, 106, 118; Applied Behavior Analysis and 104–7, 116–23; conditioning of 102–9; disabilities and 109–10, 115–18, 123; environmental factors and 50, 106, 116; mastery over 61; newborn 88; protest and 91; purposeful 36, 65, 93; rules of 40, 50, 82; self-injurious 94
behavior analysis 106, 110–12, 115, 117
behaviorism xiii, 101–10. *See also* Lovaas, Ole Ivar; Skinner, Burrhus Frederick
Berlin Exposition 21
Bettelheim, Bruno 115
between-ness 133–34, 142
Biehl, J. 185
bioecological theory (of development) 45–57
biology 4, 8, 14, 16, 58, 63, 84, 115
Bodrova, Elena 58–70
body language 142–44. *See also* language
Boldt, Gail 180–89
Bonfligi 20–21
Bowlby, J. 74, 85
Braidotti, Rosi 185
Brazelton, T. B. xiii, 87–98
Brazelton's Newborn Behavior Assessment Scale 90

Breault, Donna Adair 149–64
Bronfenbrenner, Urie xiii, 45–57, 166

capitalism 182–85
caregiving 38–39, 73, 75, 78–80, 95, 109
caring *see* educaring
Casa dei Bambini 22–23, 27, 29
Casati Law of 1859 18
Celli 19–20
Centre for Studies, Research and Institutional Training 186
change 63, 116, 185. *See also* time
Chatenay, Valentine 4
Chess, Stella 88
child care 22, 27. *See also* Casa dei Bambini
child-centered methods 22, 95, 150
children: adolescents and xix, 12–13, 32, 37, 46, 62, 65, 91; behavior analysis and 106, 110–17; choice-making and 13, 24–25, 43, 83, 110; infancy and 12, 26–28, 34–39, 63, 74–83, 85, 93–94. *See also* behavior; communication; development; language
Children's Hospital 74
Children's House *see* Casa dei Bambini
choices (students') 13, 24–25, 43, 83, 110
Chomsky, Noam 26, 105
class 20–22, 51, 53–54, 135, 161, 167, 181
classrooms 15, 24–28, 43, 45, 49, 53, 90, 94–95, 123, 152–61, 182, 186–88
codification 169, 173–74, 176
cognitive development 4–5, 7, 92, 155, 181. *See also* development
Cohen, Lynn xi, xiii–xiv
collaboration 20, 66–67, 170–72, 176–77
communication: between children and adults 8, 36, 40, 75–84, 91–94, 153; dialogic theories of 131, 137, 143, 146; disabilities and 105–11, 116, 119, 122–23. *See also* autism spectrum disorders; dialogism; language
community 36–37, 123–24, 152, 155, 158, 165, 170
competencies 42–43, 48, 63–68, 80
concentration *see* focused attention
conditioning 102–7. *See also* behaviorism
confidence 36–37, 42, 80
conscientization 172–73, 176
consequences 40, 105–9, 117–18, 123. *See also* behaviorism; conditioning
constraints 35, 65, 82–83, 183–84
constructivism 3–16, 28, 85, 95
control (self-) 24, 35, 75–76, 141
cooperation 10, 13, 76, 80
coordination (physical) 5, 39, 77. *See also* motor skills
creativity 16, 36, 132, 146
crises *see* critical periods
critical periods 63–64, 178
critical theory xiv, 166, 169–74, 178, 185, 188
crying 89, 91. *See also* newborn states
cultural-historical approach 59–60, 65
culture 6, 11, 14, 50–52, 54, 58, 60, 65, 74, 165, 181. *See also* environment; social, the
culture circles 167, 169
Cunningham, Denise D. 149–64
curiosity 14, 75, 87, 153, 159
curriculum xi, 14, 24, 27, 59, 110, 119, 150, 152, 161, 170–72, 186. *See also* pedagogy

Darwin, Charles 149–50
de-codification 174, 176. *See also* codification
Deleuze, Gilles xiv, 180–89
demand characteristics 48, 53
democracy 151–52, 155, 158, 161
desire 182–88
deterritorialization 183–84
development xi; accomplishments and 63–64, 68; autism and 74, 88–89, 111, 115, 117, 120, 122, 124; bioecolological theory of 45–57; cognitive 4, 36, 60–61, 61–68, 62–63, 88, 181; context and 55, 61–62, 151; Erikson's theories of 31–44; individuality and 29, 38–41, 55, 81, 85, 88–89, 96, 111, 120, 135, 150, 170; language and 24, 26, 136–37, 144, 151–52, 181; moral 7, 10–15, 20, 85; motor skills and 5, 7, 24, 26–27, 27, 36, 61, 77, 80, 92, 111, 119; planes of 5, 16, 23, 27; preschool age and 34–36, 40, 59, 63, 109, 160–61, 182, 186; social 46, 63–66, 75, 152. *See also* language; learning; senses; skills; writing
Developmental Approach to learning 87–98
developmentally appropriate practices 43, 74
Dewey, Alice 149
Dewey, John xii, xiv, 149–64
dialogism 131–48
dialogue *see* communication; language
differential reinforcement *see* reinforcement
Direct Instruction 106

disabilities 21, 46, 105, 109, 111–12, 115–27. *See also* autism spectrum disorders
discipline 24, 83, 187. *See also* behavior; consequences
discourse 135, 137, 144. *See also* communication
discrete trial teaching (DTT) *see* DTT
discriminative stimulus 102, 108, 117–18, 121
disequilibrium 8–9, 11. *See also* equilibrium
diversity 53–54, 132, 165, 177
documentation (of learning) 41, 106–7, 159–60, 171–72, 178. *See also* assessment
DTT (discrete trial teaching) 16, 118–20, 122
Dubnoff School 74

Early Head Start 80
early intensive behavioral intervention *see* interventions
ecological model 46–52
educaring 73–86
education *see* classrooms; development; learning; pedagogy; teachers
educators 3, 10–16, 178
ego 31, 37
egocentric thought 9–10, 13
eight life stages 32
Elkonin, Daniel 65
emergence 183, 187
Emilia, Reggio 137, 160
Emmi Pikler National Methodological Institute for Residential Nurseries 73
emotions 31, 36, 91, 116
empty vessel theory 94
endearment 91–92
engagement 15, 25, 53, 122, 137, 182
environment 182; autism and 119, 122–24; behavior and 50, 106, 116; classroom 11, 90, 158; development and 22–23, 151, 154; infants and 75–81, 89–91; interaction and 4, 7–9, 16, 92–93, 105, 183; learning and 37–38, 90, 94, 151–52, 178; organization of 24, 49; outdoor 24–25, 28, 79; physical 27, 38–39, 90; prepared 23; relations with 8, 34, 170; social 38, 63; stimuli and 61, 108; toddlers and 35, 39
epistemology 3, 5
equilibrium 8–10
Erikson, Erik xiii, xiv, 31–44, 74
Erikson, Joan 31–44
Essentials for Living 119
Every Student Succeeds Act 27
evidence based strategies 105, 109, 111–12
exosystem 50
experience 6–16, 23, 28, 48, 76, 85–94, 106, 132, 142, 151–66, 171, 177
experimental analysis of behavior 104, 115
experimentation 12, 14, 36, 159. *See also* constructivism; play
exploration 7, 12, 14, 23, 64, 75–80, 84, 92, 153–54
expression 93–94, 139, 147, 152, 154, 167, 183. *See also* language

families 38, 74, 124, 138–39, 165, 171–78
Feeley, Kathleen M. 101–14
feminism 20–22, 27, 184–85
Flagg, Ella Young 151
focused attention 25, 29, 61, 80
Foebel, Friedrich 5
force characteristics 48–49, 52
Forrest, Tom 74
free-form genres *see* genres
Freire, Paulo xiv, 165–79
Freud, Anna 31
Freud, Sigmund 4, 31–32, 37, 74, 185
functional relationships *see* behaviorism
future child 58–72

gatekeeping 95–96
generative themes 169–70, 176
genres 134–36, 140–43, 147
Gerber, Magda xiii, xiv, 73–86
Gerber, Mayo 73
Grazzini, C. 23
Green, T. H. 149
grouping decisions 26, 28, 65, 78, 80–81, 83
Guattari, Félix xiv, 180–89
guilt 35–36, 40, 42

habituation 90, 92
Hall, Elizabeth 4
Hammond, Ruth Anne 73–86
Harper, William Rainey 151
Harvard's Center on the Developing Child 29
Hatch, J. Amos xi–xii
Head Start program 28, 46, 80, 106, 161
heteroglossia 131, 133–38, 141–43, 146–47. *See also* dialogism
history (in Freire) 165, 170–72, 175–78
history (Vygotsky's term) 60
honesty 81–85. *See also* authenticity

identity 32, 50, 54, 170, 181. *See also* self (concept of)
imagination 42, 65, 68, 159
incidental instruction *see* naturalistic instruction
inclusion 75, 122–24
Individual Education Plans 119
individuality 29, 38–41, 55, 81, 85, 88–89, 96, 111, 120, 135, 150, 170. *See also* identity; self (concept of)
infancy xiii, 4–5, 12, 26, 28, 34, 36, 38–39, 63, 73–86, 89
Inhelder, B. 5, 7
inquiry-based learning 155, 158–59, 161. *See also* questioning
inside-out genres *see* genres
instruction *see* behaviorism; curriculum; pedagogy
intelligence 4–5, 7–9, 12, 61, 81. *See also* development
interactions: adults and 45, 51–52, 55, 65, 75, 80; environment and 10, 28, 49, 92; infants and 70, 81, 90, 93; language and 133, 143; non-verbal 94; objects and 14, 180; peer 13, 25, 45, 55, 58, 64, 80, 92. *See also* communication; development; learning; pedagogy; play
internal motivation 26, 36
internal operations 64
intersubjectivity 135, 138
interventions 39, 62, 81, 84, 101, 106–18, 120–23. *See also* behavior; pedagogy
intimacy genres *see* genres
involuntary movements *see* movement
Italian Pedagogical Conference 21
Izquierdo, Sally M. 115–27

Jones, Elizabeth 31–44
Jones, Emily A. 115–27
Journal of Applied Behavior Analysis (*JABA*) 104
Journal of the Experimental Analysis of Behavior (*JEAB*) 104
judgment *see* non-judgment
Jung, Carl 4
justice 12, 87–88

Kamii, C. 5
Keller, Fred 101, 104
knowledge xi, 3–11, 16, 23, 25, 28, 170, 177. *See also* constructivism; critical theory; development; intelligence; motor skills; psychology
Kobel, Caraline 115–27
Kohn, Melvin 53–54

La Borde clinic 182, 186
laboratory school 153–54, 161
Lacanian psychoanalysis 182–83
language: autism and 115–16; development and 24, 26, 40, 91, 137, 144, 151–52, 181; dialogism and 132–38, 147; environment and 6–8, 23, 105, 136, 178; forms of 138–39, 141–42, 145, 147; lived experience and 132, 134; multilingualism and 45, 165, 171, 176–78; non-verbal 40, 132, 137, 143; psychosocial developmental theory and 5, 35–36; relationships and 131; tone 137, 142, 144. *See also* communication; dialogism; play
law of cultural development 62
leading activity 64, 68, 70
Leafgren, Sheri 180, 186–88
Leander, Kevin 180
learned behaviors 87–98, 104. *See also* behavior
learning xi, xiii, xiv, 5, 8, 13, 36, 168–71, 175; active learning and 5–6, 10–11, 16, 24, 95, 155, 161; developmental approach to 87–98; dialogue and 131–48; environments and 37–38, 90, 94, 151–52, 158, 178; forms of 95, 169; infants and 77, 80; inquiry-based 155, 158–61; life-long 146, 178; occupational 150; potential 67–68; rote 8, 16. *See also* curriculum; development; pedagogy
learning how to learn 68, 77
Leonardo da Vinci Technical Institute 18
Leong, Deborah J. 58–70
level of intensity *see* interventions
Liang, Yue 45–57
Lillard, Paula 24–25
line of flight 183
listening 96, 170–73, 177. *See also* communication; language
literacy 26–27, 36, 41, 152, 165, 167, 173–74, 177
lived experience 132, 134, 150–55, 159–60, 173–78. *See also* experience
Locke, P. 185
logic 5–13, 15, 61
Lovaas, Ole Ivar xii, 111, 115–27
Lovaas Institute 117

macrosystems 50, 54
Mahler, Margaret 88
make-believe *see* imagination; play; pretending
Marjanovic-Shane, Ana 145
Marx, Karl 183
Massumi, Brian 185
materials 26, 28, 36, 53, 151, 153. *See also* objects
math 28, 37, 152
McConnell, S. R. 106
meaning 131–41, 166–67, 173. *See also* dialogism; language
mediation *see* interventions
memory 5–6, 8, 14, 16, 61, 63, 92, 173
mental structures 4, 7–9, 13–14, 60–62, 68. *See also* psychology
Merçon-Vargas, Elisa A. 45–57
mesosystems 49
microsystems 49, 53
Migration Policy Institute 178
mindfulness 25, 29
Mitchell, Lucy Sprague 166
modeling 84, 107, 118, 159
Montesano, Giuseppe 20–22
Montessori, Alessandro 18
Montessori, Maria xiii, xiv, 5, 12, 18–30
moral development 7, 10, 12, 15, 20, 85
Morris, George Sylvester 149
motivation 26, 36, 49
motor skills 5, 7, 24, 26–27, 36, 61, 80, 92, 111, 119
movement 5, 23–24, 28, 64, 73, 76–77, 80, 186–87. *See also* activity; behavior; learning
Movement for Popular Culture in Recife 169
Mozère, Liane 180, 184–88
mutuality *see* reciprocity

Nathan, Ernesto 22
National Association for the Education of Young Children (N.A.E.Y.C.) 43, 59, 80
National Institute for Early Education Research (N.I.E.E.R) 161
National League for Retarded Children 21
National League for the Education and Care of the Mentally Retarded 21
National Methodological Institute for Infant Care and Education 73
naturalistic instruction 120–22
negative reinforcement *see* reinforcement
newborn states 89–90, 94
newborns 75, 88–90, 93
No Child Left Behind 27
non-judgment 11, 25, 29, 42, 81, 84
normalization *see* self-regulation

object permanence 7
objects 7, 12, 62, 185; exploration and 23, 152; infants and 78–79; interaction with 5, 14, 49, 180; manipulation of 14, 27, 52, 64; play and 65, 70
Oedipal complex 183, 185
Oliveira, Elza Maria 167
Olsson, Liselott Mariett 180, 187–88
ontogeny 61–62. *See also* history
operant learning theory 115
Organization for Economic Co-operation and Development 59
Orthophrenic School 21–22
outside-in genres *see* genres

Pacific Oaks College 74
Palo Alto Health Council Demonstration Infant Program (DIP) 74
Panksepp, Jaak 84
parents 51, 75, 123–24. *See also* families
Parker, Francis 150
participation 58, 75, 116, 171
Pavlov, Ivan Petrovich 101–2
Payir, Ayse 45–57
pedagogy xi, xiii, xiv, 19, 21, 59; behaviorism and xiii, 101–10; communication and 8, 36, 40, 75–84, 91–94, 131, 137, 143, 146, 153; constructivism and 3–16, 28, 85, 95; critical theory and 166, 169–74, 171, 178, 185, 188; culture and 6, 11, 14, 50–52, 54, 58, 60, 65, 74, 165, 181; curriculum and xi, 14, 24, 27, 59, 110, 119, 150, 152, 161, 170–72, 186; democracy and 151–58, 161; DTT and 16, 118–22; grouping decisions and 26, 28, 65, 78, 80–81, 83; inquiry-based learning and 155, 158–59, 161; Montessori model and xiii, xiv, 5, 12, 18–30; moral 7, 10, 12, 15, 20, 85; play and 8–135, 140, 143, 180–86. *See also* classrooms; curriculum; learning; teachers
peers 12–13, 15, 28, 40, 45, 55, 84, 94–95, 116, 123
Per La Donna 20
perception 60–61, 66, 92
performance 66–68, 120, 181, 186
performance assessments *see* assessment
personal stimulus *see* demand characteristics

personality, 23, 136–37 *See also* individuality
personnel preparation programs 112
perspective 10, 14–15, 70, 75, 78, 80–81, 158, 178
Piaget, Arthur 3
Piaget, Jean xiii–xiv, 3–17, 27, 74, 85
Piaget, Rebecca Jackson 3
Piaget, Valentine 10
Pikler, Emmi 73–74, 77, 80, 85
PITC 80
planes of development 5, 16, 23, 27
play 7–15, 32–40, 64–66, 70, 76–81, 116, 119, 138–43, 180–86. *See also* development; pedagogy; social, the
positive behavior intervention and supports (PBIS) 109
positive reinforcement *see* reinforcement
post-structuralism 181, 188
Povell, Phyllis, 18–30
poverty 161, 165. *See also* class
PPCT (process-person-context-time) model 46, 49, 51–52
praise 26, 83. *See also* reinforcement
pretending 7, 9, 39, 64, 70. *See also* imagination; play
problem posing 169–70, 172, 174, 176
problem solving 15, 84
processes 60, 64
prompts 107–9, 118, 121
proximal processes 46–50, 53, 55
psychoanalytic theory 4, 31, 83, 88, 115, 123, 182–83
psychology 16, 23, 25, 31, 58, 60–61, 84, 102, 143, 149. *See also* development; *specific psychologists*
psychosocial developmental theory 31–44
punishment 26, 103. *See also* reinforcement
Pyramid Model for Supporting Social Emotional Competence in Infants and Young Children 109

questioning 3, 5, 13–15, 42, 137, 159, 169, 173. *See also* development; inquiry-based learning; learning
Quintero, Elizabeth P. 165–79

reading 26, 28, 36, 41. *See also* literacy
reading readiness *see* literacy
reasoning 5, 10–11, 13, 15, 42. *See also* intelligence; language; logic; psychology
reciprocity 12–13, 75–76, 82, 146
Reconceptualizing Early Childhood Education 180
reflection 168–70, 173
reinforcement 13, 26, 83, 103–5, 107–12, 120–21
relationships: advocacy and 43; affective 94–95, 182, 187–88; authenticity and 74–75, 81–85; autism and 88–89, 115–24; infancy and 38, 77, 85, 94; language and 131, 144, 146, 170; mental 11; parent–teacher 96; social 34, 36, 40, 153, 178; toddlers and 40. *See also* social, the; trust
Resources for Infant Educarers (RIE) 74
respect 75, 77, 169
respondent conditioning *see* conditioning
Ribeiro, C. 167
RIE 78–80
RIE Parent–Infant Guidance classes 78, 80–81, 83
Rimland, Bernard 115
Risley, Todd 115
role 13–15, 64–65, 153, 155, 184
rubric 152, 155, 160
rules 12–13, 37, 40, 51, 54, 65, 83–84, 94, 184

safety 75, 78, 84, 161
scaffolding 68, 70, 84, 154–55
schedule 13, 24, 43, 90, 119
schemas 7–9, 25. *See also* Piaget, Jean
school age 34, 36–37, 42
schools *see* classrooms; teachers; *specific models, schools, and teachers*
Schore, Allan 84
security 75, 77, 80–81, 121
Selective Intervention 81
self (concept of) 32, 50, 54, 136, 143, 170, 181
self-determination 109
self-regulation 8, 24–28, 35, 68, 75–76, 83, 89–91, 109, 141, 152
self-soothing 89
senses 6, 12, 22, 24, 26, 60–61, 92–93, 187
sensorimotor stage 4–5, 7, 12, 61, 64
Siegel, Daniel 85
Simon, Theodore 4
Siraj-Blatchford, I. 137
skills 61, 66–68, 87, 106, 110–11, 116, 119–20, 122–24, 182; target 120, 122. *See also* competencies
Skinner, Burrhus Frederick xiv, 26, 101–14
Skinner box 104

social, the 6–13, 20, 26, 38–39, 58–65, 122–24, 131–37, 145–55, 168–73, 183–85. *See also* communication; development; environment; language; peers
social-conventional knowledge 5–6, 11, 14
society of control 186
socio-dramatic play *see* play
space 13, 74–75, 78, 88, 94, 134–36, 159, 161, 180, 182. *See also* environment
Sparrow, Joshua 87–98
special needs xiii, 21, 28, 63, 74–75. *See also* disabilities
spontaneity 184, 187–88
stability *see* security
stable periods 63–64
stage theory 4–5, 8
stages of the human life cycle 33
standardized tests xiv, 29
state regulation (in infants) 28, 89–92
status quo xii, 185
Stern, David 88
Still Face Paradigm 94
stimulation 23, 61, 78, 88, 92–93, 102–3, 107–8, 118. *See also* behavior
Stoppani, Antonio 19
Stoppani, Renilde 18
Strain, P. S. 106
Strategies for Teaching based on Autism Research (STAR) 119
Strong Start for America's Children 160
sustained shared thinking 137
symbolic play genres *see* genres
symbolic representation 8, 12, 14, 64, 68. *See also* intelligence; language; psychology

Talamo, Eduardo 22
Tam, Po-Chi 142
Tardos, Anne 73
teachers xiii, 13–14, 22–27, 40–45, 55, 58, 94–95, 113, 137–41, 154, 166, 171. *See also specific teachers and theorists*
teaching methods *see* pedagogy
temperament 48, 88–89. *See also* behavior
territorialization 183–87
Thomas, Alexander 88
Thorndike, Edward 102
three term contingency 107, 111
time 47, 51–52, 54, 88, 182
toddlers xiii, 8, 34–35, 39–40, 63–64, 95, 104, 122
token economy *see* reinforcement
Touchpoints model 95
transformation 166–70, 172–73, 183, 187
trust 34, 38–39, 42, 75, 83, 94, 169, 171, 178
Tudge, Jonathan R. H. 45–57

unconscious, the 23, 28, 31, 182. *See also* Montessori, Maria
understanding 11, 137, 139, 142, 155, 167. *See also* development; language; learning
utterances 131, 133–35, 138–39, 143, 145–46. *See also* Bakhtin, Mikhail; dialogism; language

Verbal Behavior Milestones and Placement Program (VB-MAPP) 119
voice 137–38. *See also* dialogism
Voloshinov, Valentin 132–34, 145
Vygotsky, Lev xiii, 28, 58–70, 84–85, 166, 181

Waite-Stupiansky, Sandra xi, xiii–xiv, 3–16, 31–44
Watson, Johan Boadus 102
WestEd 80
White, E. Jayne 131–48
Wolf, Mont 115
World Health Organization 59
World War II 73, 103, 151
writing 8, 24, 26, 28, 37, 167, 170. *See also* language; learning
Wundt, Wilhelm 25

Zaporozhets, Alexander 68
Zone of Proximal Development (ZPD) 66